YAMSI

A YEAR IN THE LIFE OF A WILDERNESS RANCH

D1026248

NORTHWEST
Reprints

Northwest Reprints
Series Editor: Robert J. Frank

Other titles in the series:

YAMSI

A YEAR IN THE LIFE OF A WILDERNESS RANCH

Dayton O. Hyde

Oregon State University Press
Corvallis, Oregon

To all those who love the land

Publication of this book was made possible
in part by a contribution from

The Cattleman's Heritage Foundation

The Oregon State University Press is grateful for their support.

The paper used in this publication meets the guidelines for permanence and
durability of the Committee on Production Guidelines for Book Longevity of the
Council on Library Resources and the minimum requirements of the American
National Standard for Permanence of Paper for Printed Library Materials, ANSI
Z39.48-1984.

Library of Congress Cataloging-in-Publication Data
Hyde, Dayton O., 1925-
    Yamsi : a year in the life of a wilderness ranch / Dayton O. Hyde.
      p. cm. — (Northwest Reprints)
    Originally published: New York : Dial Press, 1971.
    ISBN 0-87071-522-4 (pbk.)
    1. Ranch life—Oregon. 2. Yamsi (Or.) 3. Hyde, Dayton, O., 1925- .
    4. Ranchers—Oregon—Biography. I. Title. II. Series.
    [SF197.4.H93 1996]
    979.5'91—dc20   96-25463
                                                              CIP

Preface

People new to a region are especially interested in what things might set them apart from others. In works by northwest writers, we get to know about out history and culture, and about our flora and fauna. And with time, some things about ourselves start to come into focus out of the shadows of our history.

To give readers an opportunity to look into the place where Northwesterners live, the Oregon State University Press is making available again many books that are out of print. The Northwest Reprint Series will reissue a range of books, both fiction and nonfiction. Books will be selected for different reasons: some for their literary merit, some for their historical significance, some for provocative concerns, and some for these and other reasons together. Foremost, however, will be the book's potential to interest a range of readers who are curious about the region's voice and complexion. The Northwest Reprint Series will make works of well-known and lesser-known writers available for all.

                    –RJF

NORTHWEST
Reprints

INTRODUCTION

Not so long ago many of us in the American West lived in ways driven by the ancient rhythms of seasons and weather and the doings of animals. A few of us still do. But it's a way of going to life which is clearly passing.

Yamsi is a good true telling of what that life, that way of doing things, was like. But it is not just a recounting of lost times, which is to say it is never sentimental.

Yamsi is a book which takes a clear (if almost entirely implied) moral and thus political stance. Yamsi is about taking care, of your people and your place on earth, and the creatures who share it with you. In that, it was well ahead of its time when first published, in 1971; these days, its news is more urgent than ever.

Yamsi is a book I keep on the shelf with the really fine books about the West I grew up in, like We Headed Them North by Teddy Blue Abbott and Helena Huntington Smith and Old Jules by Mari Sandoz and Wolf Willow by Wallace Stegner and Goodby to a River by John Graves and The Meadow by James Galvin.

Yamsi is a book I can't help but think about in personal ways. My brother and I spent the fall of 1967 sort of working on family properties which lay adjacent and downstream on the Williamson River from the ranchlands Dayton Hyde was buying from his uncle, Buck Williams. During the warm sweet weeks of September and early October we wandered the edges of deep timber along the swamplands of the Klamath Marsh, where the sunlight was golden all day long, jumping up waterbirds as we went, fixing some fence, but mostly loafing in the shade of great yellow pines and listening to the World Series on the radio.

Our family was going out of the ranching business. We were selling the cattle, and splitting up the properties on the Marsh. Pat and I were representing our father's interests. In November winter came down over that country like a hammer. The swamplands were frozen hard as metal. We tied nylon panty hose around our ears and went off on horseback, gathering the cattle to ship. But my brother and I didn't have much in the way of true responsibility. Clinton Bassey, as accomplished a horseman as I ever saw, had been taking care if our interests on the Marsh for decades, and he was getting the work done.

That was fine with me. My wife had taken our children and gone to California. I was burning bridges, getting up some courage to head out for a new life. It was an excuse for a lot of bad conduct. Artists didn't live by the rules, everybody knew it, and I yearned to turn myself into a writer.

What I didn't know was that there was a writer living just upstream from where we were on the Williamson River, that he had come of age in the ranch business, as I had, and that he was getting down to the task of writing a fine book about life in the shadow of Yamsi Mountain, about the men and women who'd come to the country before him , about his family and the birds and wild creatures he loved, the haying and winter feeding and horseback days in autumn, all the life I was so frantically preparing to forgo. His was an example I could have used.

Dayton Hyde was a man I may have spoken to once, or not at all. But I knew who he was. I recall waving to him, pickup truck to pickup truck, as we passed on the dusty pumice roads. Working men I knew on the Klamath Marsh said he was a rigid fellow. Dayton Hyde was taken to be a man who would never go off drinking with them, a distant man who disapproved of what they thought of as winsome cowboy barroom antics, and for reasons such as that, though they didn't know him, many of them resented him. Likely he wasn't paying them any attention at all because he had more significant things to worry about.

At that time, in that country, he was universally spoke of as "Hawk" Hyde. I imagined this nickname was a result of the strong sense of personal space and distance he carried with him; it didn't occur to me that it might have come to him because of his willingness to care for raptors.

Yamsi, I think, must be a good book for young muddleheaded Western men to read while they're trying to figure out who and what they want to be. They might learn to pay strict attention to what they love, and less heed to the fashions of the world; they might learn to nurture their willingness to care for good horses and waterbirds and the play of children, and to give up on some of their single-minded acquisitiveness and rock-and-roll buckaroo craziness.

I could have been way ahead if I had at least talked to Dayton Hyde. From what I see in the mirror of *Yamsi* he might have been able to help me with the process of reinventing my self and purposes. His example might have helped me through years of floundering, if I would have listened, which is doubtful.

Nowadays, I think, all of us in the West should be listening to Dayton Hyde. The West, everybody knows, is going through a time of unsettling change. Our frontier is turning back on itself; our territories are being, like it or not, resettled again, this time by people who often come bringing money. Many old-time Western people are feeling increasingly dispossessed, out of the loop; some are growing angry; a few threaten violence.

Westerners face two primary responsibilities as times change. We have to provide social justice for our citizens, and we have to find ways to preserve the place where we live and the creatures. These don't have to be contradictory agendas.

In *Yamsi* we see a man driven by our fundamental and commonly human impulse to take care. Our best future lies with constantly, in all our dealings, honoring that impulse. All of us in the West, particularly our lawmakers, should pay serious attention to this book. Dayton Hyde is telling us things we need to hear, through his example showing us the way. We need to take heed. This is indeed a fine book, and its time is here.

—*William Kittredge*

CHAPTER 1

I AM A SPRING MAN, NOT A WINTER man. In spring, a man is filled with dreams and new hopes. When you live on a cattle ranch as I do, winter life is *reality*. It is the drudgery of routine, the bone ache of cold weather, death of a fine young cow in the snow, and a stack of precious hay that scares you the way it gets smaller with every wagon load you subtract from it. Yamsi is our tradition-bound, second-generation, working cattle ranch, taking up the whole of the lonely valley at the headwaters of the Upper Williamson River, in the pine forests of south central Oregon. Six thousand acres of hard work and mismanaged emergencies. Derived from a Klamath Indian word, "Yamsi" means "home of the north winds" and it certainly is. We are sixty miles from town, twenty miles from our nearest neighbor, and I grumble about him.

My uncle, Buck Williams, black sheep progeny of an Episcopal bishop, traded the Indians out of Yamsi for a passel of whisky money, settled it, and made an honest living on the place, building a herd of Hereford cattle which were to be known for their quality throughout the West. Immediately before those Indians were more Indians, fat, jolly, *wild* Indians, who found this valley a happy hunting ground, buffered from warring tribes by fifty miles of virgin yellow pines, found it a lost, solitary world, but one in which Nature was especially gener-ous with her bounty.

But for this ranch, as for most, times have changed. Let us *be* senti-mental about the past, for it is lost forever. Yesterday my youngest son, Taylor, just turned eight, finding a bantam hen's stolen nest hid-den in the flour drawer of the old Bar Y chuck wagon, looked at the splintered bed, the weather-leached seat, at the worn, sprung, shrunken wheels leering from rusty rims, and asked, "What's this funny old rig for, Dad?" I could have cried! Even last week is gone. This is December, the start of my financial year, and I've just exuded so much infectious good hope to my patient old banker that he's been hooked again for another year. This year the price is bound to be better because it can't stay bad forever.

"Young man," he says, though I'm forty-three and a half, "there are two things you seem to excel at—getting enthused and spending money. A poor combination."

He wants me to keep some sort of journal this year, month by month, phase by phase, so that he can comprehend how a cattle operation like mine goes, what life on a ranch is really like, and why few ranches show profit. "Try explaining it to me, my boy, and maybe you'll end up understanding it better yourself."

Well, he's the boss—almost, that is—and a pretty important figure a banker is in the life of any cattleman these troubled days. But maybe he won't mind if I digress now and then to show him not only ranch life, but a personal glimpse of a family in action, of a rancher who is maybe a little "different," whose head is filled with nature as well as cows, whose heart runs soft to the beauties of the land about him— show him an adventure not into profit, but maybe sadness, or even pure joy. This December is the place to start; next December—who knows other than it will be a time of reckoning, a mature facing of reality?

For a rancher in the snow belt, happiness is having the barns and pole sheds full of good green hay. I haven't been happy yet, of course. In spite of my dreams, my resolutions for next year, there have always been some bents, some sections of the sheds able to hold more, lots more, and that's usually the difference between skimping in the spring (bad management) or having plenty (a lucky year). To keep each pregnant cow I own strong and in good condition, I feed twenty pounds of hay per cow each day, more in colder weather (a ton and a half a head over a winter), but each bale I flake off over the side of the horse-drawn wagon seems somehow like a defeat. We worked too hard last summer irrigating the hay, mowing, raking, baling, and hauling it on battered, worn-out trucks over thirty miles of rough roads to the storage areas here on the home ranch.

I say "we" because the whole family pitched in. Yamsi is more than just a home and livelihood for my wife Gerdi and our five children; it is for each one of us a consuming passion, a common challenge and

adventure in which we all partake. What we have in common, all of us, is our involvement with this lovely ranch and its struggle for existence midst a fast-changing rural economic picture. Nor is our struggle unique, for there are millions in our plight, living from one corner to another of America's vast productive land. But the number shrinks with every successive generation, as rural family after rural family loses its youth to the painted city.

I wasn't born to blue denim, the Western cloth. I grew up in Marquette, a small northern Michigan town, on the shores of Lake Superior. To me, Hiawatha was just a kid up the block. I would be there yet as minion of the lovely land of varying hares and timber wolves, had not my glamorous rancher uncle written from Yamsi to say that he could step out the front door of the ranch house with a dishpan and scoop out enough trout from the spring with one pass, mind you, to feed all his cowboys. And furthermore, he went on to mention in passing that his riders had just corralled thirty head of wild horses out on the wild, grassy meadows to the west. Now was that fair? Was that any sort of letter to write to a red-blooded twelve-year-old boy? I wrote back hooked (as I'm sure he guessed), timidly, conscious perhaps of my own bargaining power, asking could I please come for the summer, and *promising*, as only a small boy can promise, that I would be a most exemplary lad, with an appetite limited to hard

3

work and a willingness to undertake the most menial task, and *furthermore*—an indication of my orientation by a matriarchal society at home—that I would make my bed *every single morning* without even being told.

Once I got there, of course, caught up in a regular superdazzle of adventures, which included roping a sick pelican on a river bank (how many folks back in Marquette, Michigan, ever did that?) I never did keep my promise to make my bed, but then I never did see him catch trout in any old dishpan either, and as for wild horses, while there were some hidden in the surrounding mountain thickets, the wildest horse I ran into close up was a big iron gray named B. K. Heavy, and he was only wild the time I stopped him right over a yellow jackets' nest.

It's been thirty years since I last heard the forlorn foghorns on Lake Superior, the whistle of the ore boats, the ascendant and descendant chuffing of steam locomotives, the rumbling boom of off-shore ice breaking up in the spring, or the lovely, lonely insane laughter of a northern loon on a fog-shrouded lake. I can still get misty-eyed with memories and I'm sure that wild, forested land, once the haunt of wolf and wolverine, is lovely still, but somehow, I never went back. For almost by accident I stumbled upon the promised land.

I was a lonely boy and when lonely boys fall in love, they fall hard. My first big love affair was with the land, with the green, flower-jeweled meadows, edged with watching pines, with the quiet, unhurried Williamson, its many mirrors doubling the startling beauty of the bordering verdure of the fields. For me the greatest symphony was the *sound* of the West, the lonely call of the sandhill cranes from distant marshes, the drumming, hollow wooden bells of horses' hooves as they loped wild and free across the lava tablelands, the rumbling squeaking dissonance of heavy, iron-rimmed wagon wheels, clank of harness chain, curse of a teamster on a frosty morning, snuffle of contentment of a once-wild mustang just outside my bedroom window, or the bawl of a distant range cow, calling her calf in for supper.

Disastrous obligations such as school were always interrupting my romance with Yamsi, yet that could hardly be avoided. Turning my favorite saddle horses out for the winter, or worse yet, to another rider to use in the fall gathering, was ever a moist-eyed ritual of sentimental agony. Accepting my lot, I graduated from the Cate School, near

Santa Barbara, California, went overseas in an Army Signal battalion during World War Two, and graduated from the University of California at Berkeley. But even when I was far away, Yamsi was always home to me.

My wife, Gerdi, was a California girl, whose parents owned a cattle ranch west of Palo Alto, just over the hills from Stanford University. With nothing more than color transparencies of Yamsi, with its herds of sleek horses, fat cattle, and its great stone house, I made her captive. What I forgot to tell her exactly, or she forgot to ask, was that the ranch belonged to my uncle and not to me, and that there was the strong chance the ranch would be sold out from under me before I ever got the chance to live there with her.

Once married, we moved to the little logging town of Bly, miles to the south, where I worked as a cowboy for my elder brother, Ted, and waited patiently for my hardheaded old uncle to invite us home. But the old uncle had some strange ideas. Marriage, though not preferable to his own state of bachelorhood, was allowable as long as the consenting parties were both of mature judgment, a quality which never came before forty. I was only twenty-five, clearly too young to think for myself. Gerdi was even younger.

We then proceeded to convince him of our lack of maturity by producing three children, each one of which was a progressively greater shock to the old man, and cause for a long and tedious lecture on what would happen to the economy and to us when the Depression returned. When, at last, he allowed me to move to Yamsi as boss, having need of my honesty more than my talent when his previous man departed with a Luger pistol given him by Count von Luckner, Buck preceded my move by gathering up all his Oriental rugs into his automobile and departing with them for his apartment in Klamath Falls, with the sage advice that there is nothing harder on rugs than dogs and children.

I completely understood his worries about the rugs, for the Hyde menage then consisted of one wife, four children, two setters, and a tame sandhill crane, all of which were used to sleeping in the house. When at last, after several years of anguish on my part, he finally despaired of ever moving us off the land, and sold us the ranch, the household had come to consist of a wife, five children, two setters, six sandhill cranes, and a huge mortgage.

"You'll never make it," the old man warned as I signed my life away.

I grinned at him with all the affectionate patience the young seem to have for the old when they know they are wrong. Maybe I had the old man on knowledge, but he had me on wisdom. There followed the worst ten years in the history of the cattle industry.

And now I sit thinking about December, the first month in my banking or operational year, trying to explain it all on paper to a man who gets eight per cent for his money, perhaps even more, trying to explain my ranch and life thereon to myself, so that, one fine day, having subtracted the minuses from the pluses, I may intelligently assess the future, and decide accordingly whether to stay and tough it out, or, with my family, follow the exodus of country mice to the cities where we will all be miserable.

The inevitable hostile coming of snow will bring December and the realities of the cattle business into sharp focus. Today the fields, though brown and sere, are at least furnishing sufficient feed to maintain our herd of five hundred brood cows. But who can say what the weather brings on the morrow? After thirty days of hard riding, of wearing out one saddle horse after another, I have the cows all gathered off the neighboring open range of national forest and Indian land. Only their territorial sense kept them from wandering from a land which has no fences, no boundaries; now I have them confined with barbed wire to the ranch proper.

Scattered far and wide over the frozen marshes of the ranch, they graze on rank marsh grasses they couldn't have reached before the ice gave them hard footing in the sloughs. The experts at the state college might run an analysis and call it a disastrous ration, but the cows, shed of their calves at weaning time a month before, are actually gaining in condition. And what is very important, they aren't costing me a penny to run. In fact, every day stolen from winter, when snow will cover all remaining grass with an impenetrable blanket, is a minor triumph for us, one more day when we don't have to tap our precious hay resource. It is the expense of the long winter on hay that usually kills all profit for the northern rancher.

One day's victory over the weather slides into another, then, silently in the night, wave after wave of new snow sweeps light-footed over the somber, forested ridges of Taylor Butte to the south, and settles on the brown of the land. For a time, the large wet flakes melt on the warmer soil, but make ghostly islands in the darkness where they cling to a stump here, dead vegetation there. Then autumn is lost as the snow falls thick and fast and earnest upon the yielding land.

Even in the darkness, the restless cows, scattered northward through ten miles of Yamsi meadows, bawl instinctively to calves weaned from them a month before, which by now may have been shipped by their new owners to California or even Mississippi. Hearing no answer, heads lowered stiffly against the storm, eyes almost shut against the windflung flakes, the cows head for the protective shelter of the pine thickets. Already they are thinking about hay, and only a single fence of barbed wire keeps them from breaking in to the wintering ground.

From the bunkhouse door, the old cowboy, Slim, moves out for a moment into the darkness, stares uneasily at the starless murk above him, hunches his collar close about his neck with a forward roll of his shoulders against the maddening wetness of the flakes, kicks down with the pointed toe of one boot through the snowy carpet for one last reassuring look at the dirt before spring, then heads back indoors filled with a melancholy he cannot understand to smoke the last cigarette of the day in the comfortable overheat of the ticking wood stove.

In my stone ranch house, the wind haunts the eaves, setting up a vibration of melancholy. The flickering firelight dances on the ceiling of my study, setting alive with color the bright multicolored boards painted thus by some forgotten soul years before who dared, in a conventional age, to be different. How comfortable to be sheltered from the storm by such a strong, immutable house as this! Above the crackle of my fire, I try to hear the sounds of the weather, the drip of melting snow from the eaves where the heat has escaped the insulation, the mounting, mournful howl of the intimidating winds as a new front moves in. Instead there is only silence, a stillness which can either be of nothing, or of heavy snow. For me it is a time of decision, of trying to predict whether the snow will melt off quickly and be gone, or stay stubbornly for winter. Horses can paw down through deep snows and survive, but cattle, lacking the pawing instinct, must be cared for after more snow falls than they can brush aside with their noses.

Common sense tells me to start feeding—still, I reason, if I start now, it will mean twelve thousand pounds of hay a day, seven days a week, and no chance to stop until spring. Once you start handing a cow hay in the fall, she's hooked to the habit, and will pace the fence and bawl in self-pity if the hay wagon doesn't arrive in time. All desire to forage for herself is gone. If I need six tons a day for my herd, at twenty-five dollars a ton, that means a hundred and fifty dollars' worth of feed a day, or roughly the price of a cow. In effect, if bad weather adds fifteen days to my winter, it is like going out and shooting fifteen of my nice cows.

There is hardship not only in the strain on an already tight budget, but in wear and tear on the men. Feeding cattle is a seven-day-a-week job, come hell or high water, wind, snow, or blow. When a cowboy with cabin fever finally makes it to town you've got to figure on a good seven-day spree to drive the discouragement out of him, then another seven days before his hands and stomach are ready again for productive work.

Outside my window December is making the decision easy for me, by dumping a load of permanent snow. Nose pressed to the frosted panes, trying to see out, trying to hear out, I shiver automatically, then stare into the fire, attempting to imagine what it's like to be really warm in the heat of summer. If, just once, I could pick my climate, I'd order a late fall, a heavy winter snow pack, an early spring, and good warm rains in June. But show me a rancher anywhere who can pick his weather.

December is a month of change. The springs on the ranch subside, the river slows as the ground freezes, and becomes silent, dark, mysterious—or as my daughter Ginny puts it, "Full of water woozies." I couldn't wade the river on a dare now without feeling that an evil spirit left from Indian times might be about to get me. The great trout hug the bottom, scarcely moving, part of the ever-shifting shadows. No insect hatches, no fish rises, no bird sings. Flocks of Canada geese and whistling swans sit humped up along the ice flows, gathering strength against the day soon coming when hunger will make new demands, send them winging south, all except the persistent thousand dedicated to wintering on my feed yard as guests of my tolerant cows and my long-suffering banker.

Frost on their morning shoulders, my pair of golden eagles, circling high above the snowy fields, seems to sense an urgency, a coming departure of plenty, an ominous scarcity, and becomes more and more persistent in their harassment of the flocks of ducks and geese along the valley's river bends and marshes. The eagles dive and fail, sail nonchalantly as though they really didn't care to do more than laze upon some unseen strata of the upper air. But when they think they have lulled the sentinels to security, they try again. Soaring to heights where eyes ache and water just to glimpse them, they drop, hurtling with their distinctive wind roar at the flocks below. The ducks and geese watch for a moment, carelessly, as though calculating the exact epicenter of the plunge. Then, from the proper bend of the river or from the certain marked slough, the waterfowl lose their cool, leap wildly airborne, flashing frantic wings, slapping pinions in mid stroke, whacking feather on those of a neighbor in confused, quacking terror. Is it because the eagles lack decisiveness that they so often miss their strike amongst the teeming target, yet seem more effective against a lone bird? But, often enough to make a meal, the great talons shoot out wildly against an addled flyer in the threshing flock, a puff of sudden down marks a kill, and eagle and prey are on the river bank before the down has a chance to float to ground.

I've named the male golden eagle that haunts my ranch Hercules. He has a peculiar eagle curse for me, uttered when he sees me pass below. Ungrateful bird; he hates me because I tried once to be his friend. I kept the loggers from cutting down his nest tree, a fact he ignored. Then some crude, unthinking trespasser shot his mate as she carried a limp squirrel back to the nest. As the great male drifted down the waning thermals to look for her, perhaps the man shot Hercules himself. When I lifted her, squirrel still clutched in her talons, she was cold, stiff, beyond repair. I found Hercules only by chance, crouched beneath a dead log near the river, feathers still soaked from where he had flapped half-living from the river, with hardly a spark of life left in his tawny feathered body. He did not seem to fear me as I approached. Raising him tenderly, I hooked my eagle beak to his, sealed off his nostrils with thumb and forefinger, and breathed my hot breath into his lungs in desperate hope. Just as I thought him dead, his talons slashed spasmodically, and drove hard through my forearm. Sweat beaded my forehead as the shock hit; suddenly I knew what it was to be an eagle's prey. But I left the talons imbedded, for I was still busy fighting for his ungrateful life. Our mingled blood made a hot, sticky mess of my pants. When, at last, he was breathing once again and his great piercing eyes were wild and invincible, I pried his fetid sabers one by one from my flesh, and mended the wound in his breast where the bullet on passing through had taken out a chunk of meat.

For three long months that stubborn old eagle and I quarreled with each other. He hated beef liver; I stuffed it down his gullet by the pound as though fattening a Christmas goose. He loved the tender breast of wild duck; I forced down squirrels—hide and all, knowing better than he that he needed roughage. He sulked, too proud to swallow as long as I was watching, so out of courtesy I looked elsewhere.

But he mended in spite of himself; fifty pounds of beef liver and a hundred squirrels later, he came to be like new. Now he flies again, flies the way an eagle should, unfettered, mastering the winds, paired with a new mate that somehow found our valley isolation over the broad, forested ridges of her own. He curses me, not quite appreciating our kindred natures. As I ride my horse northward through these first snows of winter, he screams, but I stare ahead, forcing myself to ignore him. But when he mounts the winds, chasing the retreating storm, wings a bold brush of color, I forget my pride and in rapt, jealous wonder I watch him wheel, etched in silhouette, splayed pinions gap-fingered, ruling the wide earth beneath. Pensively, fingering the worthwhile scars upon my arm, I stand glad that God and I have put him there.

As I push my saddle horse northward through the snowy fields, following the thin road that threads the ranch, checking to see what heritage a snowy night has left me, I see that the cows are nervous, hungry, reaching up into the lower branches of the lodgepole pines for needles, chewing them up like hay, tossing their noses sharply to spit out the larger twigs. I shudder at the sight, for pine needles can be the bane of the cowman. If a cow eats too many of the needles, heavy with turpentine, she could easily lose the calf she carries, and might die herself. And right now even a pint-sized disaster could do me in.

There are hard decisions to make now on this December day. I look to the hills, hoping against hope to see blue sky heading my way, but the clouds scudding across the pine ridges of the horizon are darker still. Much as I hate to relinquish autumn, I must decide in favor of feeding hay.

Once I have opened the gate to the winter feed grounds, it is too late to change my mind. Within a few moments, a handful of cows, out scouting ahead of others, have seen the open gate, and are crowding through, heading expectantly for the feed areas upon which they have found hay every winter since they were born. They trot forward as though eager to catch a reassuring glimpse of the long stacks of stored hay, sheltered in sheds among the pines.

One of the cows, as though remembering past favors from some bovine friend, turns and bawls a long, low summons to the distant herd, and soon, the whole valley to the north is alive with long, red lines of Hereford cattle, drifting nose to tail from the snowy wigwams of the pines. Other cows, less hungry, or perhaps unconvinced, stare at the traveling herd in the distance, assert their independence by grazing nonchalantly where the snow has failed to hold in the warmer areas of the marsh. Soon they too, hating to be left behind when there might be the prospect of an easy meal on the feed grounds, trot hard to catch up with the others.

Some stop to eye me curiously as I ride my horse on by, heading north when they are heading south. This will be my last trip down the valley until spring, and I savor every familiar scene as though this winter will be my last. But while daylight lasts, I make a careful check of each thicket, each field, each fence corner, to make sure that all the cattle have pulled out for the safety of the wintering grounds. To stay away is to court a sure slow death by starvation. I learned this the hard way. Last year four cows, missed in the fall gather on the open range, drifted in out of the snowbound forest, trailing their big fall calves behind. They found a place where a tree had fallen on the fence and crushed the wires. One by one the cows led their calves over and were trapped in a lonely, snow-choked field unable again to find the narrow exit. Beneath the round roofs of fallen logs, or under tents of low-hanging branches, they found a few frozen grasses at first, then these were gone. Living on milk from their starving mothers, the inconsiderate calves gleaned enough strength to survive the winter, but each cow perished in her sacrifice.

As I ride on now, checking against possible tragedy, I see a late chipmunk shivering, cold-eyed, sluggish, and half-dormant upon the gnarled limb of a fallen patriarchal pine. When I pass again on my return, there is only a puff of fur on the new-red snow, and a gray breast feather to show that a goshawk, driving its swift, low, compass line across the forest floor, became the chipmunk's fate. The chipmunks worked so late this fall, it may mean a tough, miserable winter. But what good is this chipmunk's hard-earned store now? Next year a host of forgotten seeds will grow into small clumps of tiny pines where the chipmunk buried them as winter provender and forgot them in death—a small island of trees, owing their existence to a wandering goshawk from the north, which, on this bleak December day, passing through Yamsi, bound for southern climes, ate a quiet, unplanned meal, and planted a thicket of future nest trees, planted them unaware, without even trying.

Mink tracks along the December Williamson. My curious saddle horse drops his head to sniff the unfamiliar musk and sounds a nervous rattling snort. I see the mink at last, a wet black male, star of white shining upon his breast as he brings a silver shadow from the deeps, hangs fiercely to the flopping trout, then rafts him upstream to the big pine foot-log above Wickiup Springs, where he neatly fillets him out, leaving a spin of monofilament bones, decorated with beads of bright, quick-frozen blood.

Intent upon the progress of a vole's tunnel in the shallow snow, a great gray owl works his huge radar screen of a facial disk, picking up the slightest hint of a mouse's squeak. My horse is a scant ten feet away, but still the owl honors us with only the barest glance, then turns his head, studious and deliberate again about his anticipated meal. He takes not a flight but a short pounce, and the tunnel erupts in flaming red. The vole's teeth gnash angrily a moment, but its squeaks of outrage bring only further interest to the owl's yellow eyes. Holding the vole in his talons, the rare owl waits until all struggles cease, then bends his hooked beak and tears daintily at the soft gray underbelly of the meadow mouse. The huge owl is so trusting I can only hope he stays within the refuge of the Yamsi fence, for so tame is this Arctic loner's nature some unthinking hunter might clunk him with a stick just to be killing.

A mute of snow cast from a tree by the laughing wind catches my horse and me all breathless in a cloud of white ice powder. We shake the best we can, the horse's outraged shake adding to mine, then, wet and uncomfortable, complete our last circle of the ranch. There are no fresh tracks in the snow, and so, convinced finally that I haven't missed an errant cow or two, I rein my tired horse about, knowing full well the change I may expect in him.

Instantly awake, he nickers in eagerness to be gone, as though he imagines another horse ahead of him that had a head start at beating him to the barn. The wind is raw in our faces now, the wet, cold flakes which once beat unnoticed at our backs cling to our faces and all but obscure vision. A solitary mule deer buck jumps from its windfall bed, but stands immobile, reluctant to leave the comfort of its sheltered hideaway. My horse, which might have shied violently earlier in the day, pays no attention now. Instead, he has the barn in mind; now that he is headed home, he thinks only vague thoughts of rather elemental things such as where to safely put his feet. My own mind is a toss of plans. Before I quit for the night, I'll roach the manes of the old work team, May and June, so that they will be ready to hitch up to the feed wagon when comes the cold early dawn of tomorrow.

CAN IT BE THE CHRISTMAS SEASON already? The silence of my weekday bachelorhood is broken by the return of Gerdi and our five children, Dayton, Ginny, Marsha, John, and Taylor, from their winter home in Klamath Falls, where the children must go to school. Excited by vacation, they charge up the long ridge beneath Taylor Butte and, after many an argument and change of mind, finally drag in a Christmas tree cut from our timber claim.

What bustle there is, what use of each precious moment away from school. Dayton cuts huge logs of dead ponderosa pine into bass drums, splits them into short billets, and stacks them neatly in the basement as food for the voracious furnace. Ginny and Marsha round up the horse herd, saddle up their favorites, and ride until darkness, reluctant to let the day end. John watches for bird life along the frozen marshes, while Taylor gathers eggs from the chicken house almost before they are laid, feeds his geese, his pheasants, and the tame sandhill cranes. My patient wife Gerdi picks up after us all, rubs the house into a high polish, cooks up a meal for family and crew as though it were our last supper on earth.

She works too hard. I wish she knew how much less we would be happy with, that the dust on the sills doesn't really matter to us as it matters to her. Snow tracked in on her clean floors; wet clothes dumped on the hearth. Why hang them up, we reason with her, for in the morning when they are dry and warm, we will wear them again.

For the children there is too little time at the ranch. The fading of December into January means that they will all go off again, leaving Yamsi as I used to for school. A bachelor once more, I drain the pipes, pour antifreeze into the drains, and eat with the crew in the bunkhouse. A cold damp chill hangs over the big stone house; it seems so foolish to build a cheery fire just for me. I wish my banker could see how frugally I live. I can see my breath tonight in my study as I write this, but tomorrow is the first of January, that much closer to the warmth of spring.

CHAPTER 2

JANUARY IS AN HONEST MONTH. IT makes no claims whatsoever to decency, and one expects the weather to be cold, the snow endless, the cowboys cranky, rheumatism prevalent, the water pipes frozen of a morning, the chickens ungratefully to have forgotten what an egg looks like, and the cattle to be bawling hungrily for more hay a few hours after you have fed them all your budget will allow.

At least you can figure the costs without any more of a computer than a sheet of lined paper and a yellow, tooth-indented pencil borrowed from the kids' school supplies. Each day being exactly like the next, the cost factors are monotonously constant. Take any day, multiply by thirty-one, and you have the month. No machinery is going to break and need repair because you aren't using any; there will be no costs of construction you forgot to put in your budget because you can't build anything anyway in that kind of weather.

As a matter of fact, January's budget is the only one of the twelve you have ever been known to hold to. Yet January is the most expensive month since there is no way to get around pouring out load after load of costly hay, much of which just plain goes toward keeping the critters warm. While a rancher would prefer to think of more pleasant things, his banker will never let him forget that if, at the end of his financial year, the cost of what he has put into the cow adds up to be more than what he gets when he sells her calf, then there is nothing left for him but to borrow more money on his already overextended loans. The calves are the crop, and the vital questions are how many of them you can manage to coax to a weaning age from your cow herd, how much you can make them weigh, and how much money you can induce a buyer to pay for them over your neighbor's cattle at weaning time in the fall, when every other rancher in the country is helping you glut the market.

And there are losses along the way, losses from disease, from toxic plants, from rustling, from logging trucks, even lightning or falling trees. Unfortunately, the cow's mortgage lives on after her death. What other business can a man work at where his actions are supervised by a bunch of circling turkey vultures just waiting for you to make a mistake? Sometimes when I see the buzzards perched on my telephone poles I think they are eavesdropping, just waiting for my calls to the veterinarian, so that they may be first at the carcass.

From the bullet-gray skies of January comes snow on snow. The road to town is hopelessly closed now, drifted bank to bank on the high ridges which slope like shoulders from the raw, rocky, logged-over and overlogged baldness that is Calimus Butte to the west. Only the winter winds, or birds hard pressed by wintry gales, dare come in from the outside world. Ice coats the telephone poles on the windward side: larger and larger grows the icy sheath upon the sagging wires until they belly down like bent logs hanging in midair. Then with a sudden screech they snap under the tension, and we are out of contact with the outside world. It matters not to Mother Nature that I built all seventeen miles of that telephone line myself, and that I watered each pole that I planted with a bucket of sweat from my own brow. The Bomb could fall and we at Yamsi would be the last to know.

Day after day, the snow piles without mercy upon the suppliant trees, snapping them mercilessly under the ever-increasing weight. Will it never end? Is this the mighty winter of the century old-timers warn of, the one to break all existing records since records were kept, or within the memory of man? Will someone a decade hence pause in reminiscence to dwell upon the Winter of the Big Snows, when Yamsi was smothered in drifts until the following August, snowed in until the tips of the giant ponderosa pines looked like seedlings? The freak winter when the heavy ceiling beams of the stone house collapsed under the weight of snows, when the cattle suffocated in the drifts and the Hyde family lost all they had? And what but the fact that it hasn't happened before in the limited memory of man is to stop this from happening some fine year?

Beyond the Cascade Mountains, our horizon to the west, the clouds hang each winter month scheming just such a disaster, an unlimited sea of moisture stretching two hundred miles to the Oregon coast, stretching on out over the broad Pacific, stretching even to Hawaii, with a tail wind from Asia howling in garbled Chinese and Russian scudding them shoreward, pushing them east across the hills until they pile up like tumbleweeds along the fence formed by the crown of the Cascades.

To date the great body of snow has always *dumped* on the mountains, a sea of twenty feet at Crater Lake, for instance, which is only one hard day's horseback ride away. But what if the snow finds some mountain pass . . . ?

I look often to the sky thinking that one day, perhaps, it will come and we will be trapped in this lonely valley. For me survival would be a challenge, a new adventure, but for the cattle there would be no way out. In January the beasts are at the mercy of the law of averages. In the worst winter known to man, with my help they could survive; but what about the winter as yet *unknown* to man? These are the things a snow-bound rancher thinks about in a climate altered frequently by human action, and one which is yearly breaking records. I try to dream of pleasant things, of course, but I have a recurrent vision of dragging miserable and despondent into the bank, holes in the knees of my worn Levis, handing the deed to Yamsi over to a banker who looks especially handsome with a Honolulu tan, and mumbling, "Well, go dig what's left of the ranch and the cattle out of the snow. They're all yours now."

Placidly the cows chew their contented cuds and await their fate. A cow has no fear of the future, nor does she have pride in her owner, the way a dog does. The next owner will feed her, too, and perhaps better.

At night, untrammeled by worry of impending disaster, the cows group together under favorite trees, sharing the warm company of each other's bodies. They soon learn which spots catch the first rays of the morning sun, where the after warmth lingers in the evening chill, which spots the north wind never touches. There is a placid contentment about them as the calf within each rotund body grows yet is still two months short of wanting out.

With the dawn's first frosty light, feet crunching on the crisp iron of the night's crust, they move out from under the shelter of the trees to stand broadside to the sun, turning as by instinct to expose the most surface to the warming rays. Yet each cow has an awareness, an anticipation which keeps one eye turned in the direction of the barns for the first movement in the trees, the first sounds that indicate that feed might be on its way. They listen for the rumbling squeal of wagon wheels on crisp, packed snow, the clank of harness chains as the bay draft team, May and June, flashy and proud, eight white stockings on eight brown legs, matching white facial blazes like frosty lightning, eases into the collars, straightens the tugs, and starts the loaded wagon rolling and rumbling toward the feed ground half a mile away.

When at last comes this long-awaited sound of action, there is a marked stirring in the herd, and juices begin to flow in bovine stomachs. Yet, like a waiting crowd just before a ball game is about to start, there is patience, too. They stand placidly enough, knowing it will come in time. As the wagon lurches along icy ruts through the last wooden gate, the red river of cows flows forward, splits on each side of the team, and engulfs the load. The eager animals throng about, stealing a bite here and a bite there from the sweet green of the fragrant bales. Mickey, the black cow dog, dashes with teamster's legs around the lurching load, growling here, snapping there, trying to drive the cows away yet knowing that to bark would upset the cows, an unpardonable sin. As the wagon moves quickly off toward the feed ground, the cows break into a trot.

One man drives the team, picking out a clean area on which to feed. The other man feeds off the hay. Clutching a growing bundle of cut

wires in his left hand, he manipulates the wire cutters with his right. Swiftly, he severs the two wires that bind the bale, then, with gloved hand or boot, flakes the hay slowly over the side of the wagon.

Occasionally the driver hollers "Whoa!" to let the sweating horses catch their wind, or to let the feeder serve up his snarl of wires and start afresh. Once the load is fed, the men pause to sweep the rich dessert of hayseed and chaff off in a pile, to which the wisest of the cows swarm. Then back goes the wagon to the stackyard for more hay. After each load, the wire is piled in growing mountains near the stackyard in hopes that some fine day someone will arrive to haul it away for scrap. But no one ever has, and perhaps one day there will be no more room on Yamsi for the cows. If the growing piles are enough to make my wife distraught, they are heaven to the small birds, pheasants, and quail, which find this crazy man-made hedgerow a super bramble bush to which they may retreat to chatter saucily at every enemy.

The cattle are divided up between several different fields, each with feed grounds, water, and shelter. The bulls have been kept separate since the fall, so that all our calves will come between February and May, a sure way of birth control unless some unthinking soul leaves a gate open. The heifers, which will be having their first calves in the spring as two-year-olds, also have their own field, since we wish to slack off on their feed during the last two months so as to cut down on the size of the calves inside them and make delivery easier. Beyond the log corrals is the weaner lot, tightly fenced, for the heifer calves we saved at weaning time last fall for eventual replacement of cows culled from the herd. Each classification of cattle is fed and handled differently. The calves and bulls are fed in feed racks; the cows clean up well upon the ground.

Although they feed a herd of five hundred lookalike cows, the men get to know many as individuals. There are cows that meet the wagon at the gate, cows that skid to a stop at the first bale fed over the side of the wagon, and eat patiently until every wisp of hay is gone. But there are also chronic wagon followers, dissatisfied cows that sniff each bale as it drops, then follow on, hoping for one better. There are also a few hookers, hay stealers, adept at catching the dog or the cowboys unaware, bumping or hooking a bale right off the wagon when no one is looking. When this happens, there is nothing the men can do but stop the wagon, jump down, cut the wires, and flake the hay out over the snow by hand. The cow, of course, decides that wasn't the bale she wanted anyway, and while the men are thus occupied hooks off another one.

In every herd there are shy feeders and bold feeders. The weaker cows, butted aside by the more dominant individuals, stand meekly aside until the feed is almost gone, and lose strength as winter wears on. A good man flakes his hay out in long lines so that there is room for each and every cow to have her own little pile. With this system, too, less hay is trampled or fouled. Most of the cows at Yamsi have been dehorned as calves, but there are always a few horns that grow out again and these cows become bullies, driving the pariahs away from the choicest feed. A quick dehorning restores equality.

Among the herd, too, there are groups of friends, cows that plain and simple like each other's company, and that are inseparable buddies except when they are in search of a bull, calving, or exceptionally hungry. Perhaps they summered together in some sequestered mountain glade, grazing side by side, heads together, each tail doing double duty as fly swatter for two cows. There is a real peace between these friends, and when one is left behind, the other turns in her tracks and bawls soft and low. Even in a herd of five hundred, a new cow is recognized as such and is butted around until the others become used to her. Habitually, the old cowboys watch for a cow that seems a misfit in the herd; this misfit often turns out to be a stray.

After the cows have gleaned the last shreds of hay from the encrusted snow, they drift singly or in groups across the snowy fields to drink, where the Williamson flows from the base of the snow-covered hills, to begin its cold, quiet journey down through gentle oxbows, through lonely meadows that look just as they did a thousand years before, bound slowly but surely for the sea.

Fed by a multitude of springs from a fault line that borders the length of the ranch, the quiet pools boil here and there with snowstorms of white pumice, a volcanic sand blown out to cover the distant hills in the eruption of Mount Mazama, which then caved in to form what is now Crater Lake. It seems as though the welling water tries to re-enact the old eruptions by catching up the grains as they slowly settle and flinging them up again. Winter and summer, the temperature remains constant, and the stream does not freeze even in the coldest weather. Wading knee-deep into the crystal realm of trout and fairy shrimp, beaver and periwinkles, the cattle drink daintily as though afraid to wet their chins, then climb dripping to the bank to lounge about, dreaming perhaps of spring, of wild clover in the Wildhorse Meadows, of bluegrass on the Sycan.

There is a medley of sound, a rough music, coming from the placid herd—the grind of molar on molar, guttural belching as they bring up food from their false stomachs to chew as cud, the sigh of contentment as they drop hard to their knees then flop to the ground, the rattle of rough bark and charcoal as a cow rubs her nose against a burned stump and looks up suddenly wearing a fool's mustache, black on white. There is the splatter of body wastes from four feet up, and the soft lowing of contentment from one friend bidding good night to another.

If a wandering winter storm should happen by, or some errant wind slide unbidden down the mountain, tormenting all in its path with icy needles of flung sleet, they rise with dignity, grumbling, eyes blinking at the assault, then drift quietly back, trying each tree for shelter, until they are lost in their inner world of lodgepole thickets, screened from sight, where even the most mischievous winds cannot pry. Bodies lumped together again beneath the sloping rafters of a pine branch roof, which keeps the snow and frost from settling on the rough red of their coats, they settle contentedly to wait out the long, cold winter night.

In the distant bull pasture, two curly-faced old Hereford patriarchs, maddened by the dump of snow from a tree, bellow loud insults at one another; horns slap, lock, rattle; hooves scrape on ice like sandpaper on cement. One bull slides the other backwards, then is pushed back in turn. An impasse now. Each bull backs up a step, not sure what the argument was about, eyeing the tempting rack of green hay as though he would forget the whole matter to dine. But now, as one steps back, the other dashes in to win. But instead of running, the other bull stops, ducks his head, meets the onrushing crash of bone on bone. Forehead to forehead they stand in stubborn conflict, until night saves face and puts an end to such a foolish war. In the darkness, each bull bellows, nervous but triumphant, one nation shouting at another.

Into the very teeth of these first storms of winter the mule deer head, pushing hard out of the valley, threading bravely up over the shoulder of Yamsay Mountain, half swimming through chest-deep powder, until the howling winds of the upper ridges all but stifle them with flung snow. Instinct, hunger, or previous experience pushes them on to the arid desert lands to the east where snow is light and brush is plentiful. A few hardy fools among them winter along my river, but here they are at the mercy of the weather. No one will know of their plight and come bringing food to scatter on the snow, for here no man moves about. If the snow crusts with a skin of iron, they move easily, standing on their hind legs to browse on tender twigs of willow and mountain mahogany. But if there is a pile-up of deep powder, the big-eyed mule deer wallow helplessly, making aimless trails from one exposed bitterbrush to another, easy prey for bobcats and coyotes with which the forest abounds.

I regret each death, but nothing is wasted by my hungry predators. One by one they cut the weaker deer from the herd; over the hamstrung body they sing a dirge of social howls and snarls, and soon only the hair remains, scattered upon the crimson snow to tell the story.

Northward up the ranch, the freezes of January lock up the ponds of ruffled gray water, turning them to smooth gray ice, sending a host of migrating ducks and geese on their final lap to southern lands. I cherish those loyal to my valley, those that endure hardship just to stay on, willing to sit out the winter here when they could be bobbing in sunlight in the southern rice fields. Their breastbones shrink from convex to concave, on the gunpowder gray of the Upper Williamson.

Those that are left are an exclusive group. I love the tiny black-and-white buffleheads most, rafting on the upper pond, looking too small really to be ducks, seemingly too gentle to survive, yet able to flash downward in the water to escape a shotgun blast. They have come here, perhaps, from the coffee-watered marshes flowing into Great Slave Lake in northern Canada, marshes bordered with black spruce, tamarack, and aspen. They relish our loneliness. Yesterday I tried to capture one whose little wing is a jagged splinter of pink bone. He is crippled unless I splint him up, doomed to my pond forever until the last image of his northern pond is gone from his imprinted brain, while the hunter who sneaked onto my land with his filthy gun dines somewhere in comfort, the incident forgotten.

At times a clank from the feed wagon sends the buffleheads skittering from the pond, circling in tight formation right over the heads of the draft horses for a nearsighted look at what frightened them, but just as I despair that they are lost to another valley back they come, so low they panic the very horses that dared to panic them, plowing a wild, icy spray of water as they land recklessly. Then they swim merrily about their gentle winter business of survival, bothering no one.

I am not so fond of the American mergansers, unfriendly birds, wildly indignant about my very presence on *their* river. They startle me as they flush from the bend as though they enjoy their fright, delight in their harsh, grating, ghastly noisemaking. Beating the water to a froth with pointed pinions, they take off like giant jets loaded with lives, barely clearing, scaring the dining relatives watching from the jetport restaurant.

Mergansers don't care whether the morning is cold or snowy. They catch my unwary trout, so that by survival of the fittest only the wary fish are left for me to try. With fifteen of these serrate-toothed pirates paddling suspended in their sky, or submarining by in a champagne of bubbles, the trout leave off feeding and hang goggle-eyed in groups, scarcely moving a fin, hoping not to be singled out for dinner. (If I were fair, I'd admit the mergansers catch tons of trash fish that compete with the trout for the lush insect life that dimples the stream.)

Their long serrate beaks make them seem oddly streamlined, longer than they really are as they fly in slender, fast, purposeful V's up or down the frozen valley. Their croaking voices are ever harsh, unlovely, heron-like, coarse enough to send the crystal frost palaces of winter fairies collapsing along the river bank. They are fish-breathed loners, these mergansers, unbothered by eagles, ostracized by or ostracizing the happier groups of divers and dabblers. They shun even the groups of mallards common to every bend save theirs, or the stately Canada geese, which leave off their gleaning of fallen rye to try the river for a winter swim.

I live alone; but who could boast of better company than those small creatures with which I share a joint tenancy of the land? The human eye is deceitful. At first glance, the forest is silent as the snows; then suddenly a burden of snow crashes from a surrendering bough, for which, perhaps, the city visitor would blame the wind. But there's another crash, yet the high branches, where wind should show its presence first, are still. From out of nowhere comes a cheery host of avian friends traveling together potpourri in mixed species, God knows why. Mountain chickadees with a tiny white line above the eye, and with them their chestnut-backed cousins, tinier still, yet blessed with color, an uninvited tolerated relative from the fir forests of the Cascades. Not to be left behind is another set of cousins, red-breasted and white-breasted nuthatches, *yank-yanking* happily in extroverted chorus, overshadowing in sheer persistence the *dee-dee* of the chickadees. Behind them come the brown creepers, shaggy feathered, primitive, almost blending with the brown-gray of the bark. And yet they perform miracles, defying gravity, hopping along upside down on the underside of limbs, topsy turvy, finding a whole new world of bugs undiscovered by the less talented. Their voices are tiny, near indistinguishable, but still a faint part of the peeping chorus, which sounds a louder symphony through the very quiet of a winter forest.

As a cold, uncertain shaft of sunlight ventures for a few minutes through the clouds, the ruby-crowned kinglets, drunk with song, flash jeweled headtops as they transform each branch end into a bit of flame. Now here, now gone, following after the joyous group searching out the plagues of tiny forest mites that would otherwise destroy my forest land. One leaden egg, one tiny cocoon unraveled, one winter-stupid moth, one boreworm grub pale as sapwood, from his endless journey through the rot of a tree, looking out at just the wrong moment, and now fuel for the tiny feathered furnace; one moment's song, one moment's quick energy, no more.

I am glad for their help. If all my birds were gone, how long would it be before some hollowed, precarious tree, insect-ridden so only the bark held the once noble column, collapsed and buried me? How long is it since that bureaucratic bureau of forest overdevelopment, the Forest Service, with more engineers than foresters or biologists, decreed that all dead snags be felled from the forest outside my boundaries? My house is still marked with blood where desperate birds, overpowered by nesting instincts and with no place left to nest, beat themselves the next spring without mercy against shadows on the stones, or on any knothole that looked as though they could pound it open.

The hundred hollow homes I rushed up were taken within minutes, but in the forest itself there was a void unfilled, and now islands of bug-killed pines stand, rusty-needled among the green, as testimony to man's lack of understanding. Thank God for private land where I may leave the osprey's snag and the eagle's loft unfelled, where a dead lodgepole pine may, for my lifetime, raise itself in glory, holding to the sky its nesting holes. No planes will dump clouds of pesticides upon my land. My fat stay-at-home chickadees, by keeping within my fence, might well support the last uncontaminated avian gonads anywhere. But will they be that wise, poor trusting birds?

Outside my fences the planes roar, killing the bugs, killing the bugging birds, demanding new funds from taxes next year to do twice the job since all the birds are gone, forcing my land, innocent, to pay its vassal's share of tax to further the poisoning of the land. Let them kill bugs with birdhouses instead. The hairy woodpecker drummed his last Morse code warning from the naked top of my great virgin houselot pine. *"Smokey Bear is a fink!"* I think he said, speaking out for the other denizens of the forest. Anyway, this morning he was dead from such impudence, daring to criticize the hierarchy. I buried him in my woods, where in my lifetime the roaring bulldozer will never build a giant roadway over his bed.

What was God thinking when he gave stewardship of this mighty land to his most savage, his most destructive predator?

The animals and birds cannot risk accepting a human friend. They flee me, not understanding that I only want to see them better. The somber-feathered gray jays, wagging their shaggy heads at me, scold me with a derision they save especially for someone who would put out the tender nuggets of dog food unguarded in a dish. It had not seeped into their sly larcenous jay brains, tempered by the robber's world in which they live, that I could possibly enjoy their thefts. In one day they take a year's supply of rations, which they hide in every nook and cranny to be soon forgotten, pounding them even under the turned-up shingles of the roof, thinking that I am too stupid to see. Often I play a joke upon them by popping the lid upon the garbage can as they are busy with their pirate's ways inside, just to hear their fluttered protest. But they have no sense of humor. In their world, the smart guy would kill them; the fact that I turn them loose moments later, commuting their sentence, only adds emphasis to what they already know about me.

Their smarter, warier cousins, the Steller's jays, smartly crested in black, a darker blue than the Eastern blue jay, are lovely mimics. They do such a perfect valley quail that my lonely male flew to the tops of the pines to them, followed them out of the valley, and was lost to me forever on the very day I brought him home a mate from a game farm. Now it is the lonely female that breaks my heart with her unrequited love calls.

The pines are silent with anticipation as I take out a can of wheat for my tame sandhill cranes, but if I listen as I walk, I hear the faint whisper of wings as the jays follow me. Hardly have I turned my back than they are down, bright jeweled pirates in the snow. Stealing is their business, and once the cranes have wandered over to put them to flight, they chuckle happily from the needled greenery for every morsel they have managed to steal from a crane's breakfast.

Derisive too are the Clarke's nutcrackers, which nest early, when the snow still lies patchy on the ground. They love the tallest trees, screaming a harsh *kra-ah-ah* for all the world to know their presence, flashing white on gray against the dark green of the pines. High in their treetops, they catch the morning sun long before it has struck the valley floor.

Only their highly intelligent cousin, the magpie, is more conspicuous, with harsh, jabbering rattle and black-and-white formality of long-tailed frock. When he is idle the magpie proudly announces himself with much chattering; when he is silent, beware, for he is up to some small magpie mischief. Hang your beef on the screened porch, or the magpies will be up before you in the dawn, working silently, and have the tallow stripped away, and all you'll get from them will be their harsh laughter. To a magpie, happiness is a fresh cowhide draped flesh-side-up from a corral fence. Yesterday I found a magpie's nest, bushel-basket sized, left from the year before, a great, conspicuous conglomerate of sticks, interlaced, helter-skelter, complete with roof, now filled with drifted snow clear to the living room ceiling. Yet this black-and-white outrage of a longtailed crow hid it well from me somehow. How often, as I rode my horse beneath that very tree with my head filled with problems of the ground, she must have jeered at me as I passed beneath, unmindful of her treasures. Black on black, croaking ravens play the lifting winter thermals as the barn roof drives the winds aloft. For hours on end they tumble there, catching themselves just one split second short of disaster to shoot on high again, croaking aloud with glee as though it were fine for the whole world to know their presence.

Snow again today, this week. A fresh feed ground every day as God covers the stains of messy bovine eating with the pure white of a new cloth of snow. I miss the children, sixty snowy miles away in Klamath Falls. They have grown a bit each time I see them, and though they thrill boisterously to my unannounced arrival in town for stolen moments away from the cows, they are all too soon bored, having become used to life without a father. Hardly waiting for answers as they swarm me, they hurtle a thousand questions. Ginny needs to know the well-being of Bones, a horse I caught for her from a band of mustangs. Marsha wants to know that her mare, Tune, is getting a special feed of clover hay. I tease them with all sorts of grisly tales of accidents to their animal pals, but they only grin, and count the wrinkles on my face. I have fourteen when I lie.

"Are there coon tracks in the snow, Dad?" comes predictably from John, while Taylor has to know how each chicken is, each duck, each goose, each sandhill crane—"the animals," he calls them, somehow reluctant to call them birds. And Dayton, older, more reserved, feeling seventeen, waits for the silly questions to abate, then wonders, dreaming, if this time of year a trout would take a gray hackle yellow, lightly dropped, in his favorite bend below Wickiup Spring.

The ranch house is closed up now save for my corner study, where a constant fire loses its continual battle with the cold. The pipes are drained, and I am fifty years back in time, packing my water in icy buckets from the spring. Without heat, the house soon acquires an unfriendly damp, a gloomy chill, which makes it seem far colder than the out-of-doors. There is a presence here, an unseen mischief which seems to love a vacant house. Who broke the jar of jam upon the pantry floor, burst out the bottom from the mop bucket, scattered dust upon the tables? I find a window wide open; storm fingers turned the latch and let the snow sift in upon the mohair couch. A stray raccoon, sliding from pine branch to snowy roof, stepped in over the sill as though the wind had done the mischief just for him, and took up living in Marsha's room, sleeping soundly midst summery scenes of grazing horses, curled in the middle of her bed like a big, brown furry pillow, flat forehead turned under against the comforter, paws holding his ears against the possible obscenity of my discovery. He left a host of footprints in the winter dust along the halls. His busy hands shredded a winter-dormant mourning cloak butterfly found in the curtain folds, played with Taylor's marbles in a dish and spilled them noisily upon the floor. Perhaps I stirred at this, coughed uneasily in my winter lair below so that he left, unbidden as he had been uninvited, passed out the window, thankless to his host. That morning, I saw where he, on leaving, had climbed with muddy feet out of the pond and dirtied up the whiteness of the snow.

Ghost of Matilda, perhaps, a mannerly, gentle raccoon we all loved. I fell in love with her in Vermont and bummed her quite unabashedly from a friend, rationalizing that I had need of her to teach nature in the schools at home. On the plane west, the jet's roar made both of us timid.

All raccoons are devastating to live with, but Matilda less than most, having a certain rare refined sense of delicacy. I hear her voice now in the nighttime that is forever, chirping to us through the muddied pane to share some animal excitement. We went through heartbreak one winter when we thought we'd lost her, then one fine February day I found fresh tracks in the snow and trailed them to my winter-stalled cattle truck. Small, innocent black eyes peered sleepily at my voice. She lay regally upon what was once the seat but was now a huge disarray of torn-up cushion. "Come in," she seemed to chirp, with a stifled yawn. "It's warm in here."

She thrilled a thousand children in the schools, where I took her, cradled trusting in my arms, that boys and girls might see her charm.

At the ranch she had her freedom, bumbling along behind us as we walked, always too fast for her because of her many distractions along the way. And then one fall, when we were hoping she'd find a mate and bring us grandchildren to play with, a deer hunter, camped outside my fence, tossing his beer cans over into my meadow, shot her from four feet away with his high-powered rifle, as she came smiling up to play with him. Cutting off her tail as proof of his great victory over Nature, he tossed her body into the borrow pit of the road, where it was found by my children. How do I explain Man to them now? God's chosen creature! Even now, Great Hunter, the moths are at your trophy.

CHAPTER 3

As a snowbound bachelor, I take my meals with the cowboys in the cottage overlooking the big spring, a four-room house which we use as winter quarters. Blessed with a buckaroo-style barrel stove, the cottage is easy to heat, even though one can look out in places and see the sky.

My uncle built the cottage as the original ranch house, having espoused Yamsi as the perfect place to get away from people. Viewing the ranch's lonely beauty, the wild roses in the lava outcroppings, the flowers profuse in the green meadows, the trout in the crystalline stream, his friends felt the same way, and soon he had guests stacked up like cordwood in the sleeping areas. In desperation he added a wing, but this only served as an invitation to other guests who came more often and stayed longer.

One day, infuriated by the bumbling of Joe Robustelli, a cowboy he had just hired, he strode over to where the man sat astride his horse and said, "Joe, isn't there anything in this world you can do right?"

"Well, Boss," Joe grinned, "over in Italy, when I was a boy, I worked for my father as an apprentice rock mason."

Harried by a sleepless night of revelry on the part of his guests, my uncle growled, "Well, there's a big pile of rock over there by the willows. Get off that damn horse and go build me a house."

Jamison Parker, a well-known Portland architect, drew up the plans and from then on every cowboy on the place was grounded from his string of horses, and while the cattle wandered off on their own, that bowlegged bunch of sore-footed grumblers were put to packing water, cement, and lava rocks, dragging in huge logs from the surrounding forest, or hauling lumber by team and wagon down from a logging siding halfway up the side of Yamsay Mountain. In 1928, after one of the rainiest summers in the history of this semi-arid land, the great stone house was finished, a seven-bedroom bachelor retreat, which seemed to grow out of the forest, out of the gray lava rocks which had formed it.

It may have been Joe Robustelli's first house, but it wasn't his last, for the little Italian-born cowboy soon found himself in great demand to build houses for Buck's friends in the Klamath country, houses which still stand out as a curious monument to a cowboy who, as another hand once put it, was "as useless on a horse as teats on a boar."

Guests poured in from all over the land. Whisky came in by the wagon load; soon, half Buck's calf crop came to be devoured right on the place. In despair, Buck ordered a great tower drawn up on the east side of the house, where he could retreat and cast down buckets of boiling water on any of his guests who followed him there. Fortunately for his guests the crash of twenty-nine came, and from then on Buck was too busy enlarging his empire, and hiding out from bankers who arrived from time to time to foreclose, to get back into the building business. Whenever a cloud of dust showed above the trees along the road to civilization, indicating perhaps that a banker had been sent out to discuss money, he simply grabbed his fishing pole and strode off for a few idyllic days of hiding out among the willows along his river.

It was clear to Buck that to survive financially he had to get bigger. On and on he went buying land from ranchers as desperate as he, buying without money, but somehow ending up with control of more land and more cattle, until finally he owed so much money that the banks had to go along with him for their own survival. His outfit came to control twenty thousand acres of deeded land, and ran six thousand head of fine Hereford cattle. And maybe it all started with Buck being run out of his cottage by a bunch of hungry guests.

The passing of time has left an odor of age in the old original ranch house, the smell of ancient smoke from fires long cold. There is a scent of leather, too; odd bits of harness, saddles, and bridles hang among drifting cobwebs from the smoke-blackened ceilings. Reatas are coiled like sleeping hoop snakes on all the walls, along with a few faded cowboy classics such as a print of cattle shaded up in a deserted shack, or a cowboy lighting a cigarette as he urges a cow and her calf through stirrup-deep snow. Leather chaps lean wet and stiff-legged against chairs until the heat from the roaring barrel stove warms the grease and they collapse weak-kneed drunk upon the linoleum flowers on the floor. Soiled and tattered gloves, widows needing mates, hang like colonies of bats above the stove to dry from the morning's constant wetting.

A great brown pot of beans, surrounding a central island of ham bone, simmers at the back of the stove as the one constant companion to meat fried to leather, and spuds fried period.

I sit quietly, watching the meal steam upon my plate, wondering what this will do to a palate used to Gerdi's inspired cooking. But I am silent as the snows, for tradition dictates that whosoever dares complain about the food finds himself with the job of cooking. Talk is of horses and of men—the first liar hasn't got a chance. Each man has worked a hundred places, built a mental library of tales stolen from the best of a thousand other men. Figure it out; for each man to have done all he claims to have done would have taken a hundred and fifty-three years.

The magic word is "windmill" tonight, it dropped somehow out of a conversation and old John Wood picked it up. "Speaking of wind-mills," he drawls, "when I was a boy down in Texas, we had a hundred of 'em on the ranch."

"That's a lot of windmills, John," someone chides softly.

A faint twinkle, almost imperceptible, shines in the old man's eyes. "I reckon I'd know whether or not there were a hundred," he retorts. "Why, I remember on days when the wind didn't blow, my Daddy'd say, 'John, ride out there and shut off about ninety of them windmills so there'll be wind enough for the other ten.' "

Al, the old Indian, stares into his coffee cup, then clears his throat. He has the poker face of his race. "Not to change the subject, but I was driving the team past the pond and I saw a trout that weighed eight and three-quarter pounds."

"Come on, Al," I protest. "How did you know that trout weighed eight and three-quarter pounds?"

The sudden twinkle in his eyes lets me know I've been had. "Why, that trout was packin' the prettiest set of scales you ever did see. Even that trout's picture'd weigh three pounds."

One by one the old cowboys I know, respect, and love are passing on. Steeped as they were in the tradition of the ranch, as I succeeded my uncle I became, in a sense, family to these men, and they have been part of my own history. But they are being replaced by young nomads who couldn't care less about what went before. For any ranch, with each change of ownership out of the family, the past is lost until new traditions have had a chance to form. They build slowly these years, these times, if they build at all, for the new breed of young men are too much of the same stamp, the same mold, each too much like the other. Tradition builds quickest and best out of eccentricity.

With the old cowboys, the talk at each evening meal was like a review of history, and the companions of years gone seemed to come back for a moment and join up in quiet reunion before the glowing wood stove. And the young man, bored at having to listen to the same old man tell the same old tale he'd told a hundred times before, ended up in spite of himself with a real sense of the personality and tradition of the ranch, a keen insight into the people and events that helped shape the land.

But now the old men go fast. Instead of living out their days on the ranch they spent so much of their lives helping develop, they retire at sixty-five, leaning on the Social Security system rather than the paternalism of the rancher. They move away from their world and the chores that could have kept them busy to the end, and thus their best and most repetitive storytelling years are lost.

At Yamsi I am the only remaining link between Buck's three foremen, Ernest Paddock, Homer Smith, and Ern Morgan, and those foremen (if I can afford the luxury) of the future. And these men will be remembered less for what great works they performed than for whatever grist their personalities and eccentricities supply to the conversational mills, as the bunkhouse men conjure up shades of things and people past.

Ernest Paddock was Buck's first foreman at Yamsi. He was a railroad man turned cowman, and he and his wife, Etta, arrived on the Yamsi scene before there was plumbing, and moved in on my uncle in the original ranch house. Etta had a thing about cleanliness and the cowboys soon grew one arm longer than the other from packing buckets of water up from the spring, so that Etta could do an endless supply of laundry dirtied packing an endless supply of water. When Buck moved to the stone house the Paddocks were left with the cottage, and in one position or another, Ern was to stay on to the end of my uncle's days.

The Paddocks were Fourth of July people. The Fourth of July was the time when people streamed down from the mountains and from neighboring valleys, headed to Klamath for the annual rodeo. The Paddocks lived for the parade. With its hundreds of horses and riders, this was the place to show off their rich trappings, a fortune of highly engraved silver on richly embossed leather, the old-time saddle maker's craft at its finest.

Hot blood was written all over their horses. It took a good cowboy to top off Etta's horse for her before the parade so it wouldn't cause a rodeo down Main Street. "Just get on him for me a minute," she'd say with a grin to one of the men, "and ride off a little steam." More cowboys bit the dust off her horse than got bucked off the rodeo broncos.

The Paddocks were sociable and soon people were coming from far and wide to attend the Bar Y brandings. There got to be more fence sitters than workers but Paddock's hospitality was unflagging. He wasn't as direct as his Beatty Indian neighbor, old Tim Brown, who, on looking about his branding corrals as noon drew near, addressed the group in no uncertain terms: "All you fellows work, come to house and eat; all you fellows sit on fence, *sit on fence.*"

At the Paddocks' the food was ample, with neighbors bringing their specialties. Often the crowd would devour a whole barbecued beef. The roping was spectacular, especially in late afternoon when things got pretty drunk and the action got wild, if only from cowboys falling off their horses.

When Paddock moved to the B K Ranch in Bly as part of my uncle's expansion program, Homer Smith became the next foreman at Yamsi. A teamster from the days when the term meant just that, Homer had grown up driving freight wagons and passenger stages in pre-automobile Oregon. He had worked for many a tough outfit, including that of J. Frank Adams, whose horse herds numbered in the thousands and stretched over half of southern Oregon.

Homer was built like a dwarfy bull. Five and a half feet was stretching it, and that with high heels, but his massive shoulders made up for lack of height. He walked with the rolling gait of a sailor, although his sea legs had come from driving teams, and leaning back against the reins on a lurching wagon deck. Big jug-handle ears, and a bull roar for a voice. A curious enigma of a man who would fight at the drop of a hat, but was gentleness itself with any child.

Homer had a propensity for Saturday nights on the town, when he always got drunk, always picked fights with someone twice his size, always lost, and always ended up in jail, upon which my patient uncle always made the sixty-mile drive on Mondays to spring him.

I remember the excitement among us and the speculation when we heard that Homer had got himself a mail-order wife. Everyone expected her to take one look at Homer and take the next train out, leaving the rough old cowboy we loved heartbroken. But she knew something we didn't and stayed on. Only Neely and her doctor knew that she needed a strong man to care for her in her coming illness. She was sweetness itself, Neely was, a rare, gentle lady, who never spent another well day in her life after she married Homer. Homer, reformed now to match the gentleness he married, tended her with love and affection for the rest of her days. Patiently he bore the heartbreak of leaving the Klamath country that had shaped his roughness to take Neely to a gentler climate for her health. We saw him sometimes when he dropped by, wearing a white shirt and low shoes, looking sheepishly out of place. "That goddamn woman would have me wearin' a tie, too, if she could find a shirt big enough to button round my neck." Protest he had to, but his pride in her showed through.

After Neely's death, Homer came back to Yamsi to work for me, driving a battered old Plymouth as troubled with emphysema as he, the sides splattered with tobacco juice as though he had driven full tilt through a field of grasshoppers. We had a good time together, Homer and I, and I tried to make it as much like old times for him as I could. But cigarettes, whisky, and hard living had taken their toll. I told him he could die there if he wanted to and I'd take care of him, but there was too much pride in the old man. He'd always made his own way.

He stood beside me at the house spring, trying to roll a cigarette in callused fingers stiffened by what he called "arthritics," glancing about at the scenes he had loved for thirty years, smiling at the great gray pile of rocks into which his horse Tune, now long dead, had bucked him off. "God damn yuh, kid, I like yuh," he said, one great pearl of a tear sliding down the wrinkled furrows of his nose. I helped him get his old car aimed down the road to town, and in a few moments the dust from the ridgetop showed that he was gone. I never saw Homer alive again.

But I remember Homer's funeral well. In spite of my uncle's firm avowal never to set foot inside a church, I dragged him along, reminding him that Homer had served him long and well, pointing out the times Homer had driven out into winter gales at Yamsi with team and buckboard to rescue him as he sat stranded in his newfangled automobiles, stalled in the drifts high atop Calimus ridge. "Just paying the tab on his funeral isn't enough, Uncle. Nothing would please the old man more than to know that you, his old boss and friend, came here to pay his last respects."

After much prodding on my part and heel dragging on his, Buck finally settled in the back pew of the church as the sermon started, turning off his earphone with a dramatic flourish to let everyone know he hadn't gone soft on churches.

The Smith family seemed to be a big one, for the church was crowded and most of the congregation bore the distinguished stamp of the Smith nose. Midway in the sermon, my uncle, touched perhaps by the simple Episcopal dignity of the sanctuary, leaned over to me in intended tribute to the late departed, and spoke in a deaf voice that shook the church. "Homer was a drunken S.O.B., but he sure had lots of personality."

Forty-three large Smith noses suddenly homed on the back of the room like a field of weathervanes in a fresh wind. I fled the church and left the old man to his own music.

In terms of work, the foreman who did the most for Yamsi was Ern Morgan, who took over when Homer moved on after his marriage to run my uncle's Klamath Marsh operation. Like Homer, Ern was short in stature but stout as an ox. He took immense pride in all he did, and worked to excess. Four o'clock in the morning heard that dry, rasping cough typical of so many cowboys who rolled their own cigarettes, and I came to hate his shouted "Daylight in the swamp!" which meant an abrupt end to my dreams.

When he built a gate of jack pine poles, he built it to perfection; his fences marched straight and tight through the pine woods, and his ditches carried water over new and thirsty land on a ranch that had never known such energy of development. The old horse-drawn fresnos soon lay rusting and forgotten as the ranch acquired its first tractor with a bulldozer blade. Morgan hated to come down off the tractor even to eat. Perhaps because he never gave anyone, including me, credit for much sense, he developed a propensity for giving direction. He was patiently didactic, and you soon forgot to think around him for he told you in running commentary just where to put each footstep.

When I took over Yamsi, Ern left to work for a timber company and a giant log dropped from a truck crushed him to the ground. Where most men would have given up, Ern propped himself on one elbow and shouted directions to the driver just where to place his blade and how to drive his tractor to best remove the log. He now lives out his retirement below Chiloquin in a neat little house of cedar which he built slowly and proudly with his own hands. The waters of the Williamson slide by his front door, bringing him memories of Yamsi with each passing ripple.

Sometimes in my loneliness I can look out the window of my study and see them there as they looked so many years ago. I can see Margaret Biddle, my uncle's aunt and partner in his cattle company, trotting her leggy bay Standard bred, Ginger, across the frosty meadows after a cow, strayed from the herd. Tiny, slender, iron-willed, indomitable of spirit, she was beautifully in command of any horse on the ranch. Even in her sixties, she crowded wild-eyed old outlaws up against a stump as mounting block and stepped on easily, and the confused animals, reputations shattered for all time, moved off gracefully, bewildered at finding a rider without a fear scent. Many a good honest old Bar Y outlaw got a good, dishonest selling off after that, as Paddock would snort to a buyer, "Of course that horse is gentle. Why I've seen a sixty-year-old woman, hair white as snow, packing a picnic lunch on his back." When it comes to selling a horse to a dude a cowboy has no conscience, and some of those old horses eventually tossed riders clear up over the skyline of Los Angeles.

Our clashes were frequent and bitter in that her one notable failure was to get motion out of a sixteen-year-old who was helpless off a horse. But I loved her just the same, conscious perhaps that I was seeing part of Yamsi's golden age, when cowboys ate on silver plates, and Caruso recordings roared from the windup phonograph. Even today the great carved chests, the brass candelabra, the Oriental rugs, now returned to grace, bespeak her elegance.

From my study window, my dreaming glance drifts out over the meadows blue with penstemon at the pile of graying boards, now splintered and scattered by the hooves of cattle. How often my wife in her endless clean-up moods has pressed me to burn them up; that woman would burn history to make a tidy world. I hold to the past, knowing that they will have to rot, be consumed by grass before I move them willingly. The boards are all that is left of the old hay slide Morgan built to stack loose hay. Even the method is gone now, part of the past, replaced by a complicated and heavily mortgaged hay baler. We call that field the Slide Stack Field still, but only I am old enough to remember how it got its name.

Suddenly through the mists there is a stack there a-forming. A growing mountain of hay, loose, not baled, rising higher and higher with each load. My brother Ted, curly-haired and tanned, driving a team of dapple grays, Rock and Steel, pushes a load of hay on the slender ground-hugging teeth of a buck rake, slides it forward onto hay nets of rope or chain, laid on the ground, then backs the long teeth out from under the load. A figure dashes in to close the nets with a trip-latch, then a teamster, driving a team of heavy bays, hidden from the action by the growing stack, pulls the hay up the inclined plane of the slide. Up, up, up it goes. Up and over the top of the slide and across the mountain of hay. The man on the stack shouts, the tripper jerks his rope, the load dumps in position; the pullback horse pulls the empty nets back to the ground where they are set again for the next buck-rake load.

Morgan is there, sweat making a shine of his balding forehead. Like most cowboys, his face is dark from wind and sun, his brow milk white from the convent of his Stetson. He moves the mountain of hay beside him with one little pitchfork. I wallow in the hay beside him, trying to stand up, and his washed blue eyes twinkle at my ineptness. "Damn it, *roll* that hay, don't try to lift it. Let's make a stack here, not a *pile! Wup!* Make your corners first; let the middle of the stack take care of itself. Nope, take a *load* of hay on that fork, not a *wisp.*" If I went back to loose hay now, instead of baled, where would I find men like Morgan who know how to make a great stack smooth, even, perfect as a great loaf of bread? And where would I find men who could brave a cold pitchfork handle in zero weather to feed the hay out to the hungry cattle?

A horseman moves by, riding a stocky bay horse that looks rough and jolting. Homer, of course, stocky and rough as his mount. I can just hear the gruff, rolling curses as Tune shies at the ditch, then, as

Homer swings the romal at the end of his rawhide reins in one swift arc to where the colt sucks, bogs his hammer head to buck. Homer wins easily. He is headed north today, busy about his work, and the vision is so real I wonder that the line of black buzzards, making a charred cap to each fence post but twenty feet from where he rides, don't notice him. They dry their wings, holding them outspread against the new sunshine, unaware that Homer Smith is passing by.

Today Al Shadley, my old foreman of Pitt River Indian descent, came back to me out of his retirement. I need him, need his wisdom, his knowledge of cattle and their ways, as I move into the busy-ness that is the calving season. I'm fed up with men who wouldn't know a heifer having calving problems if they saw one, wouldn't know what to do if the calf was coming backwards, hind feet first, or was stuck with one foot back. Al has put on a little weight this winter; the worn Levis, clean enough yet for town, sag a little, finding it easier to hang below his stomach than to go around it, and the square old shoulders are more rounded, softer lined, under his blue denim jacket. What is there about retirement that ages men, shortens their breath, deepens the crow's-feet about their eyes, turns a strong man into a fragile one?

His sight is failing a little too. Today I rode past him as he drove the team and wagon back from the feed grounds and he failed to notice me. One eye is dimmed with a cataract, and the other with a heavy lens, distorting his face, making him wrinkle his nose to support the weight. I sat astride my horse, watching, trying to fathom the secret of how he handles the lines, makes the great bay team lean evenly into the collars, double tree straight with wagon front. One slow horse, one fast, yet they pull straight and even. He stands, I notice suddenly, behind the slower horse, giving the fast horse less rein. Necks bowed to their work, filled with more pride than any thoroughbred, the team moves past.

Some current must flow down the lines from his hands. Yesterday, before he came back, the men were complaining of having trouble controlling the team. But now they are gentle, quiet, under control, each in step with the other, each nose in photofinish tie with his mate. I hear Al's low, gruff voice murmuring like a far-off brook, quieting, soothing, calming. "Easy, boys," as they shy at the sudden sound of a pine squirrel rattling across the worn, paper-thin shakes of the old abandoned slaughterhouse.

The old man is a quiet source of strength for me. If something needs doing, he does it; no running to me with problems. Most men I hire work me to death. The last man to hit me up for a job made me despair. I took one look at him and asked, "What do you pay?" But there are no more Als to hire. He is the last of his kind, and the new generation couldn't really care less about working on a ranch.

How long will Al stay with me this time? One month? Two? Until he has need of another visit to town, and then, one morning, the crew will be on its own, the great team standing dejected in the lane, waiting for his shambling step. Gone to town and maybe this is the time that one day soon has to be forever. Quite unabashedly, I'll beg him to come back. He'll look down at his hands, paining him with arthritis, and mutter, "Get yourself a younger man. Why can't you let an old Indian die in peace?" We have been through this many times, Al and I. If, as the psychiatrists claim, old people need to be needed, then I'm doing Al one whale of a favor. All I want is that he stay around to tell my children stories, and to give me courage.

After the other men went grumbling off to work this morning, Al and I sat at the table in the bunkhouse kitchen and stared into our coffee cups in reverie. I had things to do, but somehow I feared to miss another trip into the past with him. It happened to be Slim Fields he talked about, and soon I had forgotten all about going out into the cold.

Slim worked for my uncle here at Yamsi when I was a boy, then left here to marry, to run his own cattle ranch in Langell Valley, and raise a top cowhand of a daughter. He worked during his later years on the

Oregon Desert, for one big outfit after another, then, coming full circle, came back to Yamsi.

It is tough, of course, for the old to take orders from kids they once gave orders to. Slim and I kept an uneasy truce between us, and he always had one eye down the road, ready to leave should I make one mistake, let loose one small arrow into his monumental pride. I never did. I never even dared suggest what projects I wanted done, or, except by signing his check, admit he worked here. For a tradition-bound cowboy like Slim, who had walked off other outfits for breach of cowboy etiquette, to work for a rancher like me, whose mind was tied up with birds and nature and who could sometimes be seen of an early morning dancing in a circle with a flock of tame sandhill cranes, was something that he couldn't admit to. When his friends met him on the street and asked what he was doing, Slim always said, "Oh, I'm retired now," and avoided all further reference to the subject by walking off.

But things got done, whether or not he admitted doing them. A new gate here, new corrals, new fences there. Water changed from where I, being too busy, had let it run too long. A sick cow I'd missed brought in, doctored, and turned out, unheralded, without comment. He taught my children how to rope and ride, did the things their busy father should have, and spoiled them utterly when they were in trouble with their mother at the house by being a willing confidante either on the corral fence or a bale of hay in the barn. A cowboy Mary Poppins. I told him once, "Slim, you're sure nicer to my kids than you ever were to me when I was a kid," and he replied with just a trace of acid to his twinkle, "They're better kids."

If he had to feed the chickens, pheasants, or crane he stood way back from them, grumbling, as though he were afraid they would turn on him like skunks and spray him with a permanent scent. Once after a long, tough, snowy winter, when the hay pile was at low ebb and I was aching for spring, I walked with him past the parked feed wagon and suddenly a bird flew up to perch on the Jacob staff, drenching the pine trees with a melody of pure spring sorcery. "Look !" I cried joyfully, forgetting my companion. "There's a meadowlark!"

A vague shudder of distaste shook him. "So what?" he said dryly, cutting me down to size.

But then it will be his gentle sting that keeps his name alive around the campfires and winter stoves long after his deeds are forgotten. Once Margaret Biddle, knowing and appreciating his intelligence, called him in as he rode past the ranch house to show him some antiques that had just arrived and of which she was especially proud. Everyone including the choreboy had done his duty by exclaiming over them, and now it was Slim's turn. Slim stood on one bowed leg and then the other as he heard out their history and half the history of Europe. He grinned at her politely as he climbed back on his horse. "I like new things," he said.

Although he is retired, there are miles left in him yet. He comes out weekends to visit the children but he won't stay in spite of our entreaties. Secretly, I keep waiting for the novelty of being sixty-five to wear off, hoping one day soon I'll look off across the meadows to see a brand-new gate where there was only a poor excuse for one before. I wish I could make young men out of Slim and Al, but then if they were young men, they wouldn't be working for the bird-crazy likes of me.

When Al, sipping his coffee, senses my restlessness to be about my work, he mentions Mamie Farnsworth, knowing I'll be hooked for another round of coffee. A silence falls over the kitchen and we are both in reverie, young man and old, each with his own memories.

You had to look twice at Mamie to see the faint tracings of Indian heritage, but she qualified as a member of those wealthy timber barons, the Modocs, and was entitled to their rights and privileges. She had the best of two worlds, Mamie did, being white and Indian at the same time. She had the Indian pride, the minority sensitivity, but from her white blood came a sure sense of money management, and boundless energy. Because she was careful with her money she was a pariah to the other Indians, who were still geared to the old Indian ways, where if a man had plenty of food or whisky the others moved in on him until it was all gone, and so on to another lodge. Communal living in its pure form; and in the days before refrigeration, when deer meat would spoil if it was not eaten, and food gathering was done in groups, the system was eminently practical. Mamie drank no whisky, put her money in a savings account, and kept her beef for herself and her crew.

For years after her divorce many men, white and Indian, tried to separate her from her wealth, but none succeeded. She had a way of flirting with a man, making him feel important, laying her fingertips gently on his arm, calling him "dear," and batting her lashes at him, which made for a loyal following among the menfolk and violent jealousy among the women. When she drove in periodically to the Klamath Indian Agency office to collect her money, chaos reigned as every man in the place dropped everything to bustle around her, and every secretary typed four words and erased three, trying to ignore her.

In those days, what is now Yamsi was a series of Indian claims to which the individual Indian owners had been given title, and the right to sell the land if they so pleased. Mamie was one of the Skein girls of Dorris, a California town just over the Oregon border. She married Al Farnsworth, a white man, and the pair piled a wagon high with their possessions and settled in a secluded, spring-fed cove, halfway down the valley of the Upper Williamson, at a point now known, of course, as the Farnsworth Springs.

Only the clothesline poles and a few logs of the barn and corrals remain of what must have seemed like a heavenly retreat. There was a house of sorts, woman's carpentry mostly, since Al was lazy. Through it the wind blew without effort, although a roaring fire in the stove took care of that, as long as Mamie would get the wood. Through Mamie's industry, they built a barn and corrals for the horses and thin, pinto cattle, then dammed up the spring into a large pond so that Al could sit and watch the reflection of the day, and see the double image in its mirror calm of Mamie scooping up a bucket of water to pack up the hill.

It was an ideal life of fishing, hunting, lonesomeness, and few worries. It was undoubtedly Mamie who dug the big root cellar into the hill to keep the food cool in the summer and from freezing in the winter, although Al did take a job helping my uncle, who had bought some of the claims up river from the Farnsworth place. Al hired out to help Buck hay, and my uncle never got over the experience. According to him, Al Farnsworth ranked close to being the laziest man in the world. He was always falling asleep on the mower and would end up drowsing with his team standing quietly idle somewhere off in the jack pines, where the mower had finally run into a tree too big to cut.

My uncle bought the first half of the valley, claim by claim from individual Indians as they sold out and moved to easier and more social lives in the towns of Beatty, Sprague River, or Chiloquin. For what was the use of the Indian's doing physical work when the government would give them a handout without their having to lift a finger? Out of their sense of guilt at stealing them blind, the whites were sowing the seeds for the eventual destruction of the Indians as a people by placing them on the nation's first big welfare program. The old generation were a great people; the young soon became park bears.

Yamsi would have ended up too small to be a real working unit, had not Al and Mamie split up. Al moved with the Indians to the easier life of the towns; Mamie moved north, up the valley, and built a pretty little ranch on some meadows she owned, where Deep Creek, a clear stream of melted snow, tumbles down the side of Yamsay Mountain, through hillsides of yellow pine and aspen parkland.

Perhaps it was to spite his former wife that Al sold my uncle the property Mamie had given him in settlement. This enabled Buck to march a few more miles down the valley, and made a ranch of the place. Often as I waft a fly over the splendid trout water that surrounds the great bubbling flow of Wickiup Springs, listening to the sound of sandhill cranes on evening flights over the marshes, to the Wilson snipes wing-singing a hymn to the river gods, I reflect that I wouldn't own this land today had not Al and Mamie Farnsworth divorced each other nearly half a century ago.

When as a boy I came to know Mamie, she was a plump jolly woman in her forties, given to flowered tents of dresses, and big picture hats flowing with gay ribbons. On a quiet night, her laughter still rings from the rafters of the Yamsi dining room. She came in the old days by buckboard over the winding woods roads which wandered like cow trails over the ridges, stayed a night with us, then spent the second night with her sister, Ida Corbell, twenty miles closer to town. Sometimes she was trapped at Yamsi by the snows; once her team ran away, tore up the buggy, and left her bleeding and unconscious by our gate.

But beyond the fact that she enjoyed visiting, she came often because she loved to bait my uncle, whom she never forgave for buying her old ranch from Al. Buck tried his best to ignore her but she was a force to be reckoned with in the land.

43

Even after her beauty left her, Mamie kept so many admirers that she was known as "The Cleopatra of the Reservation," and one way to make Buck furious was to suggest that he too had a crush on her. Throughout the years scores of men worked for her and for little or no wages. They were captivated perhaps by her coquettish bat of an eyelash, by her way of making them feel special. It helped too that she was rich, for who among them didn't entertain ideas of one day being master of Deep Creek Ranch? but Mamie, having once been burned, was too smart to let it happen again.

When she breezed into the ranch house, voice shrill, gay, bubbling with laughter, missing no one including my choleric uncle with her attentions, it was as though April had arrived in January. At one time or another most of Buck's cowboys were in love with her, buying her gifts from their thirty-dollar-a-month paychecks.

A great brown crank telephone graced the kitchen wall, and for all I know it may have been connected to Mamie's ranch alone, for hers was the only ring cranked over the single wire line. Since Mamie did most of the talking it was easy for the cowboys to disguise their feelings even with the rest of the crew and the cook unabashedly listening. The cowboys invented code names for her in order to throw others off the track, but everyone knew Mamie's ring and the names fooled no one. Every crew we had held bitter rivals for her favors. But however Mamie flirted with them she managed to elude them just when they grew most confident. There was safety in numbers, and numbers were what Mamie preferred to have around.

But sometimes she was trapped into being alone with one of them. One of our cowboys, full of ideas about getting himself a ranch and easy living by courting Mamie, rode out with her one fall to help her gather her cattle. In the heat of noon, he found a sequestered glade where a small brook tumbled through golden aspens. Stepping off his horse, he laid his saddle blanket out on a picnic table of pine straw, noting with satisfaction that there was just enough room for two if they didn't mind bumping elbows. When he looked around for Mamie, she was eating lunch on her horse.

For months he awaited another chance to be alone with her. The chance came at last. It was the Fourth of July, and all her swains had gone off to the rodeo without her, leaving Mamie to do her own chores.

With a nervous chuckle of anticipation, the cowboy knocked at the door. "Mamie," he said. "You're down here all alone. Is there anything I could do to help?"

"It just so happens there is," Mamie said. "The boys were just digging me a cesspool."

All day long the cowboy shoveled at the bottom of the hole, peering out only to make sure that no one else had arrived. When at last the bottom of the hole became dark with the approach of evening, he crawled out, noted with satisfaction that Mamie was still alone, and washed himself off in the brook.

Thoughts ran riot through his head. Maybe Mamie had planned the whole thing, sent everyone away so that they could be alone together. Putting off the subject of his departure, he rushed about doing her chores while Mamie watched from her yard. When it was almost dark, he sidled over to the house, almost choking with anticipation.

"I got a real problem, Mamie," he ventured. "It's miles back to the Bar Y from here, and gettin' darker than the inside of a cow. I just this minute remembered I got no lights on my pickup. Reckon I'll just have to spend the night."

"I'll fix that problem," Mamie snorted. Disappearing into the house, she came out with a couple of Coleman gas lanterns, which she lit and wired to the front of his car.

MAMIE AND MY UNCLE CARRIED ON their running feud for years. When they met head on in the ruts of that narrow, winding dustway they shared as the only way out to civilization, neither one would pull over to let the other pass, and if one gave way it was only to shower the other with a storm of dust. When Buck arrived from town with a brand-new car, we always knew that Mamie would rush to town to buy a bigger one. Every salesman in the county worked one against the other.

Whenever she swooped in at dinnertime, he was always carefully hospitable, to a point. He always invited her to stay, but with elaborate show, he inevitably reached into his vest and turned off his hearing aid.

Then Mamie would drop her voice so that only her lips moved and even the cowboys couldn't hear. On and on she would pretend to rattle until Buck became curious as to what on earth she could be so excited about. Quietly, his hand would slip to the control button of his aid; still she was inaudible. Just as he had the thing on high range, she would turn suddenly to him and shriek, *"Isn't that right, Buck?"* It drove the old man right up the wall.

Buck was proud of his Hereford cattle, as well he should have been, and was deathly afraid that a bull of another breed might come along and mongrelize his calf crop. Mamie worked on his fears to keep her own cows supplied with the finest Bar Y bulls. Every spring she'd arrive dressed to kill, with a wild tale of how she was on her way to such and such a bull sale and just thought she'd drop by to say hello. "I think I'll try some Angus bulls this time, Buck," she'd announce, and Buck, shuddering with real fear, would send her down a truck-load of his very best Herefords for the summer.

The battle soon moved into the realm of real estate. Mamie bought a piece of dry land adjoining Yamsi, and even though there was no stock water on it, fenced it up tight to keep Buck from using it. Buck ignored her, never mentioning the fact that his cowboys now had to drive their cattle an extra two miles around. But when another claim came up for sale right next to Mamie's ranch, Mamie scurried in to the courthouse in Klamath Falls, only to meet my uncle coming down the court steps with the deed already signed under his arm. "Good afternoon, Mrs. Farnsworth," he said, tipping his hat politely, and kept on his way.

Still trying to outdo him, she turned her Deep Creek Ranch into a show place. There wasn't a neater ranch in the West, and her menfolk policed the area on her orders to pick up any twig or pine cone that dared fall to clutter her domain. She painted her barn bright red, and spent thousands building a modern house around her old shack, trying to outdo Yamsi. Yet somehow the more money she spent, the more ludicrous the place became. She laid copper tubes in the cement slab of the new floor to give herself radiant heating, but they froze and broke the first winter when the beaus all got drunk in town. She installed a modern tiled kitchen, complete with stove and dishwasher, but her electric plant was grossly inadequate for the job, and she cooked all the meals out in a ramshackle little cookhouse in the back yard.

The cookhouse had a year-round spring of water gushing from a pipe in the sink, which gurgled loudly and kept up a constant splash of water on the floor. It came down a pipe from Deep Creek, and was

reported to handle trout up to three quarters of a pound. Certainly the water always had a faint taste of horses, cows, fish, bugs, and beaver musk, but I accepted it in the form of tea.

The bathroom she built was legendary with windows all around so that she could always look out and see what the men were doing, both outdoors and in the living room. It was always a little startling, for it afforded the men the same privilege.

I miss her, a character out of the past whom modern times couldn't possibly replace. Sometimes on a winter night, I can still hear her jolly laughter as she sweeps into the Yamsi living room, stamping her feet for attention, pirouetting her large body around the room with picture hat trailing from one dumpy, dimpled hand, winking at old and young alike and calling them "dear." And I can still hear my uncle's exasperated growl, "Good God! Can't that woman ever be still?"

ONLY THE TOPS OF THE FENCE posts show now as January slides into February. A pigmy owl, only a little larger than a sparrow, moves into the hayshed, glad to work under cover. His hunting is made easier by a family of least weasels, finger-sized, that have moved into the lower layers of the baled hay, and drive the mice upward to the surface where they are easy prey for the little vest-pocket owl. With a flash and flurry of feathers, the owl picks off a vole almost as big as himself, glares at me angrily as though he expects me to challenge him for his dinner, then buzzes off, rising and falling with each burst of his stubby wings, to dine in stingy solitude.

The hay in the shed is going fast, and I make endless calculations to determine if it is going more rapidly than it should, or, miracle of miracles, if we will have a few bales left over in the spring. I picture myself strolling confidently into the bank, casually dropping the bomb-shell. "Well, I've got enough hay to last until turn-out time on grass. Won't have to go over my hay budget this year by buying that high-priced spring hay." It hasn't happened yet. *It never will happen.* What is there about a banker, in a warm comfortable office in town, that makes him set up your annual budget on the basis of a ton of hay to winter each cow, when both of you know it may take two?

Until now the horse herd, a mixed variety of broken and unbroken saddle and draft horses, have wintered well by pawing the snow away from the tall marsh grasses. They have pawed holes so deep only their rumps stick up above the snow as they graze. But now an iron crust forms on the snow and in they troop, begging over the fence for hand-outs, nickering plaintively to me across the snowy fields.

Their hair is long, shaggy, and dull, and snowballs, beaded on the long hair of their fetlocks, rattle as they walk. With a look of high disdain, the work team snorts and puffs to break a trail through chest-deep powder to pull them out a wagon load of hay, ignoring the horses as though they were just another bunch of helpless cattle to be fed. But Bright, a wise old veteran of a saddle horse, now retired, raises his head a moment to watch the steam cloud about their nostrils as they strain and blow through the drifts on their errand of mercy. Bright nickers loudly in the frosty air, and to me it sounds like laughter.

CHAPTER 4

TODAY IS JUST PLAIN FEBRUARY second. I don't believe in Groundhog Day. How could the fact that a scrawny, mangy, rock chuck or Western marmot, body winter-shrunken in an overcoat three sizes too large, pokes his sleepy head from his burrow and happens to see his shadow during the one moment of sunshine in a whole week of storms, how could *that* influence the weather, and bring on another whole six weeks of winter?

Al and I were riding our saddle horses down the slope by the springs and basking in the sudden warmth as the sun broke through the leaden clouds hanging oppressively over the tops of the giant pines. I was grinning like a happy fool at a story I was telling, when suddenly I saw the old Indian's jaw tighten. He pointed down the hill.

"Look at that!"

A marmot lay stretched on a rock, his paws curled under his chest for warmth. He was in a path of sunlight that couldn't have been more than ten feet square, separated from our patch of sun by a stretch of snow.

"Six more weeks of winter now," the old man said gloomily. "You better go out and buy some more hay."

Fled was happiness. I shook my fist at the grizzled old chuck, galloped my horse at him in a mad charge, frightened him down his hole, sent him to the very bottom of his burrow with a torrent of angry invective. "I don't place any stock in superstitions," I roared. "What could that one old rock chuck have to do with the weather? It's all a pack of silly nonsense. I don't believe a word of it!"

"Then why are you so mad?" Al asked with a grin.

For the first time I realized how really nervous I was about the weather. I had had enough of winter, yet it was still too close to January for me to feel safe. One could always accept the unexpected as a rule in the cattle business.

February, at Yamsi, is usually a calm, unruffled month. Granted, the nights are apt to be zero if the sky is clear, but by noon that high-altitude Western sun is beating hard at the snowpacks, rotting the ice, and causing brown rivulets to tumble down the slope from the feed ground, forming rich alluvial deposits out into the placid crystal depths of the canal, where a host of aquatic insects farm it like water fairies.

The cows lie about after they have gleaned the hay from the snow, contentedly chewing their cud, soaking up the welcome sun, vitamins included. As they await the time of calving, their bodies are huge, elephantine, distended; their coats shine with good health, and they look as handsome and as cared for now as they will look at any other time of the year.

Were it not for apprehensions of foul weather, it would be a relaxed time for me. As long as the calves are still snuggled safely in their mother's protective wombs, barring a meal of pine needles or a rare disease causing abortion, there is not too much that can go wrong. I wait for a warm weekend when the children are at the ranch, then rouse them early in the winter darkness. It is time to vaccinate the cows.

Horses hump up against the unaccustomed restraint of saddle girths, mittened hands are shoved deep in pockets for warmth, noses buried in scarves. It is never as cold as one imagines from the warmth of a bed or stove side, but still, the seat of the saddle is a bit of a shock, and everyone rides off silently, intent upon their own sleepy thoughts. As the first rays of the sun strike the treetops, we gather the cows, drift them up the long, snow-choked lane to the corrals, then ease them as quietly as possible down through the long chute. The cows are so fat they can barely squeeze along and the frozen planks creak under the strain. We can handle fifty cows at a time in the chute. Vaccine bottles clank, cattle bawl in angry surprise as the needle hits each cow three times. Each and every animal gets not only a massive dosage of vitamin A, but also a vaccination for Leptospirosis, an abortion-causing organism spread to cattle from deer. As dessert there is a final shot against Enterotoxemia, an intestinal organism which kills off the calves that get the most milk—that is, the heaviest calves. All this vaccination is an additional cash expense I can't afford, but then I can't afford to take a chance either. Vaccine is cheap if only for the peace of mind it gives the owner. The banker grumbles about the money I spend for veterinary medicines, but he would grumble even more if I came in to his desk one day and startled him with, "Well, I just lost my whole calf crop." And this can happen to the rancher who takes the short, careless road toward prosperity.

Five hundred cows, vaccinated in little more than two hours, file down the chute to freedom only a little bit ruffled for their experience, and are back on the feed ground, the incident forgotten in their appreciation of their daily ration of hay. But the vitamin A is working in their bodies and soon their coats will shine with an added luster.

The price of hay in the county has gone up from twenty-four dollars a ton to twenty-nine. There is nervous talk of a shortage this spring which could drive the price up to forty. Carefully, I inventory my stacks to make sure I won't be caught short before the feeding season is ended, and have to buy some of this expensive spring hay.

January took more hay than I expected, since the weather was cold and snowy. Then too, before Al came back the hands fed out the hay carelessly without flaking it, causing some of it to be trampled and wasted. How does one train young men who have no tradition, no feeling for animals, and no loyalties save to themselves? In this age it is easier to hang around town in idleness, drawing welfare or unemployment insurance, than to brave the cold for a day's work. It is their life to lead, of course, but it is my nation whose future is at stake. And yet they seem to have no apprehension themselves for their future.

Joe is my experiment. I listened to the "Hire the Handicapped" advertisements on the radio one day and called up the employment service to ask for a handicapped person. Everything is new to him, but at least he tries. He was embarrassed when one of the work mares raised her tail and made a great noise, astonished that she would do that when we were actually present to hear. He thought the milk cows gave milk all year around, didn't realize that they are dry until they give birth to a calf.

I took time out to teach him how to milk our big Holstein cows. He milked one, then left the other until two days later when he had more time. By then the poor cow hated us both. To get work out of him I need to be with him every working hour of the day, for even though he tries hard he simply doesn't have the knowledge of how to use his hands, the ability to make decisions. The man at the employment service just shrugs when I ask for better men. Where are the men of yesterday who, born on a farm or ranch, knew how to improvise, to make decisions, and had certain standards of honesty and hard work that went with them all their lives?

This morning a cow slipped on the ice as she descended the ditch bank for a drink, and soon aborted her calf. It looked small but normal, although it still had no teeth. Another cow ate the needles from the top of a pine which had blown down during the night, and lost hers. This calf was small, pink, hairless, and wouldn't have come normally until late April. Both cows are sad, dejected, and bewildered. Instinct drives hard at them to mother calves that fail to respond, or to rise from the ice to which they have frozen fast. The cows bawl low, sad, forlorn; their bags swell and hurt with new milk, but for them there is no relief.

If only I had a couple of orphan calves to graft on the cows. With a little bit of sorcery on my part, they would accept the calves as their own. I could rub the smell of the dead calf on the new one, or even skin out the dead calf and place the hide on the orphan like a sweater. In time the cow would take the calf and be happy with it. But I have no orphans yet, and bringing in calves from the outside world would risk the introduction of serious calf diseases. The income from these cows is lost now for the season, although they will cost me just as much to run as the cows that raise me calves.

Checking back on my calendar of the previous year, I find that I put the bulls out with the cows on the fifth of May. With a gestation period of a little over nine months, I may expect the first calf about the twelfth of February, with the bulk of the calves to be born in late February and early March. I ride out on the twelfth half expecting to see a host of newborn calves, but there is not even one. Maybe the bulls were all sterile. Maybe the herd is infected with a new disease in which the calves fail to develop. Perhaps feed conditions were such last year that the bulls failed to find the cows in the lonely meadows and pine ridges that make up the range country.

But I am reassured by the fact that the cows do look heavy enough to burst. Their udders have filled out, plumped with health, making them pink and smooth. A snowstorm, sudden and violent, lays siege to the ridges to the south. I glance up nervously, following its course by fixing its edge on a spire of the pine forest; it *is* heading my way. The sun shines pleasantly at first, but suddenly there is a cold shadow as a cloud passes between me and the sun; the air is colder, and the sky dark and ominous. Soon the trees of the ridges are obscured, and quickly we are in the vortex of a sudden winter maelstrom.

The chickadees have disappeared into the thickets, and the wood is silent. The cattle leave the feed ground nervously, their backs already white with snow; heads lowered against the fierce assault of the wind-driven sleet, they trot on and on toward the thickets. My horse glances back at me as I sit hunched astride my saddle, my coat collar a funnel into which the flakes fall on their journey down my neck. Clearly he has visions of the barn, of a nice warm stall and a manger full of fragrant timothy hay; he is seemingly trying to influence my thought waves and convey the picture to me. I let him move into the thick timber where a tortured pine, with huge misshapen branches, forms a canopy overhead.

Here the center is surprisingly still. But cannonades of white sleet balls bounce off the sloping branches of the tree and dance on the crust of the slate gray snow. Homer Smith is dead now, of course, but I hear his gruff laugh at my predicament. Well, Homer will hunch his collar at no more snowstorms. Funny I thought of Homer here at this moment of high storm. I seem to remember being with him once, on this very hillside, riding the cows together in a spring storm some thirty years ago. Yes, yes, I remember!

To put the record straight, we weren't exactly riding together; Homer had been tolerant enough that day to let me come with him. It must have been one of my first trips out of the barnyard on a horse, and I was doing my best to sit up straight, zig when the horse zigged, zag when it zagged.

"Put one leg on one side, kid, the other leg on the other, and keep your mind in the middle." Homer grinned. I went on one day to become a rodeo saddle bronco rider, but this was my shaky beginning.

Yes. I remember—the big pine, built like a leggy woman with her head stuck in the sandy hillside, screened gently by thickets as though to protect her modesty. Homer and I rode by with averted eyes. The cattle congregated on this hillside during the calving season, sheltered from the wind, warmed by the new sun of spring. It was the place to come to find trouble, if trouble had to exist somewhere. The cows were there that day and Homer reined old Tune up to look at them. With one quick glance educated by years of experience, Homer looked over the hillside, saw everything there was to see.

He rested his elbow across the scuffed swell of his saddle, whirled Tune about so that the horse's rump weathervaned away from the trail home, and rolled a cigarette. Even in daylight, the kitchen match made a rosy glow on the rough leather of his storm-lined face. He blew out the first cloud of blue sulfur smoke through his big nose.

I caught up, eased rudely around him, and rode up the hill to where the animals lay, pretending I knew a thing or two about cattle and wanted to check them more thoroughly. Homer watched quietly, in half amusement, from his battered saddle. I was riding a big, gentle long-legged bay named Sleepy, and I was secretly pleased to be allowed him because the chore boy, who had only been there a week, avowed he'd heard that Sleepy had been a regular bucking fool in his colthood, a decade before.

Sleepy had a twinkle in his eyes whenever I rode him, as though he knew just how preposterous it was, in his declining years, that I should be afraid of him. He stumbled, climbing over a log, and I half fell off him but he shifted expertly to keep me from landing in the snow bank.

"Whoa, horse!" I said, in warning. "You'd better not try to buck with me!"

I heard a snort of disgust from Homer, and, as though he understood, Sleepy turned one big, bemused brown eye back at me. With the skilled eye of the veteran cowhorse, he had already glanced over the cows lounging on the hillside. There was only one he seemed interested in and I wouldn't have noticed had it not been for the horse.

I watched the cow as she moved quietly off up the hill, switching her tail nervously, kicking her belly now and then as though she was bothered by something she had eaten. Again and again her tail switched nervously. "Nothin' wrong, old hoss. Reckon hit's just a passel of flies abotherin' her," I advised Sleepy in my best lingo. Was it my imagination that Sleepy looked embarrassed at my ignorance? It hadn't occurred to me that there were no flies in winter. Under her tail, the cow looked all sloppy and swollen. I gasped, reining old Sleepy half around, and trotted right back to Homer.

"Hey, Homer," I called out, pleased as Punch. "I knew we should have rode those cows 'stead of just sitting there. There's one up there is plenty sick!"

Homer glanced up in surprise as he finished working a witch's knot out of Tune's mane with his gloved fingers. The matted snarl of hair floated gently to the snow. He stared for a long moment at the cow, rolled another cigarette, and lit it with a blue-topped kitchen match struck under the heavy thumbnail of one bared hand, consuming half the cigarette with the flame. Then he reined his horse around so I couldn't see his face.

"You better follow her, kid," he said with something that sounded like a choke. "And don't you dare let that cow out of your sight!" With that he disappeared into the trees.

When the cow finally left the herd, Sleepy and I were right on her trail. Up over the ridge we went, and down into the next swale. I soon noticed that the cow wanted to be alone in her illness, for whenever she drifted off ahead, she would lie down, only to rise at my approach and move on her way again. And as to direction, that cow sure changed her mind an awful lot.

But I wasn't about to let her out of my sight. I put a big log in between our line of sight, and soon she paused to rest beneath a tree. Once or twice, she looked back over her shoulder to see if we still followed, then satisfied with her aloneness, she lay down and proceeded to groan and grunt and strain.

Slapping a set of figure-eight hobbles around Sleepy's ankles, I crept up to her and was completely frightened by what I saw. She was straining her guts right out. A great sapphire sack was spreading over the ground from under her tail. Larger and larger the sack became, and, wide eyed in my fascination, I moved closer, so near that I could even see the veins. When, suddenly, the sack broke, flooding the ground with pearly fluid, I jumped straight back in my tracks, knowing she was a goner for sure.

Scared, I ran blindly down the hill to my horse and leaped into the saddle, impatient to be gone. Old Sleepy refused to move. With patient dignity, he dropped his nose to his ankles to show me he still had his hobbles on. "Sorry!" I said. I half tore them off, dreading that Homer might come along at that moment, then galloped off desperately to find him.

But there was no sign of Homer either in the thickets or on the road back to the barn. I remembered his words then, "Don't you dare let that cow out of your sight." So back I went to watch her.

For a long time I stared at two frazzled ivory objects that seemed to be progressing out of her. They were shaped like tiny hooves, but then what would hooves be doing coming out of a cow that ate nothing but hay? They seemed to wiggle now and then, and draw back swiftly, as though unhappy with the sight of the world, as though timid. Boldly again they came, followed  by what looked astonishingly like the pink nose of a calf. "My God, Homer," I mumbled. "This cow must have eaten a calf!"

Ignoring me, the cow groaned in agony, and I wished fervently I had carried a six-shooter with which to put her out of her misery.

Then my head began to swim, for now came what looked like a calf's head, and then my sudden comprehension came as a shuddering heave from the cow produced a mighty rush of fluid, plus inner mysteries, *and a calf*, all wet, stained, newborn, and lively in the middle of the whole steaming mess. The cow hadn't been mortally wounded after all, but had just given birth precisely the way her ancestors had been giving birth since the first cow tolerated the first bull.

I took courage from the fact that her breath still came in short puffs and her eyes had a look of peace in them. "Nice cow," I said, "nice bossy. I'll fix up your calf just like a town doctor would." I had rubbed the calf's severed umbilical cord with snow as an anesthetic in case it hurt him, and tied a couple of real nice granny knots in the cord, when the cow jumped to her feet, let out a loud roar of outrage, and butted me clear down the hillside. *"Hooomer!"* I screamed as I made a flying leap for Sleepy's back.

Well, Homer came that time and he had funny little tear streaks down the side of his face that made him look as though he had been crying. I told him the cow had died, hoping to fool him, but cowboys being cowboys, he went right home and told the whole ranch about seeing a calf with knots in his umbilical and they all had a pretty good laugh at my expense.

But I learned, and here I sit, thirty years later, straight in the saddle now, astride a horse that has been known to buck a little, looking over the descendants of my uncle's cattle as the owner of the ranch and herd.

I see a cow flicking her tail nervously and I am smarter now. I wish she'd wait until after the storm, but she has held off as long as she possibly can, hoping perhaps to outwait the weather. Now she moves up the hillside to seek a sheltered spot beneath a pine, where the winter sun has melted off the snow to the bare brown of the pine needles.

Screened from the others by the trees, she sniffs the ground, lies down, rises, turns around, and lies down again as though making a nest. From beneath her tail the blue of her water bag forms, glistening in the cold light. Slowly, as she strains and rests and strains again, the sack gets bigger, then bursts, inundating the brown straw of the needles. Head stretched out on the ground, eyes feverish and unhappy, the cow strains rhythmically in spasms she is helpless to control; gasping, bawling soft and low in her pain, confused at what Nature is doing to make her pay for her moment's joy.

Minutes pass like hours. There is a glistening of ivory as the front feet clear the orifice, then, resting upon them, comes the small pink nose still covered by the natal sack or shroud which has been his home. The calf's tongue hangs long and thin from its mouth; the head looks squeezed out of shape, wrung out by the pressures of her body. The cow strains, relaxes for a moment, eyes cloudy, troubled, then strains again. Fifteen minutes pass and the cow makes no progress. Now and again the calf's feet jerk spasmodically as though impatient to be out. The cow rises, sniffs the ground for a calf but finds none there. Again she lies down and strains. The contractions roll like waves through her big brown-and-white body.

Now the calf's eyes show, blink at the light it has never before seen, flinch at the pelting of the sleet which shows it no mercy. The ears show, wet and glistening, slippery with Nature's fluid lubricant that makes birth easier.

Again the cow rests. For long minutes she lies placidly, then the pains come and she groans and gasps in anger and confused anguish.

Now, suddenly, the calf's feet are sliding along the ground, next the head and shoulders, the gaunt rib cage, with no breath showing as yet, no beat of the heart; then come the hips as little by little she expels it. Quickly, in a sudden rush, calf and sack flow over the ground, and the calf lies steaming.

Enraged by smells, instincts aroused, the cow bawls in anger, rises quickly, breaking the umbilical cord which has up to now fed the calf from her body. Shocked by the rupture of the cord, the calf gasps and starts breathing on its own. Unsure whether to love it or hate it, the cow butts it angrily, sliding it clear of the clinging sack, then sniffs it in astonishment. Some odor emanating from the wet helpless heap pacifies her and she bawls a low bawl, no longer of anger but of love. Instincts have taken over as they have since the beginning of her species.

Then as the snowflakes pelt the wet, shivering puppy of a calf, she licks it dry with her long, rough tongue, rooting her offspring with her nose to get the blood circulating against the cold. Pine needles stick to the calf, making it as homely as a wet mink out of water. When he is dry, so that wild animals will not be attracted to her secret nursery by the odors of birth, she turns to eat the pink flag of afterbirth. Only when her chores are done does she flop down for a time to rest, sheltering her calf with her big warm body against the drifting snow.

The calf's breath still comes in gasps and there is a faint gurgle of fluid not yet expelled from the lungs, but his heart hammers hard against his tiny ribs. Struggling, he flops like a catfish in a drained pond. Quietly now, still weak from her ordeal, the cow rocks gently to her feet, sniffs hard at the calf to make sure he is really hers and to memorize his scent forever, then nudges him along the back to make him try to rise.

The calf struggles up, but falls, spraddle-legged as a drunk spider. Each time he falls, the impact sends blood racing through his veins, coursing through his arteries. His feet are under him now, and he is upright, but he leans too far back for balance and sprawls for his efforts. Each attempt leaves him steadier until, at last, he gains his balance.

Eyes out of focus, bewildered by the big, dim world about him, he staggers to the first upright thing he discerns, which just happens to be a tree. When chewing on the bark proves unproductive, he staggers backward in confusion, tripping over every exposed root until he nuzzles the soft warmth of his mother and chews away at her shoulder and brisket. Sniffing him, she nudges him tenderly with her nose, pushing him ever backwards, trying not to upset him, until he chews at her rear leg. It is almost right and from there instinct seems to prompt him to raise his head and nibble at the distended teat.

Soon, amidst soft sucking noises, the hot colostrum milk, packed with vitamins, antibodies, and sugars for quick energy and heat, strike his tiny stomach. For a moment, he shivers out the cold, then his tail flicks happily back and forth, as though creating a vacuum to suck the milk out of her udder.

At last, his body distended with hot milk, his tiny furnace roaring against the cold, he flops down in contentment, and soon his mother has joined him. A coyote bitch, her own body distorted by approaching birth, trots through the pines, intent upon her way. She will hunt for voles along the edge of the river; experience has taught her that the quickest way to create chaos among a herd of cattle is to approach too close to a new calf.

Luckily, the cow has brought the calf through in spite of the storm. During the night another cow calves, but this calf is not so lucky. It is a difficult birth; the exhausted mother lies too long without rising to lick her calf off, and the calf, with shroud clinging to its nostrils, suffocates once the navel cord is broken.

Each loss is a defeat for me, but the thing I hate most is seeing a life snuffed out before it has had a chance to begin. Let my banker worry about my calving percentage. I keep thinking about the maybes. Maybe if I had gotten up earlier that morning, maybe if I had made that last trip just before dark, maybe if I'd brought that cow in to calve in the shelter of the barn. But the fact remains that there will be one less calf to sell in the fall. The survival of the fittest goes on.

The storm is over as quickly as it began. More cows, after eating their fill of hay, drift unnoticed from the herd and wander a contrived but seemingly aimless course from the herd toward the shelter of the trees. The mysterious compelling force of birth is at them, the desire to be alone, screened from predators, from man, and even from fellow cows.

There is a reason for this aloneness. Cows are herd animals, and when many are calving at the same time, the urges a cow feels often

precede her own actual time of delivery. Sometimes when one cow is trying to calve, another cow, near her own delivery time, is attracted by the birth odors, and tries to claim the other's calf before it is half out of her body. Sometimes she will steal the new calf away, deserting it when she finally goes off to bear her own.

With calving season in full swing, the days are busy. I leave the barn at daylight, riding a colt that needs the riding, needs the routine of day-in day-out saddling that is the calving season. I dread the mornings the most, the ride into every thicket fearing what has happened in the cold, dark hours of the night.

Under my coat I carry a bottle of colostrum milk, warmed from a supply stolen from the dairy cows and stored in the deep freeze. If I can get to where I am going without spilling it down one pant leg I count myself lucky. In my other pockets I carry sulfa pills, a hypodermic syringe, bottles of penicillin and streptomycin, as well as a bottle of iodine concentrate with which to soak the navels of the new calves so that bacteria from the soil will not enter their bodies. The iodine stains my hands like nicotine, soaks through my Levi's to blister the skin on my leg. When my colt shies sideways at a burned stump resembling a black bear, I rattle like a drugstore in an earthquake.

I check each calf I pass on my rides. Has he sucked his mother or is her bag tight? Mother a tight-bagged cow up with her calf and you usually find the calf sick. Does the calf have diarrhea or "scours," is he breathing hard with pneumonia, is his nose pink with good health or spotted blue with fever? Are there tracks in the snow where the cow has been coming back from the feed ground to check him? Has she licked him off clean and dried him; is the hair about his muzzle curled from sucking, or are his flanks hollow from lack of milk? Some cows, through sickness or simply because they are not good mothers, do desert their calves, and by being alert the rancher can save many of these calves from death of the "hollow-belly" or starvation.

As I ride, my glance takes in the whole field as, half consciously, I watch for a calf with a stomachache kicking his belly, for a calf standing dejected, with head hanging low, or a calf lying in the exact same spot he lay on the day before. I watch a calf sucking his mother and try to memorize the pair as they stand, storing up facts in my faulty computer of a brain for future reference. If I find a sick calf standing alone some day, it may come in handy to remember just which of five hundred lookalike cows is his mother. Fortunately, cows do have facial expressions just like people, and even though the coloring is much the same, the total picture can be different. I try to identify them with people they look like; one might resemble my banker Gordon, or my sister Liza.

Finding a calf lying quietly in the woods, I get him up to check his navel against any swelling, make sure that he stands well. I find calf tracks beside him in the snow but they may have been made by another. A calf hidden behind a log remains limp as a wet dishrag, at first refusing to stand, but as I rub his back and speak in the language of his mother, he suddenly stands straight, stretches out one hind leg and then the other, then licks his chops and chews at my pant leg with interest. I see that he is in good health and am now sorry I got him up, for he refuses to lie down again. Staggering over to my half-broken horse, he investigates the colt's legs for a source of milk; the poor horse snorts, cocks one hind leg invitingly as though he would like to kick the calf into the next county. Suddenly, frightened by the calf beneath his belly, the indignant horse jumps sideways, sending the calf sprawling.

Patiently, I try again to keep the calf down, but, dim-eyed still, he trots faithfully after us. In despair, I imitate the call of a calf in distress, and from afar, on the feed ground, comes an answering bawl, as his mother leaves the hay and comes trotting over, ready to defend her calf against all dangers.

As she runs up, sniffing her calf suspiciously, she gives me a look of disgust, and the calf eyes each of us, uncertain of which to fear and which to follow. He is a little afraid of his mother in her agitated condition, but she talks cow talk to him, and as I ride off down the hill, my last view of them through the timbered aisles of the pines shows that he has found the milk supply, and his tiny tail is flicking back and forth happily. She will find a new spot to hide him now, one where he is less likely to be disturbed by nosy people.

After the calves are two or three days old, the cows bring them out of their secret places to the feed ground. Every day, new little calf faces emerge from the forest of trees to the forest of cow legs, where they wander in confusion, uncertain as to which cow is their own mother. Sucking noises excite them. Here a calf is getting his dinner and it seems like such a good idea that another calf wobbles up to join him, but the wise mother has other ideas and, with a well-placed kick, sends the stranger off to find another restaurant. Again and again the calf tries the wrong cow and with every rebuttal the learning process goes on. Then out of the sea of cows, his own mother comes with a low bawl to claim him, and, her belly full of hay, she is his to enjoy for the rest of the day and night.

She lies near him with affection, letting her strength rebuild after the rigors of birth. Slowly, her body heals from the ordeal, the dilation subsides, and her glands go from birth to milk production.

Now that calves have been born, the old cow dog knows better than to leave the feed wagon, for should he descend a mighty uproar would take place, cows bawl angrily, rush shouting for their calves, sniffing every wrong calf in the field until they eventually find their own. Frightened by the din, calves scamper madly; time and again they lose their mothers and add to the confusion. Yesterday, as I was riding a half-broken colt out through the cows, the old dog thought I needed help, and sprang from the wagon into the midst of the herd and ran to me. The last hundred feet were made with a cow just half a jump behind, and the harried dog scurried right under my horse for protection. When the cow tried to follow, horse and cowboy went down in a heap, while the dog beat it for the safety of the wagon.

The great work teams love the routine of the day. From the time the harness is thrown on their backs at dawn until the last bale is fed at noon, they step proudly, each doing his share. On the rough pulls, they lean into the collars; going down hill they lean back into the britching to hold the wagon off their heels. Ice is a constant hazard and they step gingerly over the icy spots, pulling the loaded wagon out to one group of cattle, then back to the stack for another load. Patiently, they stand while the men drop the bales from high on the stack and pile them on the wagon. The lucky horse is the horse nearest the stack, for he can generally manage a snitch of hay.

And all through the day exist the love of the teamster for his animals, the quiet commands by leather or by murmured voice, and the response of the massive animals to a man they cannot see because of the blinders placed on the bridles. In unquestioning obedience, they speed up or slow down, prance or go quietly. "Easy, May, June. Git over, Bess. You, Babe. Back, Sage; back, Sand. Baaaack up now!" The teams keep their ears turned back to listen.

By noon the sweat glistens on their long winter hair, and their hot moist breath makes clouds of fog in the frosty air. As the harnesses are pulled off and hung on wooden pegs or bent horseshoes along the wall, the horses shake, each with his own particular fury. They watch anxiously for their grain, reward for a hard day's work, and munch contentedly as the teamster curries the itch from their sweat-matted coats. Then when they are clean and the feed boxes empty they are turned out the door to roll in the snow. The snow comes slanting in from the south as they turn their rumps toward the storm and bury their heads contentedly in the mangers. Only when his team has rolled and the tired horses are heading side by side toward the feed racks full of bright hay does the teamster think of wandering up to the house for his own noon meal.

The telephone jars the stillness of the lonely night. It is my banker; it is snowing in Klamath Falls, and he's just wondering how I am getting along with my calving. I never tell him the truth, of course. If it's snowing, I tell him clear and calm. If I've lost six calves, I compromise and tell him one. He'll know soon enough when we add up the figures in the fall. And who knows, maybe some of the cows will have twins this year. Twins! I always plan on them, but recall only a set or two in the last ten years.

CHAPTER 5

MARCH COMES SUDDENLY, capricious, now sullen, now blustery, now teasing with momentary summer, now violent as any storm in winter. I would give thirty days of my life for it to be April. My eyes burn and water from the ordeal of watching the skies to catch the first flight of sandhill cranes returning from their long journey to the south. So filled are they with wild, shout-ing, joyous, irrepressible laughter, so unabashed in their happiness to be back over their nesting grounds, I stare about me in new wonder, in sudden appreciation of the fate which allowed me to be the one to dwell here.

The cranes arrive in family groups consisting of mated pairs and one or both of their two young if they have survived the dangers of winter in the agricultural valleys of California. Most fre-quently, they arrive with only one. Four miles high, they sail in wide tacks in the azure, windswept heights above Taylor Butte to the south. Shield-ing my eyes against the glare, I catch only what may be the flash of sunlight on motionless wings; then, faint from the heavens, comes the sound of sandhill trumpets from an unseen land. The cranes call out the old familiar sights below, then start the long circling glide, round and round the vortex, losing altitude slowly, cautiously, watching for change. Long black legs already trailing expectantly, they stake out the airspace above their marshy fielddom of the year before.

Towards their young they show a certain tolerance still, but let a stray sandhill so much as invade their clouds, and male and female sound their battle clarions, flooding the long miles of the valley with resounding territorial challenge. Like hedgehopping military bombers avoiding enemy radar, they fly swift and low toward the invaders, bounce to the edge of the territory, careful not to overshoot, and with nary a blow struck for glory, shout the enemy into retreat. If a male is tolerant of an encroaching female, his mate is not and drives her away in a fury. As in Homo sapiens, it is the female who keeps the husband in the straight and narrow.

The young bird wanders with his parents, probing the quickening mucks of the marshes with his sturdy black bill. He watches quizzically as his gentle parents, in defense of their nesting ground, turn savage, raucous, and nervous. He himself feels nothing, but probes the earth nonchalantly as their battles with neighbors turn to frenzy. At this period he is totally committed to a sociable existence, craving the company of other cranes. As yet, his parents are his world.

But change is not long in coming. His father's eyes, reptilian, fiercely yellow, watch him closely where before he was ignored. The young crane moves to his mother to probe beside her, secure in her benignity, but suddenly the father is there between them, stabbing at him with rapier beak. Nervously the youngster moves out of range. He follows them as they feed, trailing after them as he did as a chick. Days pass and his relationship with his father grows worse. Even his mother seems a stranger. He is now an intruder in his own family group. Suddenly the giant male is truly angry and, croaking furious curses at him, flies at him with onslaught after onslaught.

Alone for the first time, confused, the young crane flees toward a pair of cranes feeding in an adjoining marsh, calling endearments to them out of his loneliness. The great male stands at full height, astonished at his impudence, then, with a sudden squawk of rage, charges and drives him from the territory, more disturbed than ever. Circling on high, he sees pair after pair feeding together in their nesting areas. He calls to them plaintively, suggesting friendship, but if they answer at all it is with derision and anger. Croaking plaintively, with heartbreak, he sails on, solitary, confused, without identity.

Below him, his marshlands give way to vast ridges of pine, of bald lava crowns ringed with fir. Then far away he sees the shine of water and is magnetized toward it. Again and again as he sails over the marshes, he hears the mated pairs below shout warning. Timidly, he lands beside a small flock of birds feeding on a sagebrushed hillside. He feeds for a time beside the group but alone, shrinking warily from every bird that gets too close. In the main, these are juveniles like himself from one to three years old. There are a few older birds scattered through the flock. There is no thought of nesting in any of them, no stirring of instincts, hence no territorialism. In our young friend this will not come until his fourth year. Quietly, he feeds up into the group and is ignored.

The group feeds happily together, sometimes dancing, pirouetting, and leaping high in pure joy. By evening their careless flight will have taken them to yet another valley.

It would be hard to live here at Yamsi without loving the greater sandhill cranes, so much are they part of the sound, the mood, and scene of the historic West. As the marshes went, so went the cranes. Wetland after wetland was drained for agriculture. Indigenous, for the most part, to the United States, the conspicuous four-foot pearl-gray birds, with rose-red caruncular crowns, fell first to the guns of hunters, then to the guns of vandals. I took them for granted as a boy, not really appreciating just how much their raucous music from the marshes was part of my world. Year by year in valley after valley, the great voice dwindled and was no more, as pair after pair failed to return from migration to the south, and if they did return found their marshes drained. People, pesticides, powerlines, pollution, all contributed to the near demise of the species.

By chance I rescued a pair of eggs from a flood, and raised what was to be the first of a long line of sandhill cranes underfoot. The first was Sandy, a female destined to give new hope to the endangered species program. I was suddenly no longer just a rancher. Without knowing it

I had become a conservationist, dedicated to helping save the resources of my country.

By deliberate bad management and poor irrigation practices, I soon had marshes where once there were only clover and blue grass meadows. Five pair of sandhill cranes nesting where before there was only one. My banker was aghast, but I knew where my joys were.

Sometimes as I walked with him, trying to ignore his grim visage, a great sandhill with six-foot wingspread would tower above us racing the clouds, and I would feel a sudden burst of pride that perhaps I had helped put him there. I would sing out with a burst of joy I couldn't contain. Look! Just look up there My banker would look at me sadly, glancing perhaps at the crane, but then about him at the cattails where once was clover, then at me, for whom he had once held hope. And I would look at him, too, each of us suddenly very much alone, and separate.

And I couldn't really blame him, for he hadn't experienced the great, crashing insight into the future that had gripped me. Where once I talked to him of bull pedigrees, of roping calves, of the traditions of the Old West, now I was fervent, overly didactic, preaching conservation, ranting about man's terrible rape of the earth as fervently as any Bible Belt Baptist foams on about sin. If I knew now where my satisfactions lay, I also knew my angers and sorrows. Living here almost alone in the wilderness, where people expected a last frontier of normalcy, a reservoir of the past, I could see change coming fast, the destruction of our great land coming fast, from our wildlife component to the very air we were once supposed to have free forever. An asset too vast, we once thought naively, to be lost or changed.

I am sixty miles from town, yet there is often enough smoke in my valley to make my eyes water, to burn my lungs. Smoke from fields burning, from pulp mills, from wigwam sawdust burners, from forest fires two hundred miles away. And yet the great Western tradition on which I had been nursed would have me a simple cowboy, pulling the sands of history about my ears, shrugging off changes for the worse.

But suddenly I was choking mad. I choked on pollution, burned with flashing insight into a desolate future devoured and destroyed by apathetic man. I was enraged at man's conceit, that he could pollute the streams, foul the air, cut down the timber, shoot the animals and birds, cause erosion, drain the marshes, dam the rivers, bisect every empty area on the map with a road, change the stratosphere, foul earth and ocean—that he thought he had the right to do these things when I saw he damn well hadn't. Instead, as maybe the brightest animal that has yet come along, he had an obligation to himself and other species not to destroy the world, but to make it better. He is a strange creature, man. A ten per cent reduction in pollution lulls him into apathy. Yet there should be NO pollution beyond Nature's ability, with man's help, to restore all to the original.

March should be a month of new hope, of new beginning, but I am no longer sure how many Marches there will be as we have known them. Loving the land I have come to live every moment as my last, being apathetic about nothing, drinking the last dreg of pleasure from the sight of a bursting bud, or the furry mittens of the pussy willow.

THE CALVING GROUNDS ARE littered with tiny calves, and still they come. Every morning new little calf faces come in from the forest, trailing their solicitous mothers. From morning to dark, I ride doctoring wet pink navels with iodine to prevent infection.

The work teams and saddle horses are shedding now, and the hair comes off by the fistful, lining the saddle blankets, the collar pads, and the harnesses with mats of dull, lifeless hair. Soon their sleek, spring coats will show through, shiny, soft as velvet, with a sensuality that has thrilled womanhood since first horses became tame to the touch. Lady Godiva didn't ride that way for nothing.

Sprouting new hair, the teams must be roached again to prevent the collars from chafing. The teamster stands on the wagon after the cattle are fed and the team, tied short to the bulwarks, leans toward him, eyes half closed, enjoying his touch, dreaming of summer laziness. The blades of the rusty sheep shears sing at every bite as he clips the bristling blue-black mane short and even. None of the modern conveniences of power shears for us, since in the barn there is no electricity. The sheep shears will last as long as there are draft horses at Yamsi.

The snow is settling fast. The rivulets are late sleepers, but in the afternoon they descend the hills ranting and roaring, changing the face of the earth in minuscule until evening when the chill puts them back in their snowy caves in hibernation. The meadows are a sea of brown water and brown ice, and the cows tread daintily, keeping to the higher ground. Now and then a cow cuts loose from the cud-chewing herd to venture out over the drowning fields, stepping from one tilting platter of ice to another, hoping for a wisp of green grass, but she must return disappointed for it is still winter. Along the edge of retreating snowdrifts edged with mold there is only the faintest trace of the green that will start in April. Only in the river where the water moderates the frost do a few clumps of swamp grass start to show their heads, and the cows make a daily pilgrimage to them as a wolf visits his territorial scent posts.

The wind is sharp in March and the weather unsettled, quickly changeable. Ride out with a heavy coat and you are too hot; ride out boldly in shirt sleeves and the north wind comes chasing down out of nowhere to drive you home sick with cold, dreaming of a hot drink, of the desperate scalding feeling a potbellied stove gives to denim trouser legs coming suddenly up against goose-pimpled skin.

One moment the cows are too warm, seeking the shade of the pines, and the next they are covered with a blanket of snow. But neither sun nor snow stay long. Like the old saying about Chicago: "If you don't like the weather, wait five minutes."

When one calves out a bunch of cows, weather is a vital factor. Sunlight kills off soil bacteria that cause a calf a peck of troubles. If the weather is damp and wet, not only is the calf's resistance lowered to invasion by a variety of diseases, but the bacteria themselves flourish in the damp soils. After a session of rain or snow, the bill for antibiotics grows astronomically. The veterinary supply stores in town could plot the spring weather without even looking out the window by charting the fluctuations in sales of animal medicines. After a storm an infectious scour often sets in that weakens the calf until he succumbs to pneumonia or another secondary infection.

But if the weather isn't a factor, then there are other calf diseases to keep one from prosperity. White muscle disease, associated with a deficiency of the trace mineral selenium, is prevalent where hay has been heavily fertilized. Enterotoxemia affects the intestines of the calves. Just when the cowman has his herd protected against one disease by vaccination, a new disease or a new form of the old one jumps in to take a heavy toll of young calves. Once they are dead, all the science in the world can't bring them back. It's a wonder any of them reach maturity.

Drifting leisurely with the herd, prying into odd corners of the fields, I spend my waking hours riding, seldom out of the saddle except to help a calf.

If I spot a tight-bagged cow, I trail her for hours if necessary until she finds her calf. A tight udder is generally a sign of trouble—that her calf is lost, sick, dead, or hasn't yet been born. Or perhaps the wind has made the cow's teats so sore and chapped that she refuses to let her calf suck. I rope her then, massage her teats with lanolin, and milk the pressure from her distended bag, making sure finally that the calf gets his dinner without overdoing.

If a calf survives the death or loss of his mother, he becomes an orphan, dogie, or bummer, catching a meal of hot milk wherever he may steal it. It is a tough way to make a living, but he may become a master of his trade. He waits nonchalantly until another calf is busy at his dinner, then slips up quietly while the cow is lost in her dreams, and joins the rightful heir at his meal. Often he sucks from directly behind the cow, "sucking hind teat" as the expression goes. For various reasons, this is not the best place in the world to stand. The other calf ignores the thief, but when the mother discovers him she sends him sprawling with a well-placed kick calculated to hurt. She watches carefully until the bummer wanders off to try elsewhere.

Beloved of cowboys in legend and song, bummers are a sad little group. While they fare well on occasion, it is either feast or famine, and the feast can be as damaging as famine to a little tummy not used to prosperity. Gradually their hair loses its bloom, they become stunted, and resemble a bunch of potbellied little old men. The best thing that can happen to a bummer is to be found by one of my children, taken to the barn, and grafted on one of the dairy cows. These are capable of taking care of four calves at once, and during the course of the season can grow out four five-hundred pound calves, or a ton of beef.

But there is a labor factor here, since the cows must be put into stanchions twice a day while the calves suck.

What the Holsteins have that the Herefords don't is an abundance of milk. A beef cow must give just enough milk for one calf, and not too much, for then the calf would leave some in the bag, and the cow's physical processes would cut back her production. If a beef cow happens to give too much milk, then she must be milked out. Some old timers yoked the calf of a heavy producer to a bummer, so the cow would have to let both suck at once. After a time, the two calves would get on surprisingly well.

Our big black-and-white Holsteins are rather stupid. If they were very smart they wouldn't tolerate the abuse they get, the hustling, pushing, greedy calves, butting them right in the udder to knock down more milk. Instead of coming meekly in, slaves to the grain we put for them in the stanchions, intelligent cows would run and hide in the timber as far from the barn as possible.

They are probably the only cows on the ranch that make money for the management, and one has a hot source of milk ready on demand for any calf born out in the field that has trouble getting the furnace going. Many a time this little boost is the difference between life and death for a calf.

WHAT A JOY THE CHILDREN ARE IN March when they arrive late Friday afternoon for their weekend at the ranch. School is quickly forgotten, book education traded quickly for practical experience. Ginny and Marsha race each other for the corrals, tie ropes pounded into hip pockets in order to trick their unsuspecting horses into going to work. The horses stare at them as they crunch out over the snow. Heads flung high, they are wild horses watching danger from some high desert rim, ready to wheel and run. But then suddenly an old horse nickers softly, expectantly, ruining the illusion, and the whole herd is trotting forward necks bowed, noses tossing, hoping for grain.

Marsha arches the palm of her small hand. Her mare, Tune, named after Homer's gelding, sniffs suspiciously, ears laid back. Then, as she smells grain, a gentle glaze masks the meanness of her as she bares her great teeth and gulps grain from the delicate whiteness of Marsha's hand.

"One slip of her teeth and no more piano lessons for you," Ginny reminds her, then proceeds to do the same with Bones. Once their favorites are securely haltered, they worry about the problem of hurting the other horses' feelings and can't head back for the barn until each animal has been fondly scratched. When they have paid their respects to all, in they come, leading Bones and Tune, with thirty other horses nodding patiently along behind. Before the advent of the girls, it took a wrangler to corral the horses; now they come in on their own. If he could see, Homer Smith would think the ranch had gone to hell.

Great pads of shed horsehair float to the floor of the stalls as Ginny and Marsha curry a clean place for their saddles. Within moments they are on horseback and away, riding the pond field for new calves, searching out their favorite cows to see if they have calved.

A cow looks up from her scavenging about this morning's feed ground, stares at the approaching horsemen, and gives a low bawl of recognition. "It's Biddy," Ginny cries. She throws herself from her horse, dashes forward, and hugs the big cow by the neck. A wild cow would have made the treetops with her. As Ginny scratches Biddy's belly, the cow's eyes glaze with comfort; she heaves a loud sigh, belches up her cud, and chews contentedly.

"What a funny-looking cow," Marsha teases as she rides on her way, not waiting for Ginny's hateful glare.

Biddy is the prima donna of the herd. She was a bummer once, half starved, jug-bellied, head covered with manure from a meal she'd tried

gamely for but failed to get from a big short-tempered cow. For a couple of days, she had lain beside the body of her dead mother, but hunger drove her on, sucking on trees, fence posts, dry cows, anything that would stand still.

When Ginny found her, Biddy wobbled weakly away. There was a fever scab over one speckled nostril, which had been kicked half loose by the last outraged cow. Cornered against a fallen log, she sniffed Ginny's offered hand timidly and liked what she smelled. One moment she was trembling in fear; the next she was chewing Ginny's trouser leg for milk. That night, Ginny was hours late for supper, ignoring her own comfort until Biddy had a full belly of warm milk and had been ensconced in her own private quarters in the barn.

Ever since that day, Biddy has been a thorn in my side. The hostile start she had in life was more than all the tender loving care in the world could undo, and she grew from a jug-bellied, runt-headed, high-tailboned calf to a jug-bellied, runt-headed, high-tailboned heifer. That fall, when I cut the heifers for quality, saving the best for replacements, Biddy was naturally the first one I culled from the herd.

Sitting astride her horse, helping me out, Ginny stared in anguish, her big eyes filling with tears. But she kept silent and waited until I was looking up at a flock of sandhill cranes to slip Biddy back in the herd. Five times that afternoon I cut her out, until I got to wondering how I could possibly have that many bad heifers. Every time I cut her out, Biddy would go right over to stand by Ginny's horse, to visit until my back was turned.

When I finally caught on, I gave Ginny a stern lecture on achieving quality in a herd. I told her that a high tail set was one of the hardest defects to breed out of one's cattle, and how one had to be quite merciless in kicking out any animal that failed to measure up in quality to the rest of the herd.

"Yes, Father," Ginny agreed.

I left Biddy locked in the corral with the other culls that night, ordering a cattle truck for morning. But in the morning Biddy was gone, and Ginny looked as though she had swallowed a secret.

From then on Biddy and Ginny were pals. Whenever we drove the cattle from one field to another, Biddy would follow Ginny's horse everywhere, so that in a herd of five hundred cows, four hundred ninety-nine would be in front of the horses and one would be following behind. Whenever the banker would come out to see what a fine herd we were building with all the money he had lent us, Biddy, with her drooped back line, sad head, and enormous gut, would be standing right at the edge of the herd.

Biddy soon learned to open all the corral gates as well as the doors to the barn, and, being a sociable creature, invited all her special cronies in for a feast in the haymow or an orgy in the grain bin. And often as not when we were particularly interested in maintaining her virgin sanctity, her guests would include a friendly Hereford bull. So when all the other heifers on the ranch were safely protected from being bred too early and from the attendant dangers of calving at too small a size, Biddy picked herself the hugest, heaviest-boned brute of a bull on the ranch. When I blamed it all on Ginny and the fact that she had spoiled this heifer beyond all salvation, Ginny shrugged. "Don't worry, Dad. Maybe it will improve her figure."

And so, not in the spring, but right smack dab in the middle of winter, when Ginny and Marsha had invited some twenty of their girl friends up for a snow party, Biddy's hour came. Ginny came bounding in to where I was comfortably curled before the fireplace reading a good book and relishing the fact that I had to go nowhere, with the excited announcement that Biddy was trying to calve.

And so she was, poor misguided creature. One couldn't help but feel sorry for her; she lay in a snow bank with great wet flakes pelting her in the face, miserable in a pool of her own melt water, and with a genuine look of contrition that indicated perhaps that she understood that this huge bellyache she was suffering was the fault of no one but herself, and that if a certain bull came rumbling by now she darned sure wouldn't open the gate for him. Right then and there, Biddy groaned and began to strain, and twenty little girls got a lesson about life I would have kept from them if I could.

Biddy licked Ginny's face with her rough tongue and groaned in pain. Forty little hands helped shove her to her feet, and push her toward the barn, where we laid her down on a soft green blanket of hay. She groaned almost with pleasure as Ginny rubbed her down with a burlap sack.

"Will she die, Mr. Hyde?" asked a little girl, her mittened hands clutching the end of her pigtail to her heart.

"Are you kidding?" Ginny snapped, showing a bravado that was only skin deep. "My dad's really good at delivering calves. He hasn't lost a patient yet."

Actually, I'd lost rather a lot of patients, especially heifers that, like Biddy, were too young and too small to calve. But now, surrounded by a ring of intent young faces, I had to keep my own courage up. "Of course I'll save her," I promised. "This one's easy compared to some I've saved." But it soon became evident as I tried to slide the calf's head out into the daylight, that this was the hardest, tightest, ghastliest job I'd ever faced.

"Better go into the house, girls," I suggested, "and leave Biddy and me here alone."

No one moved and Biddy groaned terribly.

"You girls run to the house now and bring me a pot of hot water. Make sure it boils for half an hour," I suggested, not quite knowing what to do with hot water if they brought it.

"It will only take one of us to do that," another little girl said doubtfully, not moving her lips, as though she were afraid her braces would fall out.

"You go," a girl with a hood over her blonde hair said to another.

"No, you go. I have to stay here and help Mr. Hyde."

In the end they all stayed, every last one of them, sniffing big, wet-nosed sniffs in the chill winter air, eyes big as saucers, genuine in their concern.

I spent a desperate half hour trying every way I knew to lead the huge calf out of the small passage afforded by Biddy's pelvis. My arms ached; my fingers had no more strength left. I lay down beside Biddy, put my forehead against her fevered, heaving flank, trying to gather my own strength for her next attempt. Every time I opened my eyes, I looked right into the trusting eyes of the children. Right now I needed not hot water but a rifle with which to end her misery, for I had lost hope. Biddy herself had ceased to strain, her eyes seemed sadly glazed.

Ginny eased beside me, and laid Biddy's big bovine head on her lap. "Come on, Bid," she said brightly. "Let's get the show on the road, the troops out of the snow, and all that, so I can show my friends your calf."

Biddy opened her fevered eyes for a moment as if in surprise, then closed them. But she began to strain once more. I watched for a moment unconvinced, then once again I straightened the chains I had put on the calf's front feet, and worked the jack which was pushing on the cow while pulling on the calf. Suddenly there was a popping noise as the calf's head slipped through the pelvis. I closed my eyes and kept cranking. When I opened them again, miracle of miracles, the shoulders were through, then suddenly the hips. With a rush of body fluids and wastes, the calf slid out upon the barn floor, breaking the pink cord of his umbilical. I held him by the heels, draining the fluids from his mouth, straightened his tongue, then stretched him out, working his legs to force air into his lungs.

There was no sign of life. Desperately I worked, ignoring my audience; to have stopped trying would have been a breach of faith. What could I tell them? Even though I couldn't look at them I could tell from the nose blowing that a good share of the girls were quietly weeping.

Then, suddenly, through the gaunt rib cage of the cold wet calf, I saw the flicker of a heartbeat. Rhythmically I worked his legs, and was almost convinced that I had imagined the murmur when the calf choked and gasped in a big breath. A cheer went up for Ginny's father as the calf raised its head.

"We knew you could do it all the time," the smallest of the girls said. But she had tearstains on her face, ample testimony as to her doubts.

Biddy was up and licking off her calf properly when I finally made it back to the warmth and comfort of the ranch house.

"If she had a tough delivery, I do hope you didn't let the little girls watch," my wife said.

"Just a routine delivery," I replied. It had been a long day.

Biddy and her calf flourished, of course. How could they have done otherwise? My wife took to hiding the monthly grain bill from me, but I soon knew the truth from the way Biddy acquired a glossy coat in spite of her lactation, and the calf grew and grew and grew. It was evident that Ginny must have roped Slim in on her project, for while Ginny was in school, someone was feeding Biddy grain.

It was a good calf, too, for most of Biddy's defects were starvation-induced and not hereditary. In the fall, as I was cutting out fine big heifer calves, keeping only the top ten per cent of the calves for replacements, I nodded to a husky candidate I was just driving from the herd. "Here's the best calf I've seen yet," I called to Ginny.

"Of course," said Ginny, looking very pleased. "That's Biddy's calf."
And so it was.

Biddy still opens the barn door, still invites her friends in to feast on
the hay piles, and is more trouble than she is worth, but sometimes
when I have been off riding alone, I come around a bend to see my
daughter sitting on the lonely meadows, her horse grazing aimlessly
about her, while Biddy has come out of the herd for a visit, her shaggy
head clasped in my daughter's arms. Then I am glad that I have kept
Biddy around. Or have I? Most likely I have been had, managed, and
manipulated. Do I really have the hard practical heart I would like to
think I have, or does my family merely use me? Is this life the growing
up of children or merely the raising of Father?

WHAT A LOVE GINNY HAS FOR THE
place and for every living thing here. If a calf dies, part of her dies too,
and she spends her waking days on the ranch worrying about them.
Sometimes when things are slack she sits astride a decaying log in the
forest, enjoying her loneliness as I enjoy mine, creating out of it as I
create out of mine, writing stories, writing poetry, absorbing, trying to
fathom the not-so-silent mood of the forest.

A flock of evening grosbeaks passes over her head, drenching the
pines with music. She watches them tenderly, reminded of Alec, the
white-and-yellow roisterer who commanded the upper ranch house
for a year before his accidental death at the hands of a town cat.

He is still mourned. She refuses to remove a pile of droppings from
her window ledge, a mess of cracked seed from those long afternoons
he spent at her window, calling through the screen to passing flocks
he could never rejoin. You passed him in the upper halls and he fluttered up on you, using your limbs as tree branches, searching for
delicacies in every pocket. Ginny and Alec were great pals, and the
mess will be there next year. It is her room, her hideaway, and should
be as she wants it. When Alec was alive great flocks of evening grosbeaks descended to the pines outside the window to visit; now only
the orange crossbills come, shredding the armored pine cones with
scissors beaks, littering the snow beneath with the shards of cones
and discarded wings of seeds that flew nowhere. The skull of an old
cow, so ancient the wrinkles are falling off the ends of her horns, hangs
from a stump where the girls have been practicing their roping, and

the crossbills pick happily away at the thin bone of the nostrils, supplementing their diet with calcium.

Should I worry that there is nothing in her room that is really feminine? It smells like the harness room of an old stable. On the walls, in profusion, old buggy harnesses, collars, headstalls, haimes, horseshoes, and hackamores. Horse pictures galore, a rawhide reata given her by her friend Jimmy Rapley, and renovated by her friend Slim. Spurs of all shapes, and more than a hundred old rusty bits she found in a barrel in her grandmother's barn in California.

She is sixteen now. Will there ever be room for boys in her life? As a flock of evening grosbeaks flies over our valley bound for another, I see her stiffen, longing to fly with them. I understand. There but for the years go I.

The sound of her flute echoes in the nighttime loneliness of a world not quite waked with spring. Birds stir on their perches; owls blink at this strange new territorial song. Rabbits, and maybe fairies, come out to dance on the frozen lawn. A draft sweeps through the house as the hot air slides past her out the open window and is lost in the evening chill. She plays in the marching band at school, resplendent in uniform, regulated into conformity, dressed for anonymity. Perhaps my wife and I are the only ones who notice that her Levi's are hanging down a couple of inches beneath the cuffs of her uniform, and the clarinetist next to her is having trouble tending to both her music and her allergy to horse dandruff.

At thirteen, Marsha too loves horses, but she is not of Ginny's reflective, poetic fiber. Blonde, feminine, willowy, musical, merry, sociable, athletic yet the eternal woman. She is the one who naturally chooses a pretty dress to wear, while Ginny is happy only in Levi's with the scent of horse upon them. Marsha has the appetite of a humming bird, breaks all the dietary rules of good health, and is the only one in the family never to be sick. Give her a lecture on how she can't possibly exist on what she eats, and she goes out and breaks the all-city record for the girl's broad jump. Leaving half her food on her plate, she slips out without dessert, grabs a mane holt on her waiting horse, and gallops off bareback, scorning a saddle, blonde hair mingling with the black of the horse's mane as they race the wind.

Fearless Marsha, slender and fragile. Last summer I caught her in the corral astride a wild-eyed unbroken bay colt she'd named Jimmy.

Shaking with real fear, I charged down the hillside, running as I haven't in twenty years to save my petite little daughter from ghastly injury.

"Relax, Daddy-O." She grinned to my shouted warnings, pleased at least that I cared. "I've been riding him for two whole weeks now. Watch how well he turns." When she finally slipped from the colt's back, he turned, followed her in adoration across the corral, then stood, head draped across her shoulder, waiting to be scratched.

She too has a feeling for nature, a love of the lonely reaches of the ranch and the wild creatures with whom she shares the land. She was only eight when I gave her some duck eggs I'd rescued from the ravages of a spring flood, and told her to put them under her pet bantam setting hen. I was busy with my own egg rescue operation and promptly forgot about her eggs except to note with satisfaction that she was conscientiously busy with her project, and that whatever she was raising over there along the stream beneath the pines was getting bigger and bigger. To my surprise, I found that she had raised a brood of ruddy ducks, among the most difficult of species due in part to the difficulty of inducing them to eat. I rushed to her in excitement, begging her to divulge her secret.

But Marsha refused to be awed. "It was easy, Dad. Nothing to it and all that jazz. I just fed them Friskies dog food and milk." In such manner, in the world of aviculture, are breakthroughs made.

Marsha loves to ride alone in the pine forests, carrying on a constant stream of chatter with her horse, just as though the horse were another person—at times a warm personal friend, at times a child to be chided gently and firmly for doing wrong. And the horses seem to listen. How often do I ride through some remote forest glade l haven't seen in years, only to find Marsha's tracks where she has been exploring before me. As with many ranch families, the girls are the cowboys, and the boys have other interests.

One eye on the hay pile and the other on the weather. Will the hay last until the green grass is high enough to sustain the herd? In the Klamath valleys, hay is scarce and every day huge truck and trailer loads go out of the country to the dairies of western Oregon. As the supplies dwindle, the price rises astronomically. If I buy more, it will cost me thirty-five dollars a ton, or roughly double what it cost me in late summer. Money again. I generally couldn't care less about it, since my joys are in things money can't buy. But if I intend to save the ranch for the children, the dollar has to be a pretty important part of my life.

My wife is the practical one. She wants to know about every calf that died so that she can keep score. I dread telling her. One born backwards; head hanging down, he drowned in the body fluids of the cow when his umbilical ruptured. One calf lost through the wafer-thin ice of the ditch. One calf born at night to a cow that didn't feel up to licking it off. He was stone cold in an hour. Three dead from undetermined causes, two from pneumonia, one from navel infection, four from infectious scours, one from white muscle, two from enterotoxemia. "What does it matter how they died?" I growl. "It's too late to save them." The mothers of the lost calves look sad, but they go on eating, running up just as much of a feed bill as the cows that are raising me calves. Have they no shame?

March is the month of spring vacation, when the ranch house throws off the silence of winter and is filled with constant laughter of a family enjoying each other, of young hearts happy to be home. No longer do I feel guilty at building in the big stone fireplace a fire built of wood my wife cut, for the fire is no longer just for me. If, in my busy life, wood cutting were left up to me, we would all freeze. It is Gerdi who must do all the things I leave undone.

Dayton, a sophisticated seventeen, helps with the feeding to give the men some respite from their drudgery, then, caught teasing his sisters, is sent off to work off his excess energy in the woodpile. The house smells of new-baked bread and pine smoke as the huge furnace in the basement ticks away. Through the years, bolts have corroded, and the cast iron door has warped and cracked, looking in the gloom like some monstrous jack-o'-lantern with crooked smile. Warm freshets of fragrant air ascend to the winter-cold rooms. Icicles form along the eaves in memory of cowboys long ago who as amateur carpenter left a crack here and there to let the warm air slip into the attic darkness. How nice to have the whole house heated instead of just the room in which I live.

Now that there is no danger of pipes bursting with the frost, I hook up the plumbing, and the tin shower upstairs drums with the crash of water as children try to wash off the stain of knowledge.

Today ten-year-old John took his eight-year-old brother Taylor out to start his lifetime bird list. His first birds were a sandhill crane, a

bald eagle, a Townsend's solitaire, and a great gray owl, birds a great many serious birders don't see in a lifetime.

John has done his room in raccoon skins, rusted steel traps, and old guns. From his door hangs a beaver trap knocker on a level designed to knock out the eye of an adult trying to enter. Hanging from the ceiling are bird nests and model planes; on the wall advertisements for go-carts and engines, stickers for oil additives. A boy being a boy. All he wants out of life at the moment is a little tractor with a snow-plow. For this he shoveled snow all winter. Right now he's only $960.00 short of having earned the one he's been admiring all winter in the catalogue. I keep telling him that the fields are full of loafing work teams he is welcome to employ but it's not the same. Horses don't have engines.

Taylor's pet Canada goose is at the window every morning to greet him for the morning's adventure. But today, Taylor is too sad to play. Last night a great horned owl got his pet duck. A great problem, these super efficient owls. I made tape recordings of their territorial hoots and played them super loud, but all the recordings did was keep me awake at night and attract bigger and bigger owls.

But spring is a time of new hope, a time to start all over again. Let Taylor find the first chukkar partridge egg or pheasant egg and he'll forget his sorrow in excitement. Already there is a new apple box in the chicken house with muddy footprints on its blonde sterility, which he has been using as a scaffold to peer into nests. Even the sandhill cranes I once took to be mine alone call excitedly when they hear his voice, knowing that his pockets are often stuffed with grain. They haunt his footsteps almost sadly, as though they sense that in a few days he must return to school.

MARCH TWENTY-FIFTH. IT IS MY birthday and I'm expected to drive in to Klamath Falls for supper with the family. But here on the ranch it's just another day. One catastrophe after another. An old cow adopted a calf that wasn't hers, stole him from the real mother, and knocked me down when I tried to take the calf away. She was so sure of herself, but I had doubts for I could see the front feet of her own calf as yet unborn, sticking out from under her tail. Once her own baby was born things came back to proper perspective. But as I tried to doctor the new calf's navel with iodine, she knocked me down again.

Then in the far corner of the field, screened by a rotten log from the rest of the cattle, I found a cow straining out her insides, roped her and sewed her up again. While I was occupied, two calves died being born. I called the veterinary to doctor a sick cow but she died in treatment. The least he could have done would have been to give me a fancy name for what was wrong with her. We both admitted we were stumped and each admired the other for his honesty. But still, he sent me a bill.

Just as I was about to head for town, I found a cow having difficulties having a backwards calf. I had just delivered it when she jumped up unexpectedly, knocked me down into the puddles and standing on my middle commenced, in her excitement, to lick my clothes. I shrugged. By now the kids are probably just finishing off my birthday cake. Sixty miles left to drive. In my haste the other day I left the car lights on and the battery is dead. There is no one to tow me.

But the family understands. It is Yamsi being Yamsi, Dad being Dad.

"Which cow was it, Dad?" Ginny asks, her face tender with concern not for me but for the animals. How do you describe a certain one of five hundred lookalike Hereford cows all of which are hornless, white-faced, and red, bred to uniformity? I do my best and she says, "Oh, that must be Tweedles!" and goes back to eating her late snack.

"Going to have enough hay to last until spring, Dad?" Taylor asks, peering sleepily down through the banister. He's not much of a hand to talk and when he's only in second grade the question seems too big for him, as though perhaps he's been listening to his parents worry. Or maybe the banker stopped him on his way home from school and asked him.

I am not too happy about being forty-four. I remember when my mother was forty-four (I happened to covet a gun of that caliber) and I thought she was awfully old. And yet I still think of myself as young. I had intended by now to be financially much further along, own my own ranch free and clear. Hah! Instead I'm in the same financial jam-up I was in when I bought the ranch from Uncle Buck a decade ago.

I have a good ranch, one of the best; my family and I do much of our own work. Why doesn't the business pay off better? Why is it ranchers must be such individualists and fight working together for better prices for beef?

Every rancher knows he can't go on forever borrowing ever more deeply on his land. In terms of cash, the drivers of the cattle trucks make more than I do. By 1972 plumbers in San Francisco could be making $27,000 per year and will probably be complaining about the high price of beef. How nice it would be to go into a bank and be treated like a depositor and not just a bad risk.

The children refuse to go to bed until they have heard every detail of what has happened at the ranch in the three days since they were last there. I don't dare tell Taylor that a goshawk killed one of his hens.

Taylor knows every hen on a personal basis. "Did the little brown hen lay today, Dad?"

"Yes, of course." Hoping he will go to sleep, not knowing really which hen he means.

His face screws up in puzzlement. "Don't see how she could, really. I thought you said they don't lay when they are molting?"

Days pass. The cranes are noisier in the fields, defending their territories in earnest, driving their young away, flying low over the marshes, dropping suddenly, unobserved into the secret world of their nesting spots. Tossing their heads nervously, the Canada geese fill the air with territorial clamor, and when I pass them in the fields they slink off, heads low, trying to be nonchalant. I rescue a nest built with no discretion on a low bank where the rising stream will wash it away, put the eggs under my shirt against my naked skin for warmth. I feel real or imagined lice crawling up my belly. The young will be hatched out under a bantam and returned to the wild as soon as they are able to fend for themselves. But the bereft parents curse me angrily as though I am a predator, and I feel my guilt.

Thousands of crossbills sing merrily from the jack pines. This morning a pigeon hawk stooped at them and they rose as one in huge flocks until there couldn't have been a bird left in the trees, rose from their perches as though they preferred to take their chances in the open, as though they thought to confuse the hawk in the sheer mass of their numbers. Sweeping upward they flew as though gravity had suddenly been reversed and they were free falling into space. Then as suddenly they plunged back into a wood on the far side of the valley. All that was left in the trees for the moment was a silly, twittering club of siskins.

The children phone from town and catch me in a rare visit to the house. I can hear their laughter in the background. "What's he saying? What's he saying? Let me talk."

Ginny feigns seriousness. "Here's a letter from the bank, Dad. We opened it. The bank just foreclosed on the ranch." She pauses until suddenly she becomes frightened that she has waited too long. "April Fool!"

April Fool! Can it really be April already?

CHAPTER 6

LUSTY FROM THE HALF-SAFETY OF his willow bush throne, a Mongolian pheasant cock crows, then drums his April wings mightily against the hollow log of his wine-stained chest. He had better practice that call, for it is rusty with disuse. Two hens, pale buff, tinted with wild rose, are as unimpressed as I, and ignore him to feed on a hatch of winter-stupid beetles which have chosen the wrong hour to sun themselves dry on a wrinkled cow chip.

This morning, a blue-gray goshawk came hedge-hopping in to strafe the flock, but he was a fool to have tried. All the stupid pheasants went to the horned owls last winter, and these are corps of the elite, experts at survival, in whose pituitary glands flows the stuff of wildness. The cock leaped cackling into the air, and, with monstrous jet-roar, beat his way into the sun's rays. The startled hawk, losing all but the noise, landed confused, uncertain, exposed to the laughter of the jays, plumped right in the middle of the meadow with talons empty, while the hens sank, froze, blended with the buffy, winter-leached grasses and were gone.

The pheasants are another of my extravagances. They exist only with winter help, slaves to the feed stations I keep for them in the willow thickets. Winter has thinned their numbers, but in my pens are enough well-fed hens and roosters to save a species from extinction. While pheasants in the wild lay one clutch and go broody, by gathering the eggs as they are laid I can quadruple egg production. I store the eggs until I have enough for a clutch, then set them under a willing bantam.

Calling from the roof of the ranch house as though it were their private mountain sits a covey of chukkar partridges, pearly gray bandits with black masks and striped sides. They love each other dearly now, but soon the cocks will grow mad with jealousy as gonads swell with the breeding season, and there will be room hereabouts for only one pair. The rest will be my donation to the public. One day a covey, the next only the dominant pair remains. The remnant disperse far and wide, walking, running, flying out of the valley, gone to find a lonely rimrock canyon somewhere amongst cheat grass, fractured rock, and water. To avoid buying stock every year, I keep a few pairs penned like the pheasants for seed stock in case my one remaining pair fails to raise a family. Once I kept a covey for five years, building from a single pair each spring to sixteen or so each fall. But one day a goshawk hurtled across the meadow hard on the tail of my last hen and dissolved her in mid air, before my very eyes, in a sudden puff of feathers.

By now the great, rumbling logging trucks which ply my road to town have splashed the pavement bare of ice. Even the highest ridges show the erosion of spring. The bent, hunchbacked bushes of snowbrush, bitterbrush, and manzanita are straightening as the snow burden settles about their feet, and bare brown patches show here and there to further temper the night.

The road is a mixed blessing. Al and Mamie Farnsworth drove their laden wagon through the boggy Calimus flats and on up what amounted to little more than a dusty cow trail, and my uncle followed, first with his wagons, then with the first automobile. After a half century of dust the road is paved, a wide, luxurious strip of black asphalt, a delight to drive, but a confusion to cattle, horses, and wildlife. The ravens fly from one greasy chipmunk spot in the road to another, patrolling daily, ever less wary, and are soon themselves flattened on the grille of an automobile hurrying nowhere. The biggest buck I've seen this year lay crumpled and wasted in the borrow pit, along with a regular harvest of others; spotted skunks, blue-tailed skinks, fishers, martens, weasels, badgers, coyotes, raccoons, porcupines, and assorted birds that stopped on the smooth table of the road to gather pine seeds.

No longer do I have to plow a long cold seventeen-mile road with my tractor. Instead a great, rumbling, spark-throwing county snowplow splats the snow against the bordering trees. No longer are we snowed in for weeks at a time, which is good and bad. For down the same plowed road comes the driving public, and where once we could leave the ranch alone and vulnerable, guarded by the honor of our neighbors, now we must keep constant armed guard against thieves and vandals. The food and firewood we leave for an emergency in the Calimus bunkhouse halfway to town are now stolen within the week by people too lazy to provide their own, who can't realize that in case of someone's motor failure in that lonely land, the scant supply could save a family's life. Maybe theirs.

As the mountainous snow melts under the intermittent April sun, I am at last able to repair my phone line. Fifty-three insulators and brackets were shot off last week; maybe they looked too much like glassy-headed woodpeckers. Three hard days of nervous, rickety ladder work caused by some plinker's thoughtlessness. Once more, I am able to phone my family and the outside world.

Over the road, with the thawing of snow comes a morning rumble of Forest Service trucks and pickups, a thin green line invading the forest like caterpillars. Year by year I am less alone in the forest.

In the years when the lands surrounding Yamsi were Indian reservation, the government vehicles were darker green, radiating spokelike from the Indian agency west of Chiloquin. I remember leaning on a corral at the old Crawford ranch visiting with a gray-haired old Indian rancher. Silently, we watched as a dozen Department of Indian Affairs pickups straggled by, showering us with dust. They were heading out to Mamie Farnsworth's, Corbell's or the head of the Williamson simply because the dispatcher had told them to scatter. The old man muttered about the way the white man was dribbling the Indian's timber money away through administration.

The pickups are lighter green now that the land is part of the National Forest, and there are many more of them. It is part of the changing scene. The Forest Service is now curator of myriad forest entities, from lichens to gigantic elk, from water droplets to soaring condors. Whatever the Service does with its forest is soon felt not only by the forest community but those like me who are immediate neighbors. Personnel are transferred in for a few brief months or years, then transferred out, often before they have achieved an understanding of the land. Long after they are transferred on, I must live with those permanent changes they have wrought, suffer for their errors. I must live out my days as neighbor to this land, and what diminishes it diminishes me.

So much do we associate Smokey Bear with the obvious good he does in making people aware of forest fire dangers, that to criticize him is almost to be against motherhood (though, perhaps, as a conservationist, I must now admit to that too). But many a conservationist and wildlife manager is now having second thoughts about poor

Smokey. Oddly enough, his policy of fire prevention itself has evoked much criticism. Years ago, forest fires roamed the land wherever there was an accumulation of forest residues or brush. As a result of occasional burning, the fires were seldom extensive or severe, and production of both timber and wildlife forage was at a maximum.

Now the forests are no longer parklike, but dangerously covered with hazardous, combustible residues and overly thick stands, so that not only must we maintain a tremendously expensive fire-fighting complex, but to obtain growth in now stagnant stands of timber, we must resort to tree thinning, itself an expensive procedure. It is not only the forest land which has suffered. Vast areas of prairie and arid plain have been lost to brush species which are of little use to anyone, including wildlife. Now when a fire starts, it is apt to get out of control and destroy not only the timber but the productive capability of the soil.

I have called Smokey Bear a fink because he has all too often raised havoc with the other denizens of the forest. The Forest Service now has more engineers than foresters, and its tremendous road system, seeking to invade every untouched bit of forest or primal loneliness, emerges as one of the major conservation threats to the land. The road system is changing the ecology of the forests, destroying the very habitat of the life it holds in trust.

The Forest Service has a responsibility to the public to provide access for recreation, and for proper stewardship of the timber or land resource. But what good are the recreational roads if they destroy the very thing the public wanted to see? And as for timber access, some good roads are needed both for fire protection and for timber harvest.

What I object to are the number, the unnecessary width and standard of many of the roads, and their positioning without regard to their effect upon the wildlife resource. Moreover, a sizable acreage is taken out of timber production. A sixty-foot right-of-way, for instance, amounts to a loss of seven and a quarter acres per mile. Forever.

When I look in on the Forest Service at work, I see only dedicated men, young, eager, intelligent, a cross section of America, men who have a love for and a dedication to the out-of-doors. My enemy is not the men but the system which has fostered the overbuilding of roads. It will take Congressional action to change it.

Living in the midst of a National Forest, I've had a ringside view of change, felt the roads draw tight about me, seen their devastating effect upon the land. North of me is the Skellock Draw area. Within one year after the area was glutted with Forest Service roads, it went from a major game production area to a minor one. Had the roads been designed with the total resource in mind, and kept to a minimum, allowing the wild creatures an occasional haven in which to escape in times of duress, it might still be a productive area. Blue Jay Springs once produced more giant mule deer bucks than any area of Klamath County; now it is almost worthless as a recreational resource.

3190 is a number. It is also the tattered remnant army of branch-hung survey ribbons, and thousands of stakes, now for the most part brushed down by mule deer rubbing the itching scruff of velvet from their antlers. A host of owls, great gray, horned, long-eared, and pigmy, in command of the night, peer hungrily down at the flicking, teasing ribbons as a breeze stirs the forest. It is a movement in their territory they have yet to understand, yet to make a meal of.

3190 is a ghost road now, but once it threatened to destroy the land. It came quietly and without fanfare. I even waved as I passed a group of Forest Service pickups clustered at the edge of the forest, spotting a man or two with whom I'd fished or birded. Men with axes, men with backpacks of stakes and ribbons, men with transits. Because the land had already been ravaged with four nearly parallel roads, I did not dream they would plan yet another. At that moment, 3190 began to move off the drawing boards onto the land.

Halfway down the ranch, a lonely, long, wet meadow purple with camas and penstemon slips down from the west, a meadow long referred to as the "Bull Pasture" since the days half a century before, when Childers had fenced part of the meadow as a pasture for his bulls. In this mule deer heaven wildlife abounds since the logging roads have kept to the ridges, leaving a roadless area of jack pine thickets.

Here badgers wander from colony to colony of short-tailed ground squirrels, scarce glancing right or left for danger. Coyotes howl nightly in unpoisoned ranks, feasting on an abundance of rodents, thinning the weak and lame from the deer herd, a genetically sound philosophy of wildlife management which man, his small mind geared only to harvesting the biggest, finest animal, has failed to comprehend.

In the marshy pond where Bear Draw enters the Bull Pasture drainage, year after year a pair of sandhill cranes build their nest at the base of a stark gray skeleton of a spindly pine. Mallards fly their nuptial flights over the lush grasses of the sink; cinnamon teal court happily in and out of the sedges. A goshawk gives testimony to the loneliness by building a nest of sticks in the lodgepole thicket adjoining the pond.

It was a loneliness almost lost, for an engineer's drafting pencil, operating miles from the scene, had spelled doom for that wild land.

By acts of Congress, the Forest Service is empowered to make allowances in timber sale appraisals for the cost of necessary road construction, reforestation, and timber improvement costs. In other words, these costs can be taken out of timber sale receipts with the Forest Service sitting in judgment of itself on how much to spend. Twenty-five per cent of what is left goes to the counties in lieu of taxes for schools and roads, and the balance goes to the Treasury. The Forest Service may use all or part of the timber revenue, and does not have to defend the standard of the road to anyone.

Road 3190, costing an estimated $90,000, was to be financed from the sale of 8.1 million board feet of timber. In this area the Forest Service claims that a road cost of from four to seven dollars per thousand board feet of timber to be harvested is a reasonable figure. And yet Road 3190 was scheduled to cost from twelve to fifteen dollars per thousand.

At my request, the Klamath County Commissioners held a hearing. The logging industry admitted in testimony that even though 3190 was to be built as a timber access road, it was poorly located and would be of little use. They preferred to take the timber out over existing roads that delivered it to the top of the grade rather than at its foot. I pointed out that 3190 would adversely affect wildlife, change the ecology of the area. Gone would be the productive mule deer range; gone the green meadows and the pond, destroyed by the heavy fill which would be required over the wetlands; gone the nesting site of the sandhill cranes, and other rare species. Much of the area through which the road would run was a unique land of lodgepole thickets of little value save for the production of wildlife. The area already had sufficient road coverage for fire protection.

It became more and more evident from the testimony that Road 3190 would serve no real purpose but was being built simply because funds were available with which to build it.

Support flooded in. The road had suddenly become more than just a road, but a case in point, embodying problems which were of real concern to conservationists all over the nation. Calls came from Forest Service personnel, acting as individuals, from disgruntled hunters who had returned to favorite recreation spots only to find them demolished forever by a whole network of forest roads. Conservation organizations such as the Oregon Wildlife Federation, the Western Association of State Game and Fish Commissioners, and many others passed resolutions pointing up the havoc caused by the overbuilding of government roads. Foresters worried about the large acreage taken out of production forever if roads projected for the future in our National Forests were completed. Pessimists declared that until roads became a budgeted item, and until the Forest Service had to defend each road on the basis of whether or not it was in the best long-range interests of the land, the massive road-building program would continue.

Repeatedly I voiced appreciation of the fact that timber from our National Forests is vital to the whole economy of our nation, and that a road system is necessary or many of our trees will rot, or be consumed by insect epidemics. It is often better to control an insect invasion by logging diseased trees than by a massive spray campaign. But I also felt that often the roads could be built beside the units instead of through them, and the timber harvested with spur roads which could be closed and reseeded once the harvest was done, returning the land to production.

When the Forest Service refused to cancel Road 3190, Senator Wayne Morse and Congressman Al Ullman ordered the project halted until a complete study could be made of the situation by competent biologists. 3190 is now past history, the study completed and the project abandoned. The marshes remain lonely, the mule deer productive, and the lodgepole thickets stand as isolated nesting haunts of goshawks and great gray owls.

But 3190 is only one road; it is up to the interested citizen everywhere to keep each local construction project under scrutiny, to be the watchdog over his own back yard. Such excellent wildlife organizations as the National Wildlife Federation, the Audubon Society, the Isaac Walton League, and the Wildlife Management Institute exist to fight for conservation, but often they must depend on the alert citizen to bring local problems to their attention.

Many an existing road is now obsolete or a duplication of another. Roads no longer necessary should be closed and the land put back into production. The Forest Service should defend and justify every road they build, and decisions as to the ultimate merit of the road should be made only after consultation with local foresters and biologists, the men who will have to live with the roads long after the engineers who designed them have been transferred.

Change is inevitable, but it is up to the individual citizen to see that it is kept orderly, to lessen the impact by insisting that all factors be understood, and eventual losses minimized. Smokey Bear may be a fink, but it is our failure that we have not kept his bureaucracy more in check, that we have failed to make him aware that he is not merely a fighter of fires, a seller of minerals, timber, recreation, and grass, a builder of roads, trails, campgrounds. His responsibility extends beyond, to the future welfare of his fellow denizens of the forest community.

I should be glad that the road to town is paved, but there is sadness in anything that changes my world. Yesterday as I tiptoed my skittish colt past the road grader, which was putting some finishing touches to the shoulder of the road, I found an old wrecked buggy wheel in the disturbed earth, spokes akimbo, covered with white mold and scaly orange rust. I flung myself off my horse and rushed forward. The driver must have been startled as I cradled the relic lovingly to my chest and carted it off.

It is not history that needs this remnant but I. It is all that is left of a happening of my youth, when Mamie Farnsworth's team spooked at our brand-new mailbox and stampeded with Mamie and her current beau, Whitey Arral. First we found Mamie's parasol, then her flowered hat, then Whitey's wooden leg, then assorted parts as the buggy blew up as it caromed off a tree and scattered like the one-hoss shay. We found Mamie and Whitey out cold, each under his own tree. The team turned the corner of the fence and joined a band of wild horses west of the bull pasture, where they ran the rest of the summer with a few bits and scraps of harness still left on their backs.

That battered wheel is the only roadside litter I am going to be sentimental about. A new road, new pavement, and new problems. Already the fresh new borrow pits are a fester of broken bottles and shimmering cans. Yesterday I roped a cow and took a Campbell's Tomato Soup can off her foot. It was not the company's fault that her tendons were cut, and that she will never more than hobble again. What we need is a container that destroys itself when empty, or better yet a national conscience.

Trusting, the deer come as of old, down from the hills, bound for the salt licks in my fields, bound for sanctuary on my ranch. They try to outrace the rushing cars, but skating and falling on hard rubber hooves, they end up in pulp, exploding sacks of buckskin. Dead hawks shot from my phone line, trusting redtails and rough legs, and today a golden eagle; all protected by law. Cattle entrails where the new breed of city rustler shot and gutted a fat calf, then threw it into the trunk of his car. The crafty old neighbor type rustler knew the law better, and got rid of the hide with the brand, did a clean professional job of butchering, skinning out even the tail so that the carcass could hang in a butcher's shop without detection. Now the jobs are crude hack work at best, but the cost to me is the same.

There is more rustling now than fifty years ago, and there are more rustlers. Vandalism is rampant. Fires left burning, fences cut where snowmobilers wiped out the inconvenience of my fence to attain one last ride on a lingering patch of snow. I am frightened for myself. What made me want to gut shoot that Honda, just because the driver left a dozen gates open, mixed up enough cattle for a week of hard separating, and tried to make a break for it when I asked him to halt? Does the law really protect me as it protects him?

In desperation over a rash of petty thefts I become deputized and my first arrest is the county surveyor for littering. Ten thousand dollars' worth of copper wire are stolen from our local phone system by thieves, leaving me and my neighbors to operate our business without phones for months. Is there really such a thing as private land? I pay rent in the form of spiraling taxes, and all that keeps my land private now, protects my wildlife, is one thin little trespass law. I patrol my borders religiously, convinced that Yamsi should remain a sanctuary where wild things can live without constantly staring down the muzzle of a gun.

I was a hunter for years; but now the killing of wild things, so end-lessly oppressed, makes me want to vomit. I have more than respect for my big, gentle friend, Jim Kerns, who, one deer season, was about to fire at the biggest buck in the forest, when a fawn rose from its bed and nuzzled the old patriarch on the jaw. Jim shouldered his gun and went home. Now there is a man.

I know all the arguments. I've seen ranges destroyed for all time by over-populations of deer, aspens wiped out by too many elk, quail populations (which could have been harvested) lost to disease and starvation. Hunting has seldom been as great a decimating factor to wildlife as changes in habitat. I realize that funds from the hunting resource pay most of the bills for conservation work done in America. (The recreationalist finding for the first time the thrill of photographing a bird instead of shooting it, of watching a coyote instead of killing it, often owes the very presence of wildlife to the efforts of hunters. It is now time that he undertook to pay his share of the conservation bill.) I can admit that hunting or a similar harvest is sometimes vital to the health of both the species and the range resource. But for me—no more hunting. If it must be done let someone else do it. Perhaps what bothers me most is to be linked with the pushy, greedy army I see now in the woods.

Some hunters are fine men, with a proper regard for laws, and an appreciation of Nature—gentlemen in the true sense. Too many lack the true spirit of the hunt; too many are drunks packing guns; too many are sadists taking out their animosities on helpless creatures; too many are greedy, out for so many dollars' worth of meat, capable of flock-shooting a bunch of deer, leaving the poorer specimens to die a slow death untracked, or to rot. Too many have never had enough regard for wildlife to take the trouble to become adequate shots.

If some of the hunters could walk with me, see the living beauty of pheasant cocks resplendent at their feet, have them feed from their hands in mute testimony of trust, if they could sit of a summer's eve and watch a quail hen feeding unafraid in a scurry of chicks, have their pockets picked by a friendly sandhill crane, feel the incredible softness of a great gray owl nuzzling one's ear with huge facial disk pressed close, then they would know some of the guilt I feel at hunt-ing. There is nothing more fervent than a reformed anything, and I happen to be a reformed hunter.

Whose ranch is lovelier than mine; whose life more rewarding? Why can't I be content with being just a rancher? What is it to me if the sandhill cranes no longer call from my marshes? The Forest Service doesn't try to tell me how to run my ranch; why should I meddle in their business? Surely there is enough challenge here, adrift on a melting iceberg of a profession, trying to make a living for my family, without going outside my fence for trouble. But I want to tear the leopard coat off a woman, to protect the last specimens in the wild.

The snow melts quickly now; a hundred miles of fence to fix from winter's pummeling. So many chores that won't wait. I feel that I have better things to do about the ranch than ride the feed wagon, and this morning the team dreams along and seems unbearably slow.

Today Taylor came in with the first pheasant egg. We shared the moment, regarding the olive drab treasure from the pens, clutched in his moist palm, like a piece of moon soil. Conspiring together, we place it lovingly in a tray of damp soil. We'll turn the eggs daily, saving the gather until we have enough to set under a broody bantam hen.

Once a bantam hen has laid a normal complement of eggs, she becomes broody. Broodiness is a trance-like state which has been bred out of modern, super-efficient, high-yielding layers such as leghorns, but is present in marked degree in some of the bantam breeds. When Taylor and I slip into the dusky gloom of the chicken house we place a hand (his, though I end up with the lice) under all the hens in their nests. Picking the hen that squalls the loudest, we hide her under my coat to keep her in darkness, transport her across the meadow to a nest box, and place her on a dummy egg. This may be a real egg, a stone, or even a golf ball. By morning, if she is really setting hard, she will have adopted the egg. If not, she will fly up in my face as I open the lid of her compartment, and cackle loud and indignant all the way back to the chicken house.

However, once she is safely settled on the nest, we can give her a setting of pheasant, quail, partridge, duck, goose, or even sandhill crane eggs. These she will hatch and raise as her own, feeding the young tender tidbits with her bill, ready to defend them from danger with her very life. This works well except with the eggs of a northern duck called the Old Squaw. Often the young are so vocal and raucous in hatching that the hen becomes a nervous wreck even before they are out of the shell.

95

Marsha and Taylor run the bird department. Each morning before their own breakfast they take each hen off the nest, place her in an adjoining pen, and give her fresh food and water. When the chicks hatch they are locked in with their foster mothers until they are thoroughly "nest ripe" and have learned to answer the call of the foster mother, and to crawl under the softness of her feathers for warmth. Then they may be eased out into the world of their pen. The children's chores will not cease until fall, when the young birds can be released to the wider world of the ranch.

Two more pheasant eggs today. Perhaps the sight of one hen laying an egg stimulated another. The eggs look cold and chilled, and no wonder, for they have been laid in four inches of fresh snow. April is being April.

In the basement of the Yamsi house, the toads are piping. All winter long they have lounged about in shrunken overcoats, living on toad fat, circling like gossips about the furnace, eyes glowing like rubies in the flashing firelight as I come down to throw on another log. Grumpily, they move aside as I open the gaping mouth of the furnace. The flames make dancing mischief of every eye.

The toads are at home in a wet world, for the Williamson River starts in our basement beginning a journey of half a thousand miles to the Pacific Ocean. Along the wall we have jack-hammered a Venice of canals designed to keep our feet dry by leading the water away under the laundry-room floor and on down through the secret gardens of the willows. Sometimes a spawning trout splashes water all over me as I try to slip past him to the stair.

Capricious April. Yesterday snow and storm; today sunshine, velvety and warm. A mourning cloak, lain dormant in my jacket all winter long, has awakened now, fluttering pathetically against the windowpane for freedom. Once again I may use my jacket. His wings look summer-limber; half afraid he may return to his winter home, I open wide the window. Thanklessly he sets off upon an errant course, while the spring air sweeps pure and sweet through the whole house.

From the sloughs out on the meadow, where, in Indian times, Buck's Spring once flowed and was lost in the marshes, a chorus of tiny frog voices fills the air. Like crickets chirping in the undergrowth, they seem to sense my attempt to spy on them, and turn off their voices when I come near. Only the occasional blink of a protruding eye, like a tiny bubble popping at the surface, betrays them. Then as I sit silent long enough to overcome their wisdom, a small throat puffs out, monstrous for its owner's size, and the small shrill purling voice joins in a chorus God wrote eons back in time when music was still by bird song, wind, and rain.

MY TWO-YEAR-OLD REPLACEMENT heifers are having their first try at birthing. Hourly, I stagger from my warm bed, cover my nakedness against the inhospitality of snow, rain, sleet, or even an upstart draft of a cold breeze, and slip out into the darkness, knowing that however the night is, it won't be warm, and that one wrong step will involve the whole future color of my bedroom slippers. But I am too lazy to put on boots for a jaunt that may take minutes if the heifers are holding tight, or hours if one of them is having trouble calving.

I have a huge flashlight whose beam saves walking. Beating the gloom with a club of light, I wake the killdeer from their sleep, send the starlings clattering from the limby pine tops. Heifers ring the pines, clustered beneath in groups for warmth and company, the kindly branches protecting their backs from the early morning frost. A few push blinking to their feet, stretching their sway-backed best as though their front feet are about to walk off and leave the rest of the body behind.

The heifers are all Herefords, bred to black Angus bulls. In theory this cross produces a smaller calf more easily able to slide out the narrow pelvic opening of the heifer. Sometimes I wonder. The crossbred calves are more vigorous at birth, jump up to suck in half the time, and grow faster even though their young mothers do not give the milk of a mature cow. We keep our herd pure by selling off the crossbred calves in the fall.

The flashlight reveals a world undreamed of. First a spotted skunk, a species which hasn't been seen here for thirty years, then, wet and bedraggled, a big raccoon probes for snails along the marsh, stands on his hind legs to peer at me above the hummocks, eyes glowing like red coals. Heavy with fawn, a doe comes mincing down off the forested hillsides and across the meadow, headed for salt. Around her neck a yellow cord with copper bell whose clapper has worn itself silent; hanging from one spoonlike ear, a yellow ribbon. I'll phone the local game biologist in the morning. He will know by the color where she was tagged, whether she is a member of the migratory interstate deer herd which winters on the lava beds of Northern California, or one from the Silver Lake herd, which winters on the snow-free desert to the east. She was trapped on her wintering grounds in a small enclosure baited with alfalfa hay, and released after banding as part of a continuing management study.

The quiet, windless ponds are rippled now with the spreading V of a swimming muskrat, now with a flock of cinnamon teal that came guiding in on a beam of floating moonlight, and are determined to spend the rest of the night. It is not a very safe place, for already a great horned owl has floated out of nowhere to perch on the cathedral spire of a dead jack pine right above their heads. His hoots are answered from afar from another male. These boundaries are hooted up constantly between them; and the silent owl loses his private hunting ground to his neighbor.

My beam impales him. Eyes half closed, he seems almost to turn his throat inside out as he hoots. From the hillside thickets, a great gray owl counters with a slow, deep, reverberant "*Who; who; who.*"

I am almost ready to head back for the warmth of my bed when my beam catches a heifer stretched out low, trying to calve. Head muddy from pummeling the ground, the heifer is barely visible over the tossing, uneven sea of hummocks. I brace myself for trouble, but by the time I gingerly circumnavigate the ice-rimmed pools of water, the heifer has strained the calf out and is on her feet investigating the moving pile she has made with both fear and curiosity. Fearful of frightening her, I sit in the darkness, shivering, miserable, waiting for instincts to make a mother of her, trying to hear the low bawl of motherhood, the wet licking sounds above the froggy chorus. When finally I risk a beam her way, all is well. The calf is rough-haired with her licking, a cowlick standing in a whorl on his ribs and another on his shoulder. He stands trembling, trying to suck his mother's shoulder. Stupid heifer! Twice he almost reaches her udder, but she backs away to finish licking him, sending him sprawling in a puddle of water with her well-intentioned efforts. I can't hurry him. If it were warm the time would pass more swiftly. Maybe if I came back in half an hour . . . but no, if he failed to make it, I'd have a hard time with my conscience. "Ahhh!" I sigh aloud in my relief. From the sounds he has found a distended front teat where the milk is hot and free. As I dare to shine my light, his tail flicks back and forth like a pump handle. When his tiny belly is distended, she lies down beside him to shelter him from the night as instincts make a perfect mother of her. He is lucky for some heifers can be awfully silly. Content that I have done my duty, I head back to bed to sleep more deeply for my involvement, knowing that for an hour at least all will be well.

There are no Sundays when heifers are calving, no hours off, no nights of rest. From the first heifer to the last, vigilance is the word. Come dawn I am at my window with my binoculars, dreading trouble but looking for it.

After breakfast, as the men harness the work team to feed, I pair up the new calves spry enough to travel with their mothers and put them in the adjoining field, where they will be fed all the hay they can clean up. By keeping the new calves separate I lessen the chances of a mix-up, for a heifer is a confused welter of instincts and will often suckle any calf that comes along until her own bond with a calf has firmed.

The black coat of the Angus father is genetically dominant, as are the white face and markings of the Hereford mother, so that the hybrid calves are black where the red ought to be. I memorize each pair as I turn them out together, for should a mother desert her calf, I may have to pair them up again. These heifers are the teenyboppers of the bovine world, calving now because it is economic to make them producers as early as possible, within limits. If left unbred for another year, the mothers would be fatter and the conception rates lower.

However one conspires to make delivery easier, there are those heifers that will need help, sometimes in the form of a small pull on the front feet of the calf, but more often in the form of a big pull from a device known as a calf puller. This is like a huge metal slingshot crotch with a pipe handle up and down which shinnies a jack. The fork is

placed against the cow's rump and chains are attached to the front feet of the calf, then hooked to the jack, so that when the jack pulls on the calf it pushes against the cow. Far better it is than the old method, which was to tie a lass rope around the front feet of the calf, take a few dallies around the saddle horn, and head for town. The calf either came or the cinch broke. Calving is always chancy, but the puller has added much to the safety of the operation.

The pockets of my heavy coat are my medicine bag. I carry bottles of smelling salts, antibiotics and sulfa for pneumonia and scour infections, iodine for treatment of navels against infection, selenium for white muscle disease, as well as a bacterium for Enterotoxemia. Clanking in their glassy midst is a pill gun and a syringe. It takes a quiet, understanding horse just to put up with the rattle, and to stand still for the constant mounting and dismounting. Often as not, I have a hot bottle of colostrum milk shoved like a pirate's pistol under my belt to keep it warm with my body heat.

I wander about the calves, often leading my horse instead of riding, making each calf rise for inspection. I doctor only those in need, for often the medicines, while they kill an infection, raise havoc with the delicate bacterial balance in a calf's intestine which aids digestion. I am always vastly relieved when a calf survives my medication.

But whatever the disasters, April is a time of new hope, of birth and rebirth, of new beginning. I am filled with the excitement of it. On a rare visit to town, I brag brashly to my banker about the quality I see in the calves as a direct reflection of those bulls I paid too much for last year. In my heady moments the number of calves I report exceeds the number of cows I own, as though I were stealing from the neighbors. But I manage to blurt things out so fast he doesn't notice.

He smiles patiently, his mind picturing, no doubt, how my children will look next year without shoes, and my wife in a burlap dress. He avoids any reference that might send me off on a violent discourse on Forest Service roads.

Only a faint tinge of green on the April meadows, yet here I am anticipating a record hay crop in defense of the $5,000 I have spent for fertilizer. Sensing that the man's thoughts are not with me, I tell him about the fifteen-pound trout I saw the other day just gulping down flies, waiting to break his tackle, and as his eyes turn beady with lust for that particular fish, I come back to reality and realize I haven't even had time to go down the river to *see* a fish. I shiver with the thought that before I rise from that chair beside the banker's desk, I am going to have to say, "Oh, by the way, I need five thousand bucks to pay the Forest Service for my range leases this year. That is if they don't cancel me out."

"*Five thousand dollars!*" There, it's out. I whisper it but somehow it echoes clear across the bank and brings the president running as though I have handed the teller a holdup note. There is a glance of desperation between the two of them that denotes conspiracy, as though they had expected something like this to happen, and had plotted to turn me down.

Well, how was I to know last December when I made up that little budget estimate that the price of running my ranch would go up and the price of cattle down? That taxes would go up, that groceries would go up, and gasoline, and union wages for the mechanics who work on my trucks, and parts for engines, and clothing for my growing brood, even though the President had *promised* . . . ? "Just as *your* costs have gone up," I say appreciatively, leaning heavy on the sympathy. "Like for that secretary over there. I see she's got a new IBM machine and I bet her wages have skyrocketed but not her productivity. As well as the wages for the night watchman. And the cost of *your* money. Are you able to stick to your budget?"

A fit of coughing on that one, and suddenly I am walking down the street trying to remember where I parked my battered old pickup, hoping the police haven't towed it away again, and feeling pretty pleased with myself. I have a whole month to grow that six-inch trout

in my river to a fifteen-pounder, and I have just proven myself capable of miracles by getting the money. A whole month before I have to face reality again and admit, "Thunderation, how did that happen? I declare I've gone and exceeded my budget again!"

I should be out checking my calves, but I'm worried about the sandhill cranes down in the valley. Last year disaster struck my favorite pair. A stray dog someone had abandoned frightened the female from the nest, and both eggs were dumped into the icy water.

Riding my horse down the valley, I watch the mountain bluebirds chasing the Townsend solitaires from their nesting territories, the violet-green swallows skimming the ponds in sociable clouds, and a solitary pair of rough-winged swallows flying through an abandoned culvert. Spring is everywhere.

The cranes are silent enough to be nesting. Watching over the meadows as I ride, I see a big male standing alone, feeding occasionally but with a contentment to his aloneness as though he knew a secret. Just by looking at him, I know one too. Somewhere in the wettest marsh, his female is sitting on a great, reedy, floating nest, a crane-made island afloat in the greening swamp. It is almost evening and the male calls, tilting his red-crowned head as though drinking, rolling out a staccato outburst that caroms against the far-off pines across the valley and comes back as an echo, mellowed and lovelier still. Rising as though on signal, his female leaves her nest, slinks a few careful feet, stands for a moment looking for danger, then flies, hugging the ground until she lights inconspicuously in the meadow. Only then does she call to her mate. In a moment he has crossed the valley, even larger than she, a great gray flying reptile come to life from the Pleistocene. He lights beside her and for a moment they feed side by side, heads almost touching. Then he is off again, flying low, silent, oaring the wind with studied nonchalance, hedge-hopping over the ruin of last year's cattails. Now over the nesting area, he drops suddenly and stands quiet. All seems well and he slinks a few short feet to the nest, stands above it to rearrange a few straying rootlets with his great beak, and flops down to take his turn on the eggs.

As I ride on, I see four baby badgers wrestling and tumbling in front of their den. Three scramble to safety, but the fourth stands on his hind legs to show the others how brave he is. His courage flags as I approach and he flees for the safety of his burrow, but now the other three block the hole and won't let him in. Time and again he assaults the gate but each time they shove him back into the open, until at last the showoff glances desperately at my approaching horse, and scampers off through the brush as fast as his short little legs will take him.

The cows are tired of hay and the men of dishing it out to them. If only the weather would stay warm I could cut down on the outflow, and try to save the few bales we have left. Incredibly, it is snowing hard. Four inches of new snow on the new green. Branches break under the weight of it, hundreds and hundreds of lethal dollops of pine needles, invitingly grass-colored, scattered through the forest as though someone is trying to poison my cows with turpentine, trying to cause them to abort. A cow stands under a tree, eyeing me calmly as she finishes off a huge branch of needles, leaving only the larger twigs. Good grief! It's Biddy! Utterly no conscience, no loyalty to her human family. I shake my fist at her in despair, but she chews on, showing no concern. Desperately I gather branches by the armload, then try to burn them but they are wet with snow, and the cows follow me curiously, warming themselves by my poor fires, licking up the unburned branches as though concerned with my waste. I am poisoning my own herd!

A calf follows me about; trying to suck my knee. He is wet, miserable, deserted. Icy pearls of melting snow cluster on his back. He shivers pathetically and I open my warm down jacket, hold him to me as I crouch beneath the shelter of a pine, soothing the furlike pile of the lining close about him, trying mentally to exude warmth from my own shivering body. Suddenly there is a wet burning sensation. I don't have to look to know what has happened. He has urinated down my right leg. I limp off, dragging one leg in stiff discomfort, feeling a guilt I haven't felt since I wet my pants in the seventh grade. The storm worsens, but when my conscience sends me back to the calf, his mother lies close beside him and he is telling her of his adventures. They are both laughing.

Where is hope now? By morning all my calves will have the scours, and a half dozen old cows I cheated through the winter on good hay will lie down and quit trying to live. They are all cows I kept against my brother's advice.

"If a cow looks tough in the fall, get rid of her," he warned, mouthing the old cowboy adage as we drove through my herd, me just trying to be sociable, he on a critical binge.

"So tell me something new," I said, feeling snappish. I kept them just because I didn't like an older brother telling me what to do. Only yesterday I was thinking how good they looked and then this storm hit.

Incredibly the sun comes out, having commandeered the only patch of blue in miles just to shine on me. You can hear the snow settle. The cows seem almost to tiptoe, avoiding puddles, trying to keep their feet dry. Calves I thought were dead appear by the hundreds at the edge of the forest to soak up the sun. Then out of nowhere comes another ice cloud, stinging my face with needles. A flock of violet-green swallows, tired from long migration, funnels down out of the blue sky as it closes behind them; they swoop low over the cast-iron choppiness of the pond looking for insects that aren't. Perched on a barbed wire fence, a Western flycatcher watches the swallows to see if they are having any better luck than he. He is humped up with cold, ill with hunger, and won't last until morning. I turn over rocks hoping to find a meal for him but it is still too early, and I feel the first cool chill of night. The next morning I pass beneath his roost tree to find him dead, and half the swallows are gone. Dead, or fled perhaps across the mountains to warmer valleys to the west.

This morning a male sandhill crane flew in for a handout of corn. For a decade now this crane has made use of me whenever the weather has turned unseasonably sour, and ignores me for the gallons of cracked corn I tossed out for his pleasure. I tried to capture him once with his mate for banding by soaking the corn with a fifth of Jack Daniels, but they flew off undaunted, though a little sideways and a trifle noisy. They were back the next morning with a good start toward an addiction, but that was the last whisky they got from me. As I ride through the fields on my rounds I keep watch for his mate. I see her hunched on her nest, bedraggled and miserably conspicuous in a marsh whose grasses are now flattened with snow. Every predator in the valley knows her secret now and will include the nest as part of the regular beat, hoping to take her by surprise. I have my pockets filled with corn to scatter in her favorite preening spot, but she will have to hurry for a pair of stellar jays are following me, and once the secret cache is found it will go to a host of jays and migrating sparrows.

Today the hired men quit. They had been expecting good weather, and not only was it nasty and cold but the water froze up where the pipes are exposed in the stream, and stopped coming to the bunkhouse. I am too busy calving at the moment to locate the trouble and they are too helpless to find it for themselves. They are mad at each other too, and if one had stayed it might have been an acknowledgment that the other was smarter. And so they both caught logging trucks to town.

I find Al Shadley on the street and tell him all sorts of lies about how the deer are fat on the meadows, the trout jumping in his favorite hole. I talk on and on until his eyes shine with remembrance. He asks about the children, his eyes lighting up with affection, and I know that for him I would fix the water if only he would come and stay. I imagine him there now, sitting in his old worn chair with its guts half out, and a fire hotter than we have had all winter, telling me about a buck he and Lee Corbell shot once up on Saddle Mountain.

In reality Al stands instead on the Chiloquin street, not missing a movement up and down its length, shifting his weight first to one foot then the other as though his legs hurt on the unaccustomed pavement. He tells me about the run of suckers on the lower Williamson, and how he is going huckleberry picking in August.

I beg him to come back but he shakes his head stubbornly, secretly pleased that I have asked. He pulls out a pocket watch and looks at it carefully although we both know it hasn't run in twenty years. "I've got to go now, see," he says. "I've got a date with a rich widow."

The hay sheds, once bursting, are almost empty now, and yet the cold and snow linger on. If I had the credit to buy more hay I wouldn't know where to look, for it has been a tough winter everywhere, and in the Klamath valleys empty hay trucks from the coast side of the Cascade Range cruise the rural roads looking for hay to buy at any price. I am forced to cut rations just when my cows need it most for milk production. My banker calls asking about my supply, and I tell him I have plenty, hoping he won't show up to see. I remember hearing old-timers talk about a bad winter in the Bly valley, where cattle died by the hundreds, and ranches spent their daylight hours cutting brush in the hills and hauling it down by team and wagon to give the cows something to chew on.

The bulls are itching, scratching off great patches of winter hair against the stump villages in their lot, where years back Ern Morgan once cut corral logs. The cows in the next field look tattered as though moths have been at them. One day the green grass grows, the next it freezes down, but during the afternoon, the cows roam hopefully through the marshy areas where dampness tempers the night. They are as tired of eating hay as I am of tossing it to them. With no help available I feed alone, putting the children to work when they come for the weekend.

The last snow of April is falling now. Taylor, playing his solitary game of baseball in the front yard, hits a home run by virtue of the fact that the ball disappears into an abyss of flakes and he can't find it. Ginny and Marsha come trooping in, cheeks scarlet with the storm, tying their horses to the pines outside the house where they will be sheltered from the winds. Johnny has been afield watching a dipper, two goshawks, a conspiracy of buzzards, and a great gray owl, while Dayton has been checking the stream for spawning trout. They all troop into the house at once, driven by the storm, but no sooner have they scattered their wet clothing about the house to dry and plunked down to work a jigsaw puzzle before the roaring hearth, than my patient wife nods at the sunshine which suddenly floods the front window. "Look," she says in relief. "It's sunny now. The storm is over. May is coming."

Chapter 7

Brilliant sunshine. One of those rare mornings in May when the air is so soft and thick you can almost float in it. Six o'clock in the morning and I'm actually out of bed, and wandering without a jacket. No crashing big hurry to get the team harnessed either this morning. I couldn't sleep because the rest of the world was wide awake and noisy about the weather. Up and down the length of my valley the long-billed Wilson's snipes are making a marvel of their wing song.

A better ornithologist than I might worry whether the song were territorial, sheer exuberance, a love song, or just a lonely heart a-breaking. I care not, really, but given my choice I'd take a love song ten to one. They fly just below the level of the clouds, looking from here on Earth to be no bigger than gnats. Wings beating hard to pick up speed, they plummet a descendent course, then pull out of the dive to vibrate their slender pinions mightily, causing an ascendant hymn, a voice, a song ventriloqual, rising on the scale as they zoom back to their former heights. It is a lonely sound, a sad sound, floating ever downward to become a part of the marsh music far below. Then when they have tired, or thought their music quite enough for now, they set their wings and come planing swiftly down to some girl snipe in the grass, their voice vocal now, not of wind and feathers, piping excitedly as they drop beside some watery way.

They nest where the grass is tall, and the damp moss of the marsh cushions four olive eggs, mottled with shades of purple and of chocolate. Often now as I ride I flush them from their nest, and let them broken-wing my horse away, giving them the satisfaction of a ruse well played out. They are not hunted here, but when they fly they go careening off, twisting and turning as though to shake their shadows on the grass, calling loudly to frighten me and spoil my aim with that gun I wish they knew I didn't have.

Oh, the May morning! Frogs in more furious chorus still, swallows in skimming clouds, dimpling the mirror of the pond, bluebirds, a dash of bunting on the gateposts, searching each shadow for a nesting hole. A hairy woodpecker flies at my windowpane, hating the bird he sees there, that fat, persistent rival game as he, brave as he, which can't be bluffed or tired out or driven away. *Thunk! Thunk!* A robin now, mad as a robin male can be, pestering his image while the wood-pecker, slightly dazed by his last encounter, waits upon the jack pine trunk below for his head to clear. And now the bluebird male, playing the fool himself, while his mate looks large-eyed and curious from the branch above. I chase them all away, looking back into the glass my-self and seeing nothing to get mad about, only the soft effects of being over forty, a face that's gently going to seed, a rancher who's tired of feeding hay to thankless cows and calves.

The hay is almost gone. Out of some twenty-five thousand bales, only three lonely bales are left. So I didn't run out. The cattle are a little thinner than I'd like them to be, but I didn't run out. Anything over one bale is a triumph. I can honestly tell my banker I had hay left over. The fields are actually turning green; I knew they would in time, though some years grass comes three weeks later than in others.

Yesterday morning only a handful of cows came in to be fed, as though the rest knew how little I had left and didn't want me to feel badly about the matter.

The work team stands expectantly at the barn door, still caught up in the routine of winter, still worried about another load of hay to haul out to the cattle. It has upset them that I am late. June nips at my arm in protest, while May turns her massive rump toward me and cocks one shaggy fetlock as though to kick me, but I trust her not to. I slap her playfully on the hip, hoping she won't make about three counties with me, and she nickers to me in soft, contented laughter as she bumps the barn door impatiently with her nose, hoping to jar the latch. Needing their company more than their help, I let them in to their stalls, curry their rich, blood bay coats to a lustrous sheen, comb out their fetlocks into a fluff like cotton candy. They munch contentedly, noses buried in their grain boxes, not knowing that it will be the last time in months they'll see the inside of a barn.

Mystified that I lead them back out the door, they drag back on their lead rope to show me I have erred. Opening the gate to the pasture where all winter long the other horses have had their freedom, I stroke their necks in thanks, petting first one and then the other, trying to be impartial, as though that would repay them for a long winter's work.

The turning loose comes as a surprise to them, as the leather halters drop from their noses. For a moment, they try to follow me back through the gate, then suddenly it occurs to them that they are free and off they whirl, trembling the ground as they gallop madly down the lane, kicking up their heels as though trying to snap their spines.

The other horses stare at them, trying to comprehend the sight, then up they come, necks bowed to greet the strangers. There is a squeal or two of mock anger from June as an amorous gelding sniffs too close, then off the herd dashes in madcap play, running as one.

A few gluttonous cows bawl to me as I ride out through the fields, soaking up the warm luxury of the sun through my shirt. I open the gate, turning the cattle north, and even though they have seemingly ignored my passage they are hard on my heels, as though they suspect what I am about. Without a glance at me they flow past, minds on summer and the coming grass. Faster now and still faster, as the furthermost cows gallop to catch up, and the calves bawl and mill about in confusion. Long red lines of cattle heading north; twenty movie cowboys shooting and hollering hard couldn't move my cattle faster. I bark like a coyote, hoping to stir up some mother instinct in the cows and send them back for their calves, but today I am not even a good coyote, and I cannot raise a single bovine head from grass.

Only when they have had their fill of the tender new green succulence will they come back, bawling anxiously for a neglected child, rushing here, rushing there, sniffing this calf and that, trying to find the right one by its scent, glaring at me as though I had caused the calves to be lost. Stupid cows; if they weren't so greedy, they wouldn't lose them in the first place.

Once paired up again, they allow their calves only a few hot sucks at their udders, then back away impatiently, dragging the frothing teats from eager mouths. The calves pause to stare in surprise at the retreating mothers, then gallop after, cut under the mothers' chins, and try to stop them by placing themselves broadside in their paths. Again and again they try, but each mother has the urge to travel in her, and the calf soon learns that he'd better keep up or be left behind. By nightfall there is hardly an acre of the ranch in its long ten miles that hasn't seen a cow yet.

Once the initial craving for green grass is satiated, the cows tend to their maternal duties; for the rest of the summer they will be better mothers.

Ahead of me is a tiny figure sitting on the beetling gray outcrop of lava at Coyote Springs, watching the purling water as it bubbles from some Stygian cavern beneath the rocks. Miles from the house; it can't be one of my brood, but what would someone else's child be doing this far from civilization?

Yes, it's Taylor, and already barefoot. I see his bicycle tracks now along the road like two romantic snakes. He is hunting arrowheads in places where spring rains have washed the lustrous black obsidian, a volcanic glass, sparkling clean.

"See, Dad?" he says, triumphant, showing a hot, moist palm full of bird points. His grin makes a lively dance of his freckles. I sit on the rocks with him, relishing their warmth, soaking up the sun as it beats down on my face. Together we watch silently as the cows flow on and on, intent upon their own business, as my horse drags his reins carefully through a mud puddle, head turned sideways so that he will not step on them and jerk his tender mouth. Taylor lies back, head on my lap, looking up at a blue sky that could never have been gray. "How was it back in the old days?" he asks.

I scarcely hear him. I am thinking of time past, of Homer Smith, Ern Morgan, Paddock, Uncle Buck, and the old Bar Y.

IN THOSE DAYS, WE MOVED THE Yamsi cattle out in the fall to the winter hay supply, instead of keeping them at the ranch as we do now. In November it meant a four-day drive from Yamsi to the old Bloomingcamp ranch, the BK, on the north side of the Bly valley, and in the spring another four-day drive back to the headwaters of the Williamson, when the range was ready for turning out cattle. The fall drive was easy since the calves had all been weaned from the cows. Spring was a different matter, for we left the BK with about five hundred cows and nearly as many tiny freshly branded calves. In a May dawn, we eased them out of a holding field into the long lane formed by split-rail fences, weathered and moss encrusted, on each side of the road. Those fences were a curse, since in their tumbled condition they often let a cow cross but kept a horse from following her. From the field we left a muddy track westward, past the Fitzpatrick place, the Labores Ranch, and down the sagebrushed hill to where the spring-swollen North Fork of the Sprague River crowded itself dangerously under a flimsy bridge. If the river was down there would be fishermen on the bridge, and the cattle would be afraid to cross.

If the river was high, the torrent often swirled over the bridge as well as under, and calf after calf was crowded over the hidden edges and swept away. Some drowned; some surfaced fifty feet downstream, and were cast with the driftwood on some willowed island or another, from which it took a long rope, repeatedly tossed, to capture them and drag them ashore. I shudder to remember.

We held the herd in the lane just beyond the river to let the calves catch up and dry off from their ordeal, as well as to let the men ride for survivors down the stream. We had to guard the bridge, for often the calves would break back, bound for the point where they last sucked, and hit the angry torrent as though it were a shallow mud puddle. When you guarded the drag of a herd of cows and small calves, let but one calf turn from the herd to face you and you were in trouble, for then the rest would follow suit and run back. Once they had broken

past you, you seldom had horsemen enough to turn them, but were forced to let them run, losing the hard-won miles until you could control them again.

As we left the lane, the cows, following the road, turned northward, then westward, up over the rolling hills. Sagebrush gave way to timber as they climbed. They seemed to sense now that they were headed for the Yamsi range, for out of the dragging resisting herd came leaders, sucking the rest with them up the hillsides and switchbacks, cracking the herd behind them like a whip as they trotted down hills while the drag was laboring up. Two men rode the point, two along the flanks, and the rest pounded the drag. The timber grew thicker now with islands of impenetrable young bullpine and scratchy tangles of mountain mahogany, as we dragged along the sleeping horse form of Charlie Mountain.

The men in the drag fought a constant war to keep the tired calves traveling along, trying to keep them from lying down unnoticed in the brush while the herd passed on. Now and then a cow would drop back to the bulging rear of the herd, thick with calves, find her calf among the bawling masses, and go on ahead with him. It was easier by far for her to lead her calf than it was for us to push him.

Noon usually found us on the Blue Creek flats, near the site of the old abandoned Indian lumber mill. There was water here for the cows, and an open meadow on which we could rest the herd and not risk the calves breaking back unseen through some handy thicket. We let the calves suck so that if they broke back in the future bound for where they had sucked last, they would return here instead of heading ten miles back to the BK.

Ern Morgan and I rode point, him on one side and me on the other, steering the leaders between us up the road. If the leaders slowed down, going up a hill, it was understood between us that we'd take a bunch and push them up the incline. Going downhill we'd brake the leaders by riding ahead of them, Morgan and I, side by side, blocking the road, letting them travel or eat up just as much ground as we saw fit. Even on the flat, the point men set the pace for the whole herd, and all the men in the drag had to do was try to keep pace with the leaders.

Ern was the best point man I ever saw. He had an uncanny ability to outguess a cow. Without ever getting his horse out of a walk, he would watch ahead and pick out a place where a lead cow would naturally stray, taking the bunch with her. Morgan was always there ahead of time, sitting quietly on his horse, a Bull Durham cigarette clamped stolidly and unlit in his set lips. Only the faint trace of a smile as a cow would turn as predicted from the road, look longingly in his direction, and then, since he blocked the way, turn and go obediently off down the road. Every quiet triumph of his meant saving the rest of us ten or fifteen minutes getting the herd pointed back down the road. At the end of the day fifteen minutes might be the difference between winning or losing, getting there or being trapped by darkness on the road.

Morgan and I seldom spoke; we shared a professional pride in being able to work together without speaking. For him to have advised me of a potential disaster up ahead would have been a slight to brood about for the rest of the day. To have let one see the other at a trot would have been to admit that he had been outwitted by a cow.

A good cowboy nursed his horse carefully, for on such a cattle drive he had to make one mount last the distance, and there was no predicting what disaster might befall tomorrow, when having fresh horseflesh left under one's saddle might save the day. A cowboy lost caste by galloping a horse after a cow; he turned her back at a trot if he could— but the best cowboy would have been quietly in position and prevented the cow from getting away in the first place. The buckaroo who learned his trade by watching the unreality of movie cowboys at a constant gallop was quickly fired from one outfit after another until he learned to settle down and handle the animals in the quietest possible manner.

There were times, of course, when the men could pound, pound, pound on the tail end of a herd, and all the shouting and cursing in the world wouldn't move them. But there were times when men spoke in a whisper or not at all, and the animals watched for the slightest excuse to spook. Wise to the sounds of the trail, the cattle were moved or soothed by only a slight difference in tone in the shouts they heard. I can close my eyes now and see out of the darkness that is the past the long herd trailing through the fragrant, sun-drenched sage, see the dust billowing in beige clouds over the drag, hear the cows bawling endlessly for their calves, and the men in the drag shouting and cursing. "Yippeeaoh ! Git up there you ———!" And over it all, Morgan's call drifting back over the herd from his position at the point, chastising cowboy and critter alike, whoever felt guilty. *"Give 'er 'elllll!"*

Cattle travel best if not driven at all, and the challenge was to keep the whole herd nodding peacefully, nose to tail down the road, eating up the miles at their own pace, each cow with room to avoid eating up the others' dust, with her calf anchored firmly behind, and with no appreciable bulge of stragglers in the rear of the herd.

The sight of five hundred fine, big, uniform Bar Y cows spread over a couple of miles of forest road was something to watch. People traveled for miles to see them, often arriving at the most inopportune moments, in time to either spook the cows off the road or catch a cowboy with his pants down in the sage. Gordon Barrie would be there to count the cows for the bank; there were mortgages in those days too. There were visitors who drove out to appreciate quality, and those, wiser than we, who sensed that what they were seeing was the last gasp of an era of Western history, a scene soon to be lost, swept away by the tides of change.

Often some rubbernecking stranger would roll down his window and ask me as I rode the point, "How many cattle you got in this herd, son?" Instead of the five hundred we actually had, I'd tip my hat back, scratch my dusty head with a buckskinned glove, chew a moment on a sagebrush twig, and venture, "Hell, I don't know, Mister. Coupla thousand, at least."

And the man would say, "Well I'll be damned. Why, I was just telling the wife here there must be a couple of thousand head!" He'd go back to town a whole lot happier having seen two thousand cattle than he'd have been with just the actual five hundred.

By nightfall that first day we'd crossed the Sycan River just north of Beatty, and bedded them down in a holding field west of the bridge at Bart Shelley's place. We camped outside by choice, for Bart had only two rooms and one of these was filled to the ceiling with old magazines. He chewed tobacco, too, and wasn't overly careful about where he spat, generally fouling the shoes of the fellow he was talking to through the corral fence. When you went to sit down in a chair in his house you looked where you were sitting then plunked down fast, for he could hit the seat with a dollop faster than you could with your rear.

Bart owned a big black bucking horse named Blackhawk, which might have gone on to be another Five Minutes Till Midnight had not Bart been too proud of him to sell him to the rodeo strings. Blackhawk was well into his twenties, an advanced age, when he finally went into the professional rodeo circuit and was a great horse even then, being chosen as a finals horse in the Pendleton Roundup. But his career, late in starting, was short lived, for a cattle truck overturned with him and he had to be destroyed. I still remember Bart shuffling up to the campfire, a few scraggly gray hairs cropping from beneath his battered old hat. "By Gawd, boys," he'd say. "I got a black horse over in that corral I wish one of you Bar Y cowboys would ride. Why, he's plumb gentle." But the cowboys knew the horse and no one ever tried.

By the time the calves had been mothered up and quit trying to head back toward Bly, the chuck wagon had generally caught up to the herd. A cowboy or two slipped off toward the lights of Beatty to the south for a little fun, but most of us were too tired to do more than lie around the campfire, listening to the sounds of cattle cropping the grass, the snuffle of contented horses, noses buried deep in their burlap nose bags, and the sizzle of steaks frying atop the iron stove. The sagebrush was full of ticks, and lumpy under our bedrolls; crushed by our bodies, its perfume was too heady to be pleasant, but we slept the sleep of the dead, too tired to care.

Dawn came early and nippy with Morgan coughing up a storm with his Bull Durham hack. Other than to swear at the cold, no one talked. One by one we crunched down to the banks of the Sycan to douse our faces in the cold river water, and from that instant we were wide awake. Still nobody talked much as we huddled about, watching the cook fry eggs on a stove that had no bottom, with drafts shoveled in the dirt along the sides. The idea was to creep as close to the stove as you dared without getting in the cook's way and arousing his ire. He had a way of accidentally spilling hot water on one's pant leg. Coffee black as night, so black your spoon disappeared from sight a half inch down into the murk. Only when I left home and his coffee did I find out what had been ailing me.

From the Sycan bridge, the road bent north again, on past Tim Brown Springs, a willowy, quaking, treacherous boggy mess, lined with the bones of thirsty cattle that had waded in but never waded out. We ganged up on the spring side of the herd to keep the cattle heading down the road. From there the road slanted up the hillside and climbed over the jagged rimrocks to the broad flat top of the tableland. It was a rough place to meet a car, and we generally did. Once it was a drunk Indian in a big black Chrysler, who came down the hill leaning on his horn, scattering cattle over the edge, and once they headed down there was no stopping them. He offered us all a drink and took it as right unfriendly that we wouldn't stop and be sociable. We were two days gathering the cows and the calves.

The tableland was a vast lava plateau, whose rocky reaches were broken only occasionally by oases of sand, covered with the brown straw deposit from the thick growth of ponderosa pines that flourished in islands there. Now and then one of these islands would boast a stream of cool, milky spring water, its shores lined with groves of tremble-leaved aspens, a water source which flowed off the barren lands and left in its wake a green grassy draw or swale.

At Eldon Springs there was a log corral for our horses, water, a lovely grove of aspen, and a lush meadow on which the cattle could feed and bed down for the night. Most of the cattle stayed, but some were eager now for home, and during the evening went on ahead with their calves. We looked the other way, for it would be that many less to drive come daybreak, and they would leave a set of tracks in the road for the others to follow. In the morning a band of antelope raced smoothly across the horizon, mule deer bounded for a cleft in the rim, a flock of great sage grouse almost as big as turkeys roared in off the flats for water. We had come thirty miles from the BK and still had another six to go to the edge of the Bar Y range, at Teddy Powers' meadow.

Sometimes in the clear visibility of the early morning, before the rising heat from the rocks made the air shimmer with mirages, we saw a flash of wild horses daring the open expanse between one forest island and another, moving back into the safety of the thickets for the day. Pintos, sorrels, bays, blacks, buckskins, motley browns. For a few years there was an isolated herd of blues, the color of blue velvet. I watched them often through binoculars. You could see the old grandmother, ancient, wide-sprung in gaunt ribs, and spavined. There was an assortment of daughters of every age, and a young barrel-chested stallion, all related, all blue, broken-hooved, black manes tangled like the hair of a madwoman. But they would run like the wind over a shattering fester of broken lava rock here in this garden of the devil; their hard, flinty hooves rang like bells on the tumbled rock ocean as they fled at the first glimpse of a rider's hat on the horizon.

The Andersons, Walkers, and Crumes, Indian cowboys from the Sprague River valley, ran wild horses every winter, catching them in deep snow when hard times had starved them weak. They followed the herds through the snow on fresh, well-fed horses, letting the wild bunch break trail, roping one, tying it to a tree, and pushing on after another until the band was gone. Al Shadley once found a horse frozen solid, still sitting back on his haunches as though still alive, pulling back stubbornly on the rope as his captors had left him.

I was sorry when my blues were gone. It left that vast tableland an empty place. But perhaps it is just as well that they came to a useful end. When the Indian Reservation became national forest, the Forest Service ordered the remnant herds destroyed.

North from the meadow at Eldon Springs, the road was a tumble of rocks and washes. Mile after mile of rock flats, juniper trees, and mountain mahogany, and not a drop of water for a cow to drink. After three miles of the rocks, the scenery changed rapidly as we entered a land covered with a deep layer of pumice sand, which soaked up water like a sponge and supported solid, uniform forests of ponderosa pine, beneath which lay an understory of bitterbrush and wild currant. But still there was no water. The pumice dust rolled upwards in dense clouds, obscuring the sun. The cows walked with their mouths open, long strings of saliva streaking the dry sands over which they passed.

Then suddenly, a quiet breeze from the north, coming first as a coolness in the air, wafted the scent of water to the leaders, and from then on it took both Morgan and me to hold them back. We were aided for a time by the steep rimrocks, which kept the cattle from charging down into the canyon, but when we got to the point where the Sycan opens into the broad meadows of Teddy Powers' old deserted ranch, we could manage them no longer. The herd simply flowed around our horses on both sides, and raced down the long hillsides toward water.

The first cattle stopped at the edge of the swollen Sycan, thrusting their noses deep, ignoring the pushy pileup of cattle crowding in from behind until the second and third waves of cattle literally shoved the first wave into the drink, and they were no longer drinking but swimming hard against the current for the opposite shore. It took a couple of cowboys to swim their horses across and get them back, no easy task since by now the cows were afraid of water, and sometimes had to be roped and dragged back across. If a calf or two had crossed with them, a cowboy roped one and dragged it into the water bawling for its mother. Mother instinct would make the cows forget their fears, and they would charge right in behind, bawling angrily, sniffing the calf to determine whether or not it was theirs.

Teddy Powers' meadow was the southernmost limit of our range, and thus the end of the long spring drive. We held the cattle along the river until the calves had found their mothers and sucked them dry. We left them then, trotting our horses the last seven miles up over the ridges and down the long shoulder of Taylor Butte to Yamsi and the headwaters of the Williamson.

From Teddy's the cattle scattered themselves, moving on to some special lonely glade which had summered them the year before, and to which they were especially attached. Within three days' time, only about a hundred and fifty of the original cows would be left to summer on the Sycan. The rest drifted on to Wildhorse, Bottle Springs, Buckhorn, Bear Draw, Telephone Draw, and Haystack. A hundred square miles of ponderosa and lodgepole forest threaded with long grassy meadows some of which were ten miles long. My cattle summer there still.

The flat at Teddy Powers' was always a good place to show the summering cattle off to the banker. Here the Sycan, winding from the east through steep canyons, turned south through a broad grassy meadow, thronged with bush willows and wild currants, cut deep with potholes left from the spring floods, tiny ponds on which the many waterfowl raised their broods. It was a natural lounging area for cattle, which came in from all directions to noon in the shade of the willows, away from the torment of the woodland mosquitoes.

Teddy Powers was a long, tall beanpole of a man, married to an Indian woman, who must have had a rare sense of scenery for he built his cabin on a lovely point overlooking the river and the pine-clad lava buttes across the way. Snowed in from December until May, he wintered there many a long winter, then moved on in 1914 to Cherry Creek south of Sprague River. But the cabin still stands, a fireplace of rocks holding up one end and the hewn door frame the other, weathered, rotting, caved in by last year's snows, but there, a monument to someone long ago. Sometimes of a summer's eve I ride there just to smell the scent of pine trees, the odor of hoof-crushed sage rising heady in my nostrils, and to be alone with the past.

The roof of his little covered well, made with shakes hand split from a local pine, has been flattened by a giant falling tree, but the well is there, neatly done in flat stones, set up in an era when men still took pride in what their hands could fashion. Years back rustlers used the abandoned well as a secret place to sink their weighted hides. Now it is filled almost to the brim with hunters' garbage.

Here and there sprawl a few old horse-drawn mowing machines, gap toothed, blades rusted to guards, to chatter through the grass no more. A pine tree with the waist measurement of a portly man grows up through the spokes of an iron wheel from a hayrake, torturing the spokes, growing around them as a fat man embeds his belt. Only a few teeth left unbroken, the machine itself, rusting slowly, shows only

the spring seat over the top of the encroaching sagebrush. Here part of a singletree, its iron hand-hammered by a blacksmith long ago; here the broad iron rim of a wooden wagon wheel; there a haimes strap, leather black and brittle. Now and then I find a part I need on my own harness or machinery and I use it proudly. Nothing but a few warped gray boards left of the outhouse. Some winter past, a bull trapped by winter crawled into the root cellar for shelter, not knowing it was to be his tomb. All that remain now are the horns and a scattered pile of white bones.

He had a dream, Teddy did, to carve a ranch out of the wilderness, and he had the naive confidence of youth that if he worked hard he was bound to be successful. He engineered a ditch along the hillside east of the river, dug it from gravel and rock with horse and scraper, and led the water out over the thirsty land. The rock flats were bone hard in their resistance to his attempt to set fence posts, and what posts he managed to set in summer and fall fell over when spring turned the clay flats into little more than a bog. The raging torrents of the river took out his ditches in moments. When the water subsided he tried again.

His gaunt face and scarecrow body were in odd contrast to his fat, moonfaced Indian wife. Silly Hicks was so broad of beam she took up the whole front seat of the Studebaker wagon, and Teddy had to stand the long road to Beatty, driving the team with the reins held over her head. She had to turn sideways to squeeze through the front door of the cabin, and one spring when she had an attack of appendicitis they had to tear down the front end of the cabin so that four men could carry her out.

Teddy lived there early, of course, at a time when the country was still being named. Many a richer, wiser, more educated man than he has gone unheralded by history, but Teddy Powers came to be as much a landmark as a man, and got his name on all the area maps and signs without even trying. But times are changing. Already the Forest Service has put up a sign in the middle of the meadow calling it Teddy Power Meadow, although his name was Powers.

The river and the long harsh winters proved too much for Teddy, and the high water, heartless and impersonal, washed away his dreams. When he made his last wagon trip out over the long tablelands, he left the valley as silent as he had found it. He spent his old age in the Sprague River valley, and when he died, the Indians buried him unheralded and unsung on a ridge overlooking the valley. No one returned to the grave, for he had yet to become a part of history.

REALITY AGAIN. WAS IT THE Steller's jay splashing noisily in the spring brought me back, or was it the YZ cow bawling for her calf and the plaintive, neglected, answering of that confused bovine urchin of hers from the timbered slope right behind me? Maybe those fine old Bar Y cows are gone, sold in my uncle's last years, but in that cow out there flows some of the old blood, making it a second-generation herd. Taylor sleeps quietly, head still on my lap, his bird points clutched tightly in his moist palm. There is a sudden rush of wings as a golden eagle breaks over the top of the rocks above our heads and folds on a brush rabbit who had crept from the wild plum thicket beside us. The eagle allows the rabbit only one squeak, then flaps heavily to the jutting pinnacle of the landmark snag that in my boyhood, before it lost its top in a wild winter storm, held an eagle's nest. "Look, Taylor," I whisper, not wanting him to miss the sight. A puff of brown rabbit fur, light as thistledown, floats gentle upon the thermals from the rocks. The eagle follows it with his great brown eyes, bobbing his head up and down as though to better focus on what has escaped his grasp, then goes back to tearing off chunks of flesh, bone, and hide, rejecting nothing.

Alone again at Yamsi, with the family back in school. The frustration of being alone is that my day is filled with such beauty, from the whispered, plaintive silver voice of the hermit thrush to the sight of sandhill cranes etched like pewter mobiles against the rushing clouds, and there is no one with whom to share.

But I should not be taking time to enjoy it either. I am still suffering for the moments lost in March, in April. The May rush is upon me. I must take the tractor and clean the irrigation ditches, but before that I must fix the tractor. To fix the tractor I need power with which to drill out and remove a bolt broken last fall. Before I can have power I must fix the light plant, and to fix the light plant, since there are no mechanics available, I must study the maintenance book. Then too I need a part from the parts house sixty miles away. I phone, giving them the serial number of the machine. Only last year that outfit sold me the plant as being the very latest in power equipment. Now the parts man clucks sadly. "*That* old model? Gee, I don't even know if we can still get parts. Maybe if you phoned around to some of the junk yards . . ."

I hang up the phone, trudge to the blacksmith shop, build a coal fire in the long dead forge, and make the part myself. I seem to imagine that the light plant now runs better for my ingenuity than it did before. As I come in for a lonely bowl of soup at noon, convinced that I am finally able to fix the tractor, the telephone jangles angrily.

"Ignore it," a little voice tells me, but I am too curious. After all, even *bad* news has to come a long, long way. The stationmaster at Chiloquin informs me that I have a carload of fertilizer at Lenz siding near Klamath Marsh, and I must pay demurrage after tomorrow for every day I leave the car loaded. I need a fertilizer spreader from town but my pickup won't start. There is no one about to give me a pull. I almost replaced the battery the last time I was in town, but the banker had just given me a lecture on economy, so I tried to make it last. And even if I started the pickup, I discover that the gasoline tanks are empty; I have forgotten to call the gas delivery man. The nearest gas station is thirty miles away.

Of course there is fence to ride for winter damage, over a hundred miles of it, but that too takes the pickup. *I could* get the team back in and hitch up the old fencing wagon, but I'd sort of promised them the summer off. I try to fix my tractor, only to find that I need a special wrench from town. Also my winter men have departed with my bolt extractors and my Stilson wrenches. The phone chooses this moment to go out of order so I can't call for help. A flash of inspiration. There is gas in the hay trucks. One lacks a coil which I borrowed for my tractor on the Marsh ranch. The spare tire for the second hay truck is flat, as is the front tire. I start the cattle truck in triumph, but a pack rat has built a nest on the engine which soon catches fire and burns up the wires. So I can at least look at the cattle, I run in the only saddle horse I can catch, fully expecting him to drop dead beneath my saddle. But he needs no battery, and no gas. He eats hay but gives most of it back in fertilizer; and after all it is the barn and not the tractor shed that yields the makings of my wife's garden.

But fertilizing a ranch such as the Marsh with animals would be a hopeless task, and I have to rely on commercial fertilizer in concentrated form. If I am to grow a hay crop there this summer to tide my cattle through next winter, I must sacrifice five solid days of my busy life, unload a railroad car of heavy sacks of fertilizer, dump it into the hopper of a machine, and scatter it evenly over three hundred twenty acres of broad, flat ground. Then for the summer I must send a man to irrigate the meadows so that the hay will grow.

Madhouse May. Thirty-hour days wouldn't be long enough by half. Perhaps if I moved faster, if I didn't stop constantly to watch a chipping sparrow build its nest in the hawthorn, if I let it untangle its own snarl of horsehair from the lilac bush. Perhaps if my ear weren't constantly attuned to every sound from the far-off racheting cacophony of the cranes, to the faint chattering of the Vaux's swifts searching for nesting cavities in the decaying landmark pine, I would get more done, and wouldn't fall so desperately behind.

Each broken part I find I need means sixty miles to town. To stop the bulls from rubbing down my fences I plan when I have time, *if* I have time, to spray the bulls for lice or mites. I take time, only to find someone forgot to drain the sprayer last fall and the cylinders are cracked beyond all use.

Today I turn the water into the irrigation ditches to flood the fields, but the culverts are still washed out from winter and water floods from a big break in the ditch, so that I have to turn it off again. I need the tractor to bulldoze up the breaks, fill in the washed-out culverts. It needs only a bolt this time. Having had a flat tire, I arrive in town at 5:05; the stores all close at 5:00.

How easily I lose track of the days. Is it really Friday? I count the pairs of dirty socks beside my bed, a pair for each day since Monday. It *is* Friday. That means the family will be out and I'll have to find time to wash a sink full of dishes before my wife sees what a disaster I have made of her nice clean kitchen. This week I had steak for ten meals; but the week before I had spaghetti for *thirteen* meals including three breakfasts.

Thinking of her now, I recall faintly her saying something as she left about having put some potatoes in the oven to bake. They are still there, or rather there are five little hard balls of charcoal the size of golf balls. Into the willows behind the house they go. Mickey, the cow dog, thinking I am playing games, lays one at my feet on the back porch. Spotting the abandoned plunder, a Canada jay flies down to feast, is driven off by a Stellar jay, who is driven off by a magpie, who is driven off in turn by a cock pheasant, who decides he didn't want the thing anyway. It is finally gobbled up by my huge old Irish setter, Red, who would eat anything with my scent upon it. This morning as I was throwing him his complement of sourdough hotcakes on which he has become hooked, I dropped my buckskin glove. *Slurp.* Before it had time to hit the ground Red inhaled it, than sat wagging his tail for its mate.

I have barely finished washing a dish I dirtied somewhere back about Tuesday when the frenzied, joyous barking of the dogs announces the family's arrival. A hundred stray cars can go by on the road and the dogs sleep through all of them, but let our car crest the hill five miles away and the dogs are prancing at the big log gate.

The ranch wakes up with excitement. Biddy bawls to Ginny from the lane; out on the meadows horses spoiled rotten with attention nicker for their grain. The girls race past me, heading for the barn. "Hi, Dad," Marsha calls, almost knocking me off the bridge. "Are we going to brand tomorrow? I hope, I hope?"

"We might," I reply, but she is already vaulting the corral fence, heading for the pasture.

CHAPTER 8

ONLY A FEW OUTFITS IN OREGON still rope their calves at branding time, and if it were not for my insistence that the children know the old historic ways, I too would have yielded to that faster and more efficient device known as the "branding table."

The Second World War had a great deal to do with spreading the popularity of branding tables. Good hands who could handle a rope became increasingly scarce, and there was need for a device which would lay a calf on its side and hold it tightly for branding, vaccinating, earmarking, dehorning, cutting fleshmarks, and, if the animal was a bull, castration.

Faced with wartime scarcities of help and the reality of branding three or four thousand calves, my uncle cast about for a better method than roping and came up with a device that worked, but was far harder on men than it was on the calves. At the end of a long chute he built a slippery, slanted bottom, so that when the calves came to this spot, their feet would fly out from under them. They would slide out into the open to be pounced upon by a couple of hefty cowboys, who held the calves down bodily until ropes could be put on front and back feet and the animal stretched out on the ground. This "hand-mucking chute" as it was called, with its galvanized tin bottom, died a quick, unmourned death, for my uncle soon found that his cowboys would go off on a drunk just before the branding season and not show up until after it was over.

He would have been forced to give up branding his calves entirely and throw himself on the mercy of rustlers, had not someone invented the calf table which, only slightly improved, is with the industry still. It is fast, efficient, easy on calves and cowboys, but thoroughly despised by cowboys still of the roping tradition, to whom roping at a branding is the only fun left to the working man.

The calf table, made of steel, sits upright as an extension of a short plank chute. One by one, the calves are shoved forward onto the table, caught around the neck by a stanchion, gripped in a sandwich of steel walls, and then laid flat on their sides with the rotation of the table from vertical to horizontal. A slip loop on a rachetted drum stretches the hind feet out behind. In less than a minute the calf is branded, earmarked, dehorned, castrated, vaccinated, the loop on the hind feet removed, the table returned to upright position, and the calf's head released. The main drawback is that you have to pay the crew wages to run the thing.

Just to show the world that we are as efficiently modern as the next outfit, we own a perfectly good calf table, but it will stay rusty and unused as long as we can sound the call and come up with a good showing of ropers who will work hard all day for nothing just to get to rope calves. All we are out for labor are some good thick steaks cooked in the open, baked beans, cherry pie, and a few cans of cold beer at noon.

While we still turn out cows and calves on the open range, it is not the procedure it was in the days of the Bar Y when the cattle were driven in from a wintering area. Wintering them right here on the ranch not only gives them a sense of a home to return to in the fall, but simplifies the spring turnout, since the range is just on the other side of a six-wire fence. But the calves still have to be branded, for to turn an unbranded calf out on the range would be rank foolishness. As the wise old Sprague River Indian Hi Robbins once said, "There are thieves amongst us."

Our brand, a YZ on the left hip, and our earmark, an under bit in the left ear, is recorded for us in the State Brand Office, a division of the State Department of Agriculture. It is a penitentiary offense for someone to butcher one of our animals without a bill of sale, and any of our cattle shipped out of the state must first be inspected by a state brand inspector. But in spite of such stringent measures rustling remains an annual loss which is often greater than the annual profit. In one county in Northern California, in 1968, losses to one operator amounted to over $15,000, and this was only a fraction of the rustling loss for the county.

Anyone willing to pay the recording fee may own a brand, but the state must first approve its design and the position in which it is to be placed on the animal. Not only must the intended brand be properly designed, so that it will produce a legible mark instead of a blotch, but it should also be a mark which could not be mistaken for any other state brands. Another person might be allowed a YZ, but he would not be allowed to place the YZ on the left hip as we do. Since there are more than eighteen thousand recorded brands in the state of Oregon alone, the problem of keeping them straight is monumental. Figuring out how to alter one brand design into another will always be a popular pastime among people whiling away time in the local bars.

Ginny is the member of the family most bitten by the roping bug. At sixteen, coached by Slim, she handles a rope well. I hear her boots, purposely loud, long before dawn, clumping over the upstairs floor. She is impatient that we sleep when there is so much to be done. Marsha at her heels, she stomps down the stairs, pretending to be quiet. Like children on Christmas morning, they are in a sweat to get going.

I am sour and difficult. I already know how the day will pass with those prima donna ropers taking over and me stuck with working on the ground. I roll over to try to sleep, try to forget how tired I'll feel at the end of the day. But my wife, a morning person where I am a night person, opens the door to the kitchen and lures me from bed with the smell of frying bacon.

Two hissing Coleman lanterns flood the kitchen with yellow light. A fire roars in the wood stove, coffee steams, filling the air with fragrance. Chairs I haven't seen in ages, pulled out of storage, all occupied by men I thought were dead. Here and there a young face, on whose shoulders will rest in future years the whole tradition of roping. I wish I owned a hundredth of the cattle they have roped in a lifetime.

Slim is back, lured by the one thing that could bring him out of retirement. With him are his pretty daughter and her husband. Top hands, both of them, used to heading and heeling. Clint Bassey, is there lean, tall, high cheeked and lank jawed, hard to beat; Gordon Barrie, my banker friend, who seldom misses, whether roping or judging men. Two or three others whose shy silence as they nurse their coffee shows them to be of the cowboy tradition. I cheer up perceptibly. Maybe, before the day is out, someone will say to me, "You rope. Let me work on the ground awhile."

We plow through great stacks of sourdough hotcakes, biscuits, bacon, platters of fried eggs. The chickens haven't laid that many this week. It makes me tired just to see my wife, a superefficiency of a woman, flit from one place to another. Lunch all ready to cook, the kitchen clean, and her horse will be the first one saddled and out of the barn to help gather the calves and the last one to lie down and roll tonight. My eggs are only half eaten and already Ginny and Marsha are signaling me with their eyes to hurry. My stomach has a hard knot in it and I wonder to myself what an ulcer feels like.

As we ride north, I huddle along in my saddle, immersed in my jacket, thinking how warm and nice that bed was, and how in another hour the sun will be up and the jacket superfluous and tied behind my saddle in a huge lump I can hardly get my leg over. I am cursing the ropers again. Their horses go at a jig trot, while my ranch horses are studiously trained either to walk or trot. I have pounded it into my kids that no horseman worth his salt lets a horse jig trot, and here these stray cowboys with their fancy horses, whom my kids will automatically revere more than me, are making my gospel seem suspect. How do I tell these men who *volunteered* to help me today that I just don't allow jig trotting on the ranch, and that I don't even want my horses to see it, misbegotten gait that it is?

Slyly, I ride up beside one of the cowboys and try to shame him without hurting his feelings. "That horse of yours jig trots, doesn't he?" I venture.

"Shore does. Trained him myself."

My own poor ranch horse tries to adjust to the in-between gait and stumbles.

"You ought to trim his feet," the man suggests.

I stare off into the distance as though I am appraising the way the herd is scattered. If I ride at a walk, I get left behind; If I ride at a trot then I am too far ahead. As Al would put it, those quarter horses walk so slowly they can make two piles in the same heap.

Ginny and Marsha are entranced. I've never seen a horse they didn't like, but I've tried to make them appreciate thoroughbreds. I grumble as I ride beside the girls. "Doggone pony types, those quarter horses. No withers and so muscle-bound they can't walk a step. Just fit for corral work, not riding the range. And rough enough to break a man's back."

"I think they're groovy, Dad," Marsha replies.

I am a little hurt that Gordon Barrie doesn't comment on the new gates I've built that really work, and the ditches I've cleaned and mended. Then I realize that it isn't necessary to point out anything. He was my uncle's banker before he became mine; he knows every detail of the ranch and misses nothing. By nature he only comments on the things he sees wrong, and so perhaps his silence is to be wished for.

One by one the cowboys peel off out of the formation and ride alone, circling the cows and pushing them in toward the Kay Davis corrals. The cattle are nervous, sensing that since they haven't seen this many horsemen gathered together in some time something unusual must be happening. It's usually just Marsha, Ginny, or I smoking the air, trying to move the whole herd by ourselves.

"Who was Kay Davis, Dad?" Ginny asks.

I have been feeling left out and drop my cows to explain to her, while one of the stray cowboys gallops over to see if anything is wrong.

"Kay Davis was an old Indian from whom my uncle bought this field, Ginny. Kay hit him up one day on Main Street, Klamath Falls. 'You know that claim I bin leasing you, Buck, at the head of the river? I need money bad. I sell it for eight hundred dollars, and buy new automobile.'

"'Hell, I don't want to steal it from you, Kay. I'll give you three thousand.'" Buck was a fine man. Anybody else would have stolen the fields for eight hundred. He stole it for three thousand. It was cheap at any price, for claim by claim Yamsi was moving up the valley.

We head the cows and calves for the old log corrals in the distance. They look much better when one is far away from them. Up close they show their half a century and more of hard use. Gravity has sagged the rotting logs in the middle, but the lurching, leaning gateposts seem to defy it. The first gate falls with a crash on the man trying to open it, and Gordon looks grim. It has become a thing of sentiment, a fetish of mine to use them one more year. But how long is too long; when will this one more year end?

A decade ago, I did make a sporadic attempt at rebuilding the corrals. Old Charlie Tucker was my hired hand then. We planned our attack on the corrals for a month over constant cups of coffee, but when we finally got around to starting we couldn't find a ladder.

"I'll build one," volunteered Charlie. It took him four days to build a really fine ladder, and he had just leaned it up against the first gate we had singled out for replacing when a gust of wind blew the ladder over and it hit me on the head. Knowing that ladder had done that on purpose, I whirled, administering a kick of revenge that broke it right in the middle. The old man quit right on the spot.

I spent one more day on the renewal project, and had just completed a tight new woven wire fence right down the middle when a cowboy, working a cow, headed her in the direction of my handiwork. I could see when she was twenty feet out that she wasn't going to stop and she didn't.

I am letting the corrals rot. Some year when it is physically impossible to brand another calf in them I promise I will rebuild them to their former splendor. I tell my banker that I keep them because I am sentimental about the past. He says I am just lazy. Busy would be a kinder word, and I wish he'd learn to use it.

As the scattering of cows and calves tightens and is compressed by the force of cowboys into a compact herd, the green meadow, awash with seas of yellow dandelions and buttercups, turns red and white with cows, already slickening with the loss of winter coats. I'm proud of them, but I groan as I notice that Biddy with her awful back line seems determined to travel along right in front of Gordon's horse.

The ground trembles as the cows funnel through the gate. Cowboys are stirrup to stirrup now behind the calves who drag behind. Romals pop like gunfire on leather chaps as they try to keep the calves pointed ahead. A calf streaks between the legs of Ginny's horse and dashes for freedom. Her jaw clenches angrily, and her arm blurs. So swift I hardly saw it, her rope tightens around the calf's neck and she leads him dancing like a puppet on the leather string of her reata, back into the bunch.

We crowd the herd into the furthermost corral, then let the cows dash back for freedom as we hold back the calves. The cows have run this gauntlet many times, while the calves are confused, cooperating without knowing any better. Dust hangs in a pall over the corral; the din of calves bawling for their mothers and the mothers bawling for their calves is deafening. Clint Bassey cuts fifty head of calves into the big round corral, and looks askance at the rotting logs, as though doubting they will hold.

Shifting from east to west, a mischief wind fans the branding fire, hurtling the black, sooty sting of pine pitch smoke into my eyes, and wafts the heat right up the handles of the branding irons. My wife sterilizes the tools in a pan of green soap, then tests the edge of her knife, frowning because since Al left there hasn't been a sharp blade on the place. When the irons are hot, the four ropers saunter forth to do their work. They are reata men to the man, and are as cranky about them as any possession they own.

The calves pile up against one side of the corral. A cowboy swings an easy loop, settles it about the neck of a surprised calf, jerks up his slack in a smooth back sweep of his arm, coils up the excess rope as he trots toward the bucking, bawling calf. Then comes the blur of his hand over his saddle horn, as swifter than vision he takes his dallies or turns about his saddle horn, and leads the calf out of the herd. As the calf hangs back against the rope, another roper bends a graceful loop just in front of the calf's hind legs, pauses a split second for the calf to step ahead into the trap, then jerks tight the noose and dallies. Cool and calm, the two rope horses, facing each other, back up, tightening the rope, stretching out the calf between them. Grudgingly I admit to myself that I am impressed.

One of the ground crew flips the calf over so that the left side is up. Holding the front leg pinned to prevent him from rising, he takes the rope off the calf's neck as the roper yields him slack, then places the loop on both front feet as the horse leans back and tightens the rope again. As the man kneels on the calf's neck to prevent him from struggling, Dayton takes one of the hot branding irons from the fire. Smoke fogs up in a yellow acrid cloud, as the iron singes the hair and turns the hide to the color of toast. A perfect YZ and the iron is once more laid in the coals.

I earmark the calf, cutting a V or underbit out of the bottom edge of the left ear, then, using a dehorner, scoop out the tiny horn buttons. Johnny smears the head wounds with fly repellent, Marsha vaccinates the calf with blackleg and Malignant Edema serum, and if it is a heifer calf, it is released. If the calf is a bull calf Gerdi castrates it, making it a steer. She cuts the end of the scrotal sack off with a knife, then cuts the cord of both testicles with a special crimper to prevent bleeding, and drops the testicles into a clean can. These will be stripped of sinews and fried up for supper, a delicacy most enjoyed by the crew, who refer to them as "mountain oysters." The ordeal has taken a little over a minute of his life, and the calf scoots back to the other calves.

With four good ropers working there is always a calf before the fire, and those not roping work as part of the ground crew until their turn comes.

Slim's calf kicks one hind foot out of the loop and his daughter teases him for getting old. She then makes a pretty catch of both hind feet, which puts a grim set to her father's jaw, and ruins his day. On her next throw she misses completely, but there is an impish smile on her pretty face which hints that that throw might have been one for the old man's pride. Clint Bassey makes a wild catch from forty feet away, one of the spectacular desperation shots he's famous for. Ginny trots up on Bones, misses, whips out another loop and catches both hind feet in mid dance. Her face is masked, but as she rubs her cheek on her coat I catch the flash of a triumphant smile. Slim's smile is out in the open, for he spent many a summer evening teaching her how.

By noon arms unused to roping are sore, and the horses have lost their eagerness. Somehow, in between bull calves, Gerdi has managed to start a fire of her own outside the dusty corral, and the smell of barbecuing steaks, hot baked beans, and steaming coffee floats over

to mingle with the smell of burning hair. A hundred calves done; a hundred fifty more to go before we can call it a day.

"Chow!" Gerdi calls as we release the last calf of the group, and we turn the newly branded calves back to the care of their mothers.

It is a welcome break. A light spattering of rain moves in from the west, streaking the dust on our faces, but the men ignore it to loosen the cinches on their saddles, and turn the horses loose to graze among the buttercups. As the sun comes back out there is a smell of freshness from the steaming damp of the ground. A horse rolls over on the ground, bringing a roar from his master and laughter all around. Hunkering down before the fire, the crew help themselves to food. In scattered groups they lounge about, talking between bites about ropes, and saddles, and horses they have owned, about old friends back upon the trail they wish were here.

The food tastes good in the open air, and there is a festive air about the men, but there is an impatience too, to be back under way. A roping is what they have looked forward to the winter long, and they relish every minute of it. For this the tall, graying cowboy, Bert Schroeder, has driven three hundred miles from the eastern Oregon town of Burns.

Slowly the afternoon wears on. Seventy-five more calves done. With ever increasing frequency, I glance at the adjoining corrals to see how many calves are left. My back aches from bending over, my hands from gripping the dehorning scoops. Only a few more calves left and we'll be done for the day. Clint Bassey seems to sense my fatigue and spells me off. "Here," he says, leading my horse into the corral. "You rope awhile and let me work the ground."

Now that I am faced with the prospect, I am nervous. I have visions of missing, of dropping my rope, of catching my horse around the neck, getting the rope under his tail, of having the saddle turn. My horse seems bothered by the presence of all those fancy quarter horses, and turns awkwardly. To make matters more difficult, Ginny makes a magnificent shot, and I am stuck with hind-footing the thing. I pretend to be having trouble with my bridle, hoping someone else will move in and make the catch, but they all sit around like lumps and wait for me to do whatever it is I'm trying to do. I close my eyes and make my throw, jerking my slack automatically.

"You got him, Dad!" Ginny calls, glowing with pride.

On the next cast I catch one neatly around the neck; no one but me guesses that it wasn't even the calf I was throwing at. Duane Quimby, riding a buckskin with a black stripe down his back, makes a swift catch of both hind feet, I almost lose the calf's front feet before he is half branded when my horse starts watching a mountain bluebird perched on a gatepost. There is an audible snort of disgust from my banker, to whom tradition and ability are everything.

Five straight I've roped and haven't missed a shot; I keep my head down so no one can see how damnably pleased with myself I am. This is *fun!* But I can feel a miss coming up. I ride up to the corral gate.

"Feels like my horse is favorin' his right hind foot," I lie to Bassey. "I'll trade you places."

I would like to brag a little about my roping but with that gang I don't dare. I look modestly at the ground, fishing hard for compliments. "Sure am out of practice today," I venture to Slim.

"I've never seen the day when you were in," Slim replies.

Another day of branding. Gerdi rides her old thoroughbred, now twenty-seven, a grandson of Man O'War. She ropes a calf and drags him to the fire. I've aged her; this life has aged her. Was it really so long ago I saw her break this horse, saw him jump out thirty feet and try to buck while she stepped nimbly on, hardly noticing?

She had a way with him, since first she took him as a week-old wire-cut colt no one had much hope for. He broke Jimmy Rapley's leg, bucked with me across the old BK corral until blood ran from my ears, a ding bat, prancing, jittery spook of a horse who took eighteen years of hard riding before you could throw a rope off him and not land in the next county. A great horse, though, if you could stand him; add up all the long trail drives he's been on, the cattle he's separated, the cows he's gathered off the range, the long weary traveling miles he's packed a man, the calves he's roped, and he's got to go down as one of the great ones. Her, too.

On the second day, we run out of calves in mid afternoon. There just aren't any more. After all you can't brand a calf that died in the spring; you can't brand a calf that isn't yet born; you can't brand a calf out of a cow that somehow didn't get bred last go-round. I had expected more calves; my banker had expected more calves. Gerdi looks haunted and discouraged; Gordon looks embarrassed and ill-at-ease; I look off into the distance and watch how a red-tailed hawk fingers the thermals, etched dark against the silver of a cloud, searching perhaps for the first brood of short-tailed ground squirrels to come, stupid and unwary, out of their burrow. I have escaped reality because some wisdom deep inside tells me that if I faced it it would destroy me.

"Well, there will be lots more calves born on the range this year," I assure them brightly. "Enough for another branding later on."

Everyone has gone home and I am left with the silent empty corrals, useless for another year. Will there be another year for them, or will the snows of winter flatten the rotten wood into little more than a brown scattering on next spring's grass?

The cows and calves are silent now, each family reunited. The calves are sick from their shots, sick from their operations, but they will mend in time, and within days will be romping again across meadows rampant with wildflowers. My horse nickers to me across the corral, wondering perhaps why I alone have remained, reminding me that he has better things to do than remain here, his supper to gather out in his grassy pasture.

TURNOUT DAY IS THE HAPPIEST DAY. The Forest Service range technician inspects the range, determines that it is ready, and counts the cows and calves as they throng past him out the gate. Within minutes the fields are empty and the cattle have disappeared into the surrounding forest. Biddy turns, bawls as though asking Ginny to come with her, then trots off with her calf to join the rest.

"Wait and see, Dad," Ginny boasts proudly. "This fall, she'll come in with the best and biggest calf in the herd."

After a few days the children and I will fan out over the range, making sure that the cows aren't concentrated, but are uniformly scattered. There are no fences to limit their wanderings. Cattle lack the pronounced sense of range shown by horses, which on escaping will often return hundreds of miles to where they were foaled. But the cattle do have an affinity for where they wintered last. In the old days, when my uncle purchased stacks of hay at various localities, then moved the cattle to the stacks, the cattle scattered badly, especially in the fall. Because my cows winter here, they feel anchored to the valley of the Upper Williamson. Even though an occasional animal may turn up in the fall sixty miles away, most of the herd stays within the natural boundaries of arid forest or steep ridges which separate my range from others.

In many range areas, the absence of available salts in the soils and a cow's natural metabolic craving for salt combine to give the rancher a useful range management tool. He may provide salt for its own sake; he may use salt grounds as a treat to lure cattle into areas they might otherwise neglect, or, conversely, by not salting in certain areas, to discourage heavy use in problem zones; or he may use salt as a carrier for medicines, or other supplements he wishes to add to a cow's diet. Given free choice, a cow consumes a fairly consistent amount of salt each day, so that by adding salt to vitamins, minerals, protein supplements, or medicines, one can regulate each cow's daily intake.

Generally, range salt comes in fifty-pound blocks which may be white (plain), yellow (sulfurized), or red (iodized). Over half the salt I place on the range is utilized by deer and other wildlife, including birds such as the crossbills, which flock in to the salt blocks by the hundreds. Deer lick tiny cups into the salt, while cattle lick larger ones, giving the block a weird appearance as it is consumed. We now hide the blocks in the woods, since salt is a costly item, and there are people who would rather gather salt blocks off the range than buy their own.

I once rode up on a fashionably dressed woman struggling to carry a well-worn salt block through my barbed wire fence to her waiting car. She was so excited to have found "such a pretty rock" that I didn't have the heart to tell her that it was nothing but a commercial salt block and the indentations caused by animals. Instead I said in my best drawl, "Ma'am, that shore is a museum piece you got there. If I were you I'd take it right home and put it in your birdbath." Having put out this pan of water for the raccoon stealing sugar lumps, I rode on my way.

In the days of the Bar Y, before the advent of those modern, sanitized split-level cow apartments known as livestock trucks, cattle were driven in large herds to the railhead at Chiloquin, or were driven to the ranch from the railhead in the spring.

Since the thirty-mile drive from Yamsi to the railroad corrals at Chiloquin took two days, requiring a stopping place to feed and water large herds, Buck purchased a set of Indian claims at the foot of Calimus Butte, a thousand-acre tract of lodgepole forest, well watered, and interlaced with lush meadows. For years he had observed that the cattle he picked up in the fall on these meadows were fatter than the rest and had a lustrous bloom to them. Then, having made his purchase, he set out to fence the field as a holding area. Since his boundaries sawed back and forth across the best potential road right-of-way, the Indian Service permitted him to fence in an additional thousand acres of his leased range land, in exchange for a grant of right-of-way through the area.

The Calimus Ranch still exists today as part of our operation, though it is no longer used as a resting place for trail herds. Here we summer our replacement heifers, breeding them to Angus bulls, for calving the following April.

Not only are there seventeen miles of fence to check every spring, but also it requires a twelve-mile cattle drive from Yamsi to Calimus in the spring, and Calimus to Yamsi in the fall.

These drives are the children's drives, no adults allowed, with Ginny as trail boss, Marsha and Dayton flanking, John and Taylor bringing up the rear. In the tradition of the past, they hold the cattle up for rest, and eat their lunch on the same hillside on which cattle have been held up for fifty years. Still scattered through the woods are blackened stumps where cowboys long dead built their warming fires against the chill of spring or autumn.

There are grins of surprise as passing drivers ease their cars through the herd on the road, and see that there isn't a grownup in sight. They probably figure the old man is either lazy or off drunk somewhere. A driver rolls down his window and addresses Ginny. "How many cattle you got here, young lady?" Keeping tradition alive, Ginny replies, "Oh, about a thousand."

"That so ?" the man replies. "I was just telling the wife here, it looked to be about a thousand." People haven't changed much from my generation to hers.

When the drive is over, and the cattle counted into the field, the children unsaddle their horses and turn them loose on the open range. Wearily they load their saddles in the pickup and tumble in after. The sorrel mare, Skeeter, Roman nosed from having been shot in the face by a hunter spotlighting deer, leads the way, in a hurry to get back to Yamsi. She has made the trip back many a time. The band of horses

stops to water at the Bar Y Spring atop the mountain, but the small patch of grass tempts them only for a moment and their strides are fast and straight for home. The same automobiles that drove out through the forest that morning are headed back for town. Avoiding traffic, the horses race through the bordering forest, and many a tourist goes home convinced that he has seen a band of wild horses.

With the conclusion of the Calimus drive the chores of May are almost done. The cows and calves are turned out on the range, the heifers are at Calimus for the summer. Only the bulls remain. Restive, grumbling, and argumentative in their field, they leave great swatches of dull, lifeless hair on the tree stumps where they rub, and their velvet hides shine with good health and condition. Ready and eager to breed, they paw the earth, bellow, and lock horns with adversaries. The most cowardly bellow the loudest. Sometimes the fights are in earnest; horns rattle, heads clash together until the scuffed, curly hair of the foreheads is red with blood. When suddenly one is whipped he turns and gallops off, sometimes trampling a spectator without even seeing him, in his haste to flee.

But we keep them away from the cows from December until the first of June. The main reason for this is that it makes our calves more uniform. But it also prevents calving in winter, and gives the cows and bulls a chance to heal up from a sometime venereal infection called Vibrio, passed from cow to cow by the bulls, which results in widespread sterility. Keeping the bulls out of the cows is the rancher's method of family planning. Perhaps someday someone will question our right.

From one end of Yamsi to another, the vast meadows are deserted now, save for an occasional band of retired saddle horses, and the herds of mule deer. The gold of buttercup and dandelion is giving way to the blue of wild iris, penstemon, and camas lily. The grasses are lush, waiting to be eaten. But the land is too rough to hay, and my only choice is to market the grass by grazing it, and converting it to beef. But I lack the animals, and now must enter the scary and speculative phase of my ranch operation which begins with the purchase of pasture cattle.

The spring market for cattle to go on pastures is characteristically high because there is so much demand from ranchers like myself who have no other way of utilizing their grass. But the scary part of the operation is that one is forced to sell the cattle in the fall, when prices are characteristically low, due to heavy marketings by ranchers like myself faced with the coming of winter, who have no other choice than to sell.

Motels are lonely places. Why is it that I'm never so lonely at the ranch, however much I am alone there? One night I am in Madras, in central Oregon, the next I am five hundred miles south in Cotton-wood, California, following the weekly livestock auctions, buying fifty here, three hundred there, trying to put together a thousand steers that will fit my ranch and slender budget, make me a pasture bill without losing me my ranch.

At Cottonwood, I sit nursing my lunch at Ellington Peek's auction yard. All morning long I have been wandering about the holding pens inspecting the pen lots that will be run through the auction that afternoon. The end of the day will have seen over four thousand head of cattle change hands.

There are types of cattle for everyone, shipped in from ranches in three states. Old bulls for the bologna trade, old butcher cows to go as hamburger, baby calves for veal or to someone with feed, spare time, and patience. Heifers to replace the old cows weeded from someone's herd, heifers for pasture, fat heifers for slaughter. Steers so big they are ready for the feedlot, steers so light they should go to grass in pastures such as mine. Now and then a horse some cowboy can't ride; retired saddle horses for fox feed. Twenty donkeys from Nevada. Hogs, sheep, goats. Who'll buy? Usually somebody does—at a price.

Besides managing the auction yard, Ellington Peek is an order or commission buyer. If a feedlot needs five thousand steers it is often cheaper to hire a commission buyer to put them together than to run a set of tires right off an automobile scouring the country. A professional buyer not only knows what cattle are for sale about the country, but also knows their quality from past experience, and having bought the cattle last year, generally has the refusal of them the next.

Ellington is typical of most big-time buyers. He has a radio phone in his car, is one of the telephone company's biggest customers, flies by light plane from one auction or ranch to another, and has a wife as patient as a sea captain's who becomes at times little more than an answering service for his telephone.

Ellington has bought me three hundred steers for which I have paid him a commission. He has also offered me a purchase contract on the steers for September delivery at $30 per hundredweight. The steers, averaging 500 pounds, have cost me initially $172.50 per head. To that I add $4 for transportation, $5 for interest to the bank on my borrowed money, $20 per head for pasture for the summer, since this is what I could get from someone else without my owning the cattle, and another dollar for salt and medication.

If I sell the cattle, weighing seven hundred pounds, at $30, they will bring me $210. Subtracting costs and expenses, I find that if the cattle gain two hundred pounds, and if none of them die, I will only make $7.50 per head, out of all that risk and all that investment.

I am between a rock and a hard place. Expenses at Yamsi are fixed. They will not be covered by taking in pasture cattle at twenty dollars a head, nor is Ellington's offer attractive. I can't just let the pasture grass grow up and die without any income from it. My only chance for a reasonable profit lies in gambling that the steers will bring *more* than thirty dollars in September. But what if they bring *less*? Can I afford to gamble on an agricultural commodity known for the instability of its prices? Can I expect an upturn in beef prices when the government is committed to keeping the cost of living down? Since I must borrow close to $175,000 to purchase the thousand steers I need for my pastures, it is a nervous business. One little mistake can cost me my ranch. I have a vision of someone else taking over, draining my marshes, depriving my sandhill cranes of homes, selling lots on the river, destroying everything I have labored so hard to keep pristine and primitive. I could sign the contract at the thirty-dollar figure, and get Ellington to agree to take the balance of what I purchase at that figure too. When the bidding starts, at least I would know exactly how high I could go to make a pasture income.

The sale pavilion is thronged with people. There are cattlemen who have come to buy, cattlemen who have come to watch their animals sell. There are regulars like Ellington who have come to buy on order for someone else. There are feedlot men who are buying their own, grass men like me who need animals through which to market their grass, packers who need animals for slaughter, farmers who just need a couple of calves, and city people who have time to spare to enjoy the country fair excitement.

I sit in the audience, waiting for the big bunches of light steers to come, musing how incongruous it is that my five children are sitting calmly in school two hundred miles away, while their father faces making split-second decisions which may affect not only their future but the future of the ranch they love.

The auctioneer sits on a dais above the ring, facing his audience. He wears a kerchief protecting his valuable throat, for his voice is his business just as though he were a singer or radio announcer. Above his head is a closed circuit television set showing the weights as they are recorded on the scales. Beside him sits a secretary who records the highest bidder. In the ring below are men who bring the cattle in, take bids from the audience, then push the cattle onto the scales.

The ring men, out to squeeze the last dollar out of the cattle, since the auction yard gets a percentage, know each bidder and his individual style of bidding. Not caring to have the world know he's even interested, he has his own secret way of communicating with the ring men. Some wink, some nod their heads almost imperceptibly, some wiggle a foot, a finger, or their sales record card. When the price has gone higher than they want to pay, they shake their head or merely look their disinterest.

I sit dreaming, watching an endless stream of butcher cows go through the ring, punctuated by an occasional saddle horse. I watch the horses curiously, knowing there must be a hole in them somewhere or the owner wouldn't be running them through the ring. A lovely sorrel mare with colt at side goes through. She would make a good one for Ginny, but while I am trying to make up my mind someone else takes her, and she is gone.

Then suddenly, the door to the alleys comes open and in flood the steers I want. I hope fervently that all the other buyers are out having coffee. "Lookee here," the auctioneer whistles. "Now these are the right kind for anybody." I slink down in my seat, wishing he would quit the advertising. He looks at his papers. "There are two hundred of these little moneymakers," he goes on, "all one-iron cattle right off the Nevada desert, and it shore looks like they could use some groceries." (To me the cattle look full, as though they have tanked up on water and chopped hay.) "Now let me tell you—these cattle are hard to come by this time of year.

"Who'll give me thirty-five for them," the auctioneer says, starting his chant, starting them at thirty-five dollars a hundredweight. There are no takers and he backs down to thirty-four.

"*Yes!*" a ring man screams, pointing to someone up there in the rafters, who may well be imaginary. The auctioneer runs wild.

"Thirty-four, now thirty-four ten. Now ten, ten, ten, now ten, ten, ten." A ring man glances at me. I nod imperceptibly to let them know I'm bidding. "*Yes!*" he shouts, and I'm in.

"Now twenty, twenty, twenty, *now* twenty, twenty, twenty."

"*Yes!*" I'm out and someone else is in.

"Now thirty, thirty, thirty, *now* thirty, thirty, thirty."

"*Yes!*" I'm back—if only the guy bidding against me would quit.

"Now forty, forty, forty, *now* forty, forty, forty." "

"*Yes!*" The ring man throws me out.

"Now fifty, fifty, fifty, *now* fifty, fifty, fifty." I've reached my limit, and a shiver goes through me. I nod for my last time. I am in at thirty-four fifty.

"Now sixty, sixty, sixty, *now* sixty, sixty, sixty." No more bids. "Sixty once, sixty twice . . ."

"*Yes!*" The man upstairs decides to go and throws me out.

"Now seventy, seventy, seventy . . ." I huddle in my seat. They are watching me. What an awful price to be paying for those steers. I need them. It will be a mighty empty-looking ranch this summer if I don't buy. I could get into trouble if I don't contract; if I do there isn't much profit."*Now* seventy, seventy, seventy. Seventy once, seventy twice—"

Yes! Yes! Yes! The hell with it. I'm in.

"Now eighty, eighty, eighty, *now* eighty, eighty, eighty." No one bids. "Eighty once, eighty twice. *Sold!*" Thirty-four seventy to Yamsi Ranch, way up there in southern Oregon.

The steers go on the scales thirty or forty at a clip. I watch carefully, signal them to cut out a steer with a swollen knee, another that looks staggy, with maybe one testicle they didn't get when they castrated him, still up in his belly somewhere.

I record the weights. The legal limit for trucks in California is forty-eight thousand pounds. I am overweight, so will have to get another bunch weighing about forty-four thousand pounds. A bunch of light steers comes in, but the buyer above me can't be shaken and once I have bowed out, the bidding stops at thirty-four eighty.

I steal the next bunch at thirty-four ten, but they are heavier than I wanted. It is the last bunch I get, for the buyer behind me has decided to make his purchases at any price and outbids me every time. But I have bought close to three hundred cattle this afternoon, and with what Ellington Peek has bought me now have six hundred of the thousand I need.

I feel a little better now even though the steers won't make me money. Eighteen donkeys in the ring now. One of them seems to look up in the audience at me. The kids would love it and the bid is only seven dollars. I'll get the bid, take my pick, and the rest can go on the block again. Each donkey has a printed number stuck to its back.

I nod. *"Yes!"* Just one little donkey won't hurt me.

"Now seven ten, ten, ten, *now* ten, ten, ten. Ten once, ten twice. *Sold!* Seven dollars each. Eighteen donkeys to Yamsi Ranch."

"I'll take number two forty-six," I call.

"Sorry, Mister. You just bought 'em all. You should have been listening." The donkeys are gone and in their place a pen of heifers.

Eighteen donkeys! What on earth am I going to do with eighteen donkeys? I spend the rest of the day finding them homes.

Before I leave, I give the auction yard a draft for fifty-two thousand dollars and arrange for trucking to the ranch for three hundred steers and one burro. Then being a coward, I contract the steers I have bought to Ellington for fall delivery. It will hardly pay me to run them but it will still be better than leaving the ranch unstocked.

As I drive through the Yamsi gate, Johnny meets me. "You've got to come quick, Dad. The dam has broken and the water is flooding out a sandhill crane's nest." Together we race off. Since there is no way of saving the nest, I wade out chest deep into the marshes and rescue the two big brown eggs. They are the size of goose eggs, mottled as though with all the colors of the marshes. Hugging them to my bare skin for warmth, I head for home. In the distance, above the pathetic rachetting of the parent cranes, I hear the rumble of arriving cattle trucks at the corrals, and the blat of an air horn, strident and impatient. The drivers will have to wait until the eggs are safely under a bantam hen.

Chapter 9

In January, toes frozen in my boots, I wonder if I am a fool to live thus. In March, a cold rain trickling down my collar, I am certain of it. But in June, I stare about me in real awe that, of all the world's teeming millions, I am the one born to the royalty of living here.

But the ancient tools scattered along my river—arrowheads, net weights, fleshing knives, cooking stones, and grinding rocks—keeps me ever mindful that I am but one of many, the one who is here now, but that for thousands of years before me man summered in my valley. Time and again he was driven away by giant lava flows, which turned the land to a raging furnace, a charred desolation where nothing lives. Time and again the few trees which spread quietly back to form a thin, scraggly forest on the rolling grassy hills were blackened by fires caused by lightning or small volcanic action.

As the Cascade Range thrust ever higher into the air, sucking the moisture from the coastal winds, the land became more arid, and the grasses were replaced by rabbit brush and sage, tough plants, able to exist without much moisture on the thin, rocky clays. Shooting stars turned the flats pink in springtime; composites such as tarweed turned them yellow and blue in the summer. The very hardship of their nomadic hunting and seed-gathering existence discouraged the weak, and turned the Indians by necessity into an active, vigorous people, who took pride even in the simple tools basic to their existence. The pride is easily read into the exquisite craftsmanship found in obsidian points of the era.

About seven thousand years ago came another great upheaval. For months on end Mount Mazama spewed forth great gray clouds of ash, which, blowing northeastward with the prevailing winds, covered the land with several feet of porous pumice rock and sand. The vast cavern formed by the sucking away of lava collapsed in upon itself, forming the thirty-mile sink now known as Klamath Lake. Mount

145

Mazama, too, collapsed leaving a gigantic hole. Snows came to the shattered peaks and melted, came and melted as the crater filled to become the exquisite jewel that is Crater Lake. The land was a desolation. For centuries time seemed to have stood still; in all that vast barren sea of volcanic ash, nothing lived, nothing grew.

Winters came and went; moisture saturated the sands, percolated deep into the caverns of the earth, and arose at last as springs of crystal water. Over the mineral soils, grasses spread along the bottoms; brush came to the hills, then lodgepole pines, their seeds blown like tiny helicopters on the wind. Following the hardy lodgepoles came an invading army of long-lived ponderosa pines, cedars, and white fir. As the lodgepole died of old age, the young lodgepoles failed to compete, and the species was driven from the ridges to the moist bottoms and the harsher sites. Aspens and bush willow worked slowly up the rivers to their very sources; bog birch fought with willow for the moist bogs in the hills. Whenever an accumulation of snowbrush, manzanita, and bitterbrush moved in beneath the pines, the pine straw built a layer of inflammable duff, catching like brown bird's nests in the thick branches of the encroaching understory, and lightning fires moved unchecked over the land. Insulated as they were by thick, scaly bark, the trees survived with only minor damage to their lower trunks, and the land beneath became open, parklike, a sea of wildflowers and waving grass.

The pumice rocks, filled with air cells, floated down the stream in rafts until they finally became waterlogged and sank. Along the bottoms of the streams moved constant inner rivers of sand, making a bar here and there for a day or season, but soon moved out again by the very eddy it had formed. Eventually the deep and sparkling lakes filled in, died, and became marshes, profuse with insect life, rank with vegetation.

Fish flourished on the insect life; waterfowl bred in prodigious number, and soon a rich, black layer of organic ooze formed along the bottoms. Attracted by the rank abundance of food to be had for the taking, the Indians came back in throngs. It was a gentle, easy existence. They caught and dried great quantities of fish, filleting it and hanging it from the limbs of dead trees to cure in the hot mountain sun, building a few fires to keep away the buzzing bluebottles. They gathered huge heaps of wocus seed from the yellow water lilies that floated in vast oceans on the marshes. From the rough, gray lava at their feet they made pestles and mortars, rubbing rocks, and platters. From the grasses and tules of the marshes they wove clothing, baskets, sandals, and mats to cover their houses. From the pines they gathered the white cambium layer for food and fiber, and feasted upon the pine nuts they reaped by handfuls from the nests of squirrels. Even in winter the rotting logs were filled with great yellow boreworm grubs.

Starvation was unknown, but as the old men passed away and were placed on platforms on the mountainsides, with them went the pride and know-how that had crafted the superb tools of their ancestors. Within a few generations their own points became clumsy and crude.

But however much primitive man loved my valley with its natural abundance afforded by the marshes and the river, he was both smarter and more mobile than I, for he knew enough to live elsewhere during the hard cold winters. He moved with the deer, at the first snow, up over the ridges of Yamsay Mountain toward the snowless deserts to the east, or followed the migrating herds south to the lava beds, or to the Klamath and Lost River area where steaming hot springs bubbled and not only kept the Indians warm but cooked their meals for them. In winter my isolated valley existed only as memories told beside the lodge fires.

In spring, as the migrating swallows skimmed a few early insects off the steaming waters and were gone, restless for the higher valleys, so migrated the Indian, his winter-empty belly eager to be feasted by June's plenty. He followed the trails broken for him by deer in the late mountain snows, deer migrating northward from the lava oceans south of the great lake of tules. He followed their trails from the open deserts up over the forested shoulder of Yamsay, mountain home of Kmukamtch, the supreme being of the Klamaths who had once hurled thunderbolts at the god of Mazama and broken down his mountain. The pregnant does ahead of the Indian were weak from eating the washy spring grass, and fell easily to his crude arrows, as did the foolish grouse, which hooted from the ridges, called out to him their strutting grounds, and often pecked angrily at his moccasins to drive him away.

If winter had dimmed his faith in himself as a hunter, and made him feel neglected by his gods, June restored his ego. The same complaining, black-eyed woman whose skin had hung in crusty folds about her a month before now chuckled a come-on to him in fat-cheeked joviality.

It was good that she became strong and patient, for when they arrived in the valley of the upper Williamson, to her would fall the job of erecting the lodge, tying the woven mats over the bent willow poles on the open sand spit that jutted out into the marsh. Hers would be the task of gathering duck eggs in her baskets, of wading the icy waters to net the darting silvery trout in the river bends, of digging ipos in the hard clays of the sun drenched flats, of curing the hides of deer and bear the men stalked in the tall reeds of the marshes, of gathering the stone eggs of obsidian on the rock flats of the Sycan, of gathering the red clay to make paint for the bodies of warriors; clay which they burned in pits, at the bottom of which formed the mercury which they described as "silvery water one can't pick up." Hers the job making tools, of lifting the great mortars from the river bottom where they had been hidden the fall before, hers the long tedious mud-covered days in the leech-infested marshes, pushing a log canoe before her, filling it brimful of wocus seeds sieved from the surface with a skimmer woven of grasses. Hers the job of grinding the wocus on platters, and making it into gruel or cakes. And hers the welt from the flung billet of firewood, when her buck bit into the cake and found it gritty with ground stone from her coarse, primitive tools.

But there were good times, too. The children entertained themselves and did no whining about the lodges, but played along the streams sailing canoes of floating pumice stone in endless races. Even as they worked, the women were rarely silent, but chattered and laughed together all the day long. All the days were not work days, for there were feast days when friends came even from the great marshes to east and west, to gamble in jovial circles, winning and losing fortunes in stick games, or the hiding of the bones, a "guess which hand it's in" game still played in elementary form by modern children.

It was a noisy valley. Dogs barked incessantly at chipmunks and badgers under logs, small boys shouted gleefully as they chased ducklings in the marshes. Whole families at a time took steam baths in the wickiups, huts built by the springs, poured cold water over hot stones, steamed themselves free of itching vermin, then ran naked and squealing to plunge into the icy waters. Everywhere the calling of myriad ducks and geese, the constant din of protesting marsh birds such as the killdeer and the willet. Women shouted their gossip across the narrow marshes and bogs to others on the far side. In the bends splashing, noisy flocks of white pelicans beat the water to a froth, driving the fish to the center of an ever-closing circle, then filled the huge pouches of their bills from the boil of fish. Sometimes women and children drove the competing birds from their work and waded in from all sides to imitate the fish drive of the pelicans. In similar fashion they tightened the ring about their prey until the water was black with finny backs. Nets flashed and silvery trout rained upon the banks as children shouted and screamed as they tried to keep the bouncing, flouncing trout from sliding back into the river to safety.

They were a social people, a group people. What was the need of going off on a lonely, risky hunting party, when here was food in abundance for the taking? The river was awash with spawning trout come up from the vast marshes and streams below. There were not enough Indians alive to make a dent in their numbers. In the end it would not be the harvest that ruined the fishing but the destruction of the wetlands by the white man, the dams he would one day put across the rivers, the pollutants of heat and chemicals that would make the water unfit for life.

Now and then a war party, tired of traveling and seeking to restore its provisions, descended from the hills, seizing food from the first camp and taking a few captives.

But warnings shouted up and down the river, from one camp to another, drove the rest into hiding. Scattered through the valley and lining the waterways were vast seas of bush willows, whose intertwining canes made cavernous tunnels through which a horseman could not venture and an enemy could not walk upright. No one old or young was more than two minutes away from a hiding place rich in food and water. Once the hidden eyes in the willows had seen the raiding party on its way, a call went down the valley from one throat to another, and once more campfires sparkled like fireflies along the bends of the river. There was little call to travel outward to avenge a raid that had been unsuccessful, to avenge a killing when there had been none. Or, indeed, why should they travel when they were already there?

High atop the buttes, the young men sat in solitude to prove their manhood, piling up cairns of rock to show their elders they had been there. As a means of hardening their bodies, they ran to the top of the ridges, then raced back to plunge in the river. They made games of jumping the great gray lava rocks tumbled from the rimrocks. They shot their arrows into the soft pumice hillsides, practicing for some future war which seemed never to come. For it is hard to fight a war when everyone has plenty to eat. Through the long years it became easier to avoid conflict by simply hiding in the bushes. Now and then in a place where the pumice had been washed away, exposing the pre-Mazama clay, they found the lovely, precise, serrated knives, arrowheads, and spears of those who had lived before the big explosion. They were delicate, pridefully crafted, but since it was bad luck to touch them, they were left undisturbed. If the Indians wondered about the tools, they soon shrugged them off, knowing neither who had cached them there nor how long ago they had been left. A hundred years or a thousand made no difference to these timeless people. They knew merely that someone else besides themselves knew about this lonely valley of abundance, and they hoped that whoever had left the points would not be back to bother them.

But times changed even for the timeless Indians. The white man came, forcing the Klamath and Modoc people to share a reservation. Led by Captain Jack, the Modocs bolted, only to be forced into the bitter Modoc Wars. Captain Jack and his handful of Modoc braves holed up in the labyrinthine lava cracks and tubes south of Tule Lake, and held off the might of the United States Army. But in the end, they were defeated by their own hollow bellies. Descendants of those chiefs became the first Bar Y cowboys.

The Indians ended up with a vast, rich, fifty-mile-square land of forests and grasslands, which would have boded well for them had they been allowed to manage it for themselves, and been forced to work the land to make it yield.

But thinking that the land would go to ruin, the white man moved in and managed it for the Indian, harvested the timber, leased out the grazing lands to cattle and sheep, and paid the Indians money. The Lincoln and Cadillac dealers prospered. The grocers allowed the Indians to run up large debts for food, then seized their private claims in payment, claims rich in water and timber, worth many times the debt.

Al Shadley once gave his aging parents several milk cows with which to make their living, and was startled to see the cows a month later in the grocer's corral. Worth five hundred dollars, they had been taken to pay a twenty-dollar grocery bill.

To keep them scattered, the Bureau of Indian Affairs tried to make ranchers of the Indians, settled them on good claims, issued them cattle branded with the ID of the Indian Department on their ribs. They were to pay for the cattle out of the calf crops.

But the Indian was a social person and the ranches were often isolated and lonely. Some of the ranches were on the Sycan, the Williamson, and the Sprague, and he might have fished and been happy, but the power company put dams in the rivers, water was taken for irrigation, and soon the fish which had been for his people an inexhaustible resource were no longer able to spawn. There was not much to keep him on the land. If he was not off visiting friends, they were visiting him. If he was one of the few who worked, and tried to save his money, then the rest moved in on him, or gave him the silent treatment if he wouldn't share. If he had a herd of ID cattle, it was as if he had brought a deer home to his tipi. Friends moved in and lived on the animals until they were gone. After all, his friends reasoned, "The cattle have the ID brand on them; therefore they belong to all of us." They were, however, unwilling to share the unsecured debt which remained with the demise of the herd. Once the herd had been eaten, or sold for whisky money, the Indian merely turned in a report that the cattle had died. Which was true.

One by one as ranches were sold, the Indians moved into the sociable life of the towns of Beatty, Sprague River, or Chiloquin. A few like Ora and Martha Summers and Mamie Farnsworth kept their ranches and cattle and became wealthy. But it was at the expense of their real acceptance by the other Indians. An Indian once told me, "That Mamie Farnsworth got lotsa money. But she don't share it with nobody." He was resentful, but did not realize how his pride in her as a fellow Indian was showing through.

Al Shadley told me of the old Indian couple who had sold their ranch and decided, "Now we have plenty money, we take nice trip like white people." And so they rattled south on a passenger train. But going through the Sacramento Valley the old man got thirsty. Taking a cup from his suitcase, he handed it to his woman and said "Water." He drank thirstily and again and again sent her for more. She trotted up and down the aisle patiently as was her way. But at last she came back with an empty cup. "No more water," she said sadly. "White lady sit on spring."

When many of the Indians voted to terminate the reservation, the land became national forest. Each Indian that sold out got forty-three thousand dollars in cash. Some invested it quietly and wisely; others went through it in a hurry. And after all, how many white people could have held onto that much cash? One woman carried the whole sum around Klamath in a paper sack. I was a stranger to her but she collared me and tried to buy me a new saddle. When I next saw her, she had left the bag in a bar somewhere and was trying to remember where.

Car dealers bought cars by the trainload and hired extra salesmen to sell them. In a glassed-in showroom, an Indian carrying a sack asked the harried salesman, "Say, buddy, this pickup ready to go?" The salesman nodded. While his back was turned with another customer, the Indian counted out the money in cash, set it on the floor, weighted it down with a half-filled beer can, and drove right out through the show window.

But for every Indian who made the newspapers, there were a dozen who stayed quietly at home. The older Indians were a fine people; the younger ones were confused by prosperity and idleness. Now that they have spent their money and must work again, they, too, are beginning to show their worth.

In my childhood at Yamsi, a few Indian families still came out of habit in buckboards and automobiles to camp along their historic fishing grounds. But the artifacts they left have no place with those of generations before. A few bottles, faded by the sun, tin cans rusted thin, a crumpled automobile fender and headlight from some jewel of the twenties, a battered toy truck.

I played with the last of the children along the river, capturing the baby ground squirrels for pets by packing water from the stream in five-gallon cans and pouring endless rivers down the holes. In an age-old, splintered dugout of an Indian canoe, I balanced precariously with the blue-eyed, fair-haired great grandson of a chief. We fished on opposite sides to keep the craft from tipping, but we only caught one fish an evening, for with that first fish the dugout would tip over, spilling us into the drink. Shouting and laughing, we would swim the fish to shore. At night, the beams of spotlights impaled the sky as the Indians ran the forest roads in pickups, hunting deer by flashing the beam in their eyes. It was a rare morning in the camps when there was not at least one fresh new hide draped like laundry to dry over the nearest windfall, and by fall the drying hides might number a hundred.

Soon those families, too, were gone and the campfires cold and forgotten. Along Wickiup Springs there are a few fire rocks left from the last of the wickiups which disappeared in my uncle's time; not long ago I picked up a mighty fish spear made of pitchfork tines, rusty but eloquently expressive of a time when fish were larger by far than they are today. But the traditions of living off the land faded; fences went up, and the ranch became lonely once more, more lonely than it had been since the great eruptions six thousand years before.

How swiftly the times changed and were gone. Tainted as was her Indian blood with that of the white man, Mamie Farnsworth was the last gasp of the valley's Indian history. I wonder if, as she built her sprawling ranch house among the pines and looked out past her big red barn at the lush green meadows, filled with fat, sleek cattle, she ever saw her place in history as the last of the Yamsi Indians.

However much the life of the Indian has changed, his isolated paradise at Yamsi has remained uniquely primitive. If elsewhere total numbers of wild species are down, drainage of wetlands has concentrated the pitiful remainder on land such as mine. It is good that wildlife has somewhere to go; but in being concentrated, the remnant population is far more vulnerable. The scarcity of water on this semiarid land further concentrates life on those oases where water exists, and by far the most prolifically productive of any land is the marsh, for in the marsh exists cover, food, and water in untold abundance. However vast the national forests about me, it is generally the watered agricultural land which produces the food.

On these watered bottom lands, insects feed on minute micro- and macroorganisms in the tepid shallows. Larger insects eat the smaller ones and are in turn food for fish such as roach or trout, animals such as skunks, coyotes, and bear, and birds such as blackbirds and meadowlarks. A percentage of those large or small that come to the valley to eat end up being eaten. Both man and disease figure in the chain of predators.

Just as the Indians flocked in June to harvest the abundance, so do the wild things, for June is the recovery month from unproductive winter. Animals and birds not only restore their numbers lost to migration, old age, disease, and predation by raising new litters, new broods, but also restore the body strengths of the parent. Cattle, too, have a place in the chain. They are rebuilding their numbers from losses suffered when, last fall, I made off with their annual calf crop. And fantastic Mother Nature has cooperated with amazing coordination, by building up the protein yield of the land to its yearly zenith at the time when it is most needed.

June is the time of the black drake hatch, a small purple forked tail which abandons its nymphoid case on the bottom, wings up to the surface, and flies off as though the air were just another liquid. In the trunks of trees bordering the river they cluster in teeming billions; over the sliding river, dimpling its surface, frustrating fly fishermen, they do their dipping dance and die, their spent wings turning the calm surface of the water to silver.

Each backwater forms a floating island crust of them over which mince song sparrows, Audubon warblers, rails, and wrens, picking and choosing, devouring from the black, encrusted mass what still looks appetizing, or can be passed on as such to a voracious and unfastidious brood. Trout feed until gorged, selecting lazily from what pleases them from the great mass sliding endlessly overhead. If there is no hatch in this bend it slides in from another. But only a minute percentage of the abundance can be harvested. The rest performs its function, then sinks to a final resting place to become part of the black ooze on the bottom.

Through the long days and balmy evenings of June, the grass grows succulent, nutritive, and lush. For a few days the cattle stay ahead of the supply, cropping it as it comes. Then, almost overnight, it runs away from them and they are knee-deep in forage. Wherever they have lain at midday to chew their cud, in the sea of timothy, bluegrass, and clover, they leave pockets or depressions.

Now to my other frenetic duties I add irrigation. Systematically, I run the cold, crystalline water down ditches plowed in Buck's time, and out over the thirsting land. I watch the spreading lines of blackbirds to tell where the front of water advances, for the clever birds have learned to use the water to flush insects from the grass, just as the Indian once drove animals with fire.

I am not above learning from a bird. The next day I am out there with the blackbirds, gathering insects into cans, for this morning I heard a strange, querulous pair of pipings from beneath a setting hen. The hen was a bit confused, but not I. The sandhill crane eggs I rescued are hatching, and the chance of an idle moment fly fishing on my river is lost for the summer, as I take on the demands of parenthood.

A tiny hole in the enlarged end of one mottled egg shows the tip of a tiny, rubbery beak, capped with a minute egg tooth of ivory. The tiny head jerks back spasmodically as from a hiccup, the egg tooth raps once against the shell. Again and again, between leisurely sleeps, the head jerks and the tiny pick flakes off a piece of shell, as slowly the body revolves within its cramped confines. Finally a trap door is cut and falls open, and the wet, bedraggled chick struggles out. A day later and the second chick repeats the antics of the first. They lie quietly for a time, ripening in the nest, learning the unfamiliar calls of the strange foster mother. Two more days pass and the chicks are demanding food from my hand.

I had intended to pass the chore of gathering food off on Johnny, but he has problems of his own. Today he found a rare great gray owl chick, fallen from its nest, an abandoned goshawk's nest in a lodgepole thicket. The owlet is cold, weak, sick, and its chances for survival are slim.

"Don't worry, little owl," Johnny says confidently. "My father can fix anything."

The owl opens one yellow eye, looks me over, and closes it as if to say, "You must be kidding!" It helps matters by refusing to eat.

I cut up a handsome little white-footed mouse and force it hide, bones, and all down the owl's throat, then follow it with a squirt of water, which the owl swallows gratefully. His head and body are covered with gray down like a dandelion gone to seed. If there is a sadder little face than John's it is the owl's. Mouth half open, panting thirstily with fever, the owl works his head and neck as though adjusting the contours of the mouse to his gullet.

In the morning John pulls me from the bed. I am aware that he has been trying to wake me for some time. "Come quick," he says. "Alexander is trying to vomit." At least the owl will not die unnamed.

Trying my best to forget that I am an evening person, I stagger after John to where he has built a nest for the owl on the warm griddle of Gerdi's new kitchen stove. The owl bobs its fluffy head up and down convulsively as though retching and I am about to panic when out pops a quite normal, healthy, great gray owl casting, a large, oblong gray pellet showing the outlines of fur and bones, all that is unused from last evening's mouse. The owl is suddenly stronger. *"Eeeeek?"* he calls, looking about him for another mouse.

Once a drug on the market, mice are suddenly hard to come by. Word goes out, perhaps, that there is a useful purpose they can perform, so they decamp from the pantry. John suddenly finds out how hard a mother owl has to work. Nor can he rely on me. In addition to irrigating, building fences and gates, getting some obstinate and obsolete machinery ready for haying, salting the cattle, patrolling for rustlers, and fixing ditches with the tractor, I must also find time to feed my little sandhill cranes, which follow me tirelessly about, devouring a seemingly endless amount of bugs, crushed earthworms, and sliced calf's liver, and demanding tender loving care. One tiny chick attacks the other and for long hours I soothe the emotionally troubled chick until I get him used to another foster mother. In the end it is poor Gerdi who is stuck with their upbringing as an additional duty beyond caring for an indigent husband and five active children.

Screened from the rest of the world by thickets of bush willow, Taylor and Marsha work hard at raising ducklings, goslings, chukkar partridges, and pheasants. Under one hen Taylor has a woodpecker's egg (fortunately sterile); in the oven of the kitchen stove, couched in my winter hat, he has a naked brood of starlings (as though the world didn't have enough starlings). The baby Canada geese have adopted him as mother, and follow happily about stepping on his shadow. When he goes indoors, they throng frightened and complaining on the porch, standing on tiptoe to see him better through the dog-slobbered panes. They have a perfectly good foster mother who will do everything for them but swim with them; but they somehow prefer Taylor, who wades happily beside them in the stream, as they dive for fairy shrimp stirred up by his toes. Today John and Taylor made a wiggly raft out of a gas tank perched on some inner tubes and, drifting lazily on the pond, played at fishing until a friendly Canada goose from last year's hatch climbed onto the raft with them and upset the works.

During the night clouds creep in over the valley, low, heavy, ominous. Flashes of lightning make an instant brilliance of the sky, and the rumbling thunder echoes and re-echoes from mountain to mountain, ridge to ridge, building to building as though the first terrifying clap were not enough. It is a dry storm, the kind the fire watchers fear the worst. In Indian times the forest floor was kept clean by random fires which burned unchecked, but left only a few cat-faced scars on the butts of trees. But the white man with dubious wisdom kept the fires in check; the brush, the duff, the dead grasses and rotting wood have accumulated to create a frightening hazard. Now when a fire escapes, the forest goes with it.

Taylor and Marsha dart from the house to cover their chicks from possible rain. We need rain so badly that I somehow resent their action, as though in being prepared they have somehow guaranteed that that rain won't fall. They stare for a moment at the skies, then scamper toward the protection of the house, as the lunch bell tolls faint above the answering thunder.

As I slip from the blacksmith shop where I have been welding a broken rocker arm on a mower, lightning strikes a jack pine not twenty feet from me. A steaming, angry scar of yellow wood spirals down the tree; the smell of sulfur is a smell of closeness to death I'd almost

forgotten. I go back into the shop and sit on a tire casing while I try to remember. We were in an old hay barn on Klamath Marsh, Whisky Jim and I, a couple of brash kids trying to put up the hay when everyone else had gone to war. Glad to be sheltered from a rain that was making a soggy ruin of the hay, we were sitting tete-a-tete on blocks, slicing the cable which draped from the floor to the hay carriage along the ridge pole. We had just got into a wrestling match over how to splice the thing when *bam,* a massive blow staggered me. "Now, Jim," I said when I had managed to recover, "you didn't have to go and hit me that hard. I was just about to agree to do it your way."

"No, let's do it yours," Jim said, rubbing his head and looking at me with a respect he'd never had.

But the respect was short-lived. Lightning had struck our cable and burned a black stripe up the floor of the barn and fire was even now licking at our shirt tails. By the time we'd gotten the flames out we were back being friends.

Not long after that escape from lightning, I was stealing a ride on a miserable, cantankerous, pink-nosed, spoiled old horse named Spot, on which the Bar Y had given up, when thunder rolled as we rode through the Sand Creek field. The more that thunder crashed, the crankier old Spot became, and the more I thought maybe I'd like to get off and lead the old boy the seven miles home. But I should have jumped for it right then, for the horse jerked his head down some-where below his knees, and exploded into a wild sunfish that climaxed halfway to the pine tops. Right in the middle of that awful jump light-ning splintered a tree, and Spot, who had never known a scared moment in his hateful career, made up for it now and stampeded for his salvation. In three minutes he made three fields with me.

When I finally got the old devil stopped, I leaned over in one stirrup so I could look him in one crusty eye and said, "Spot? That's what happens when a hoss tries to buck with me." He must have believed me for from that day on he became gentle as a dog, and the Bar Y sold him to an almond knocker down in California to irrigate on.

BACK TO REALITY AGAIN, I SIT IN the musty gloom of the blacksmith shop trying to convince myself that I am not superstitious about someone who has *almost* been struck by lightning three times now, and am really just watching a golden-mantled ground squirrel digging in the dust, emptying his cheek pockets of wheat he has stolen from the chickens. But suddenly the ground squirrel peeks out, glances at the sky, then cuts and runs as though he has seen something I haven't. Just then lightning hits a tree right next to the first and I am headed across the flat for the house.

"Didn't want to get wet," I explain to Taylor, as I make a wild slide for the porch.

"Didn't know it was raining," Taylor replies.

Uncle Buck always claimed a June rain was better for the grass than a big winter snowpack, but the weather is being difficult. From the covered porch I glare at the clouds. Heavy with moisture, a massive cloud hovers over the house so close I can almost touch it. I stick Buck's old shotgun out from under the eaves and discharge both barrels. There is a sudden answering rattle of hailstones big as marbles, smashing Gerdi's delphiniums, and for a moment I am afraid I've shot God.

Through a gap in the overhanging clouds, I see smoke billowing from the dog's-hair thickets of young pines on Taylor Butte, and the pink glow of flames reflected on the clouds. Fire is everybody's busi-ness. I phone for help but naturally the phone is dead. Moments later, I am headed up the mountain on my tractor. My wife sighs and puts away my lunch, uneaten.

The tractor crashes like a slow tank over the brush, bucks wildly over a fallen log I didn't see, and takes forever. I have visions of my being forced to spend the rest of my days in a fire-blackened valley. A coyote trots past me, glancing back over his shoulder in the direction of the fire. He seems hardly to notice the clanking, pounding machine. The fire is running wild. I bulldoze the brush and duff back into the fire, leaving a sterile swath of pumice. With a hideous, crackling, roaring boom orange flame towers suddenly through the green branches of a massive sugar pine; a shower of burning bark rains on the hood of the tractor. The heat is so intense I turn my face away, stealing quick glances to avoid the falling trees which come swishing down in a pall of ashes and smoke, piling like jackstraws into the fire. The fire crowns again, jumps my fire line and races up a small pine. If I can doze the tree back into the fire I have a chance. My tractor grunts and almost dies as I raise my blade and hit it high; if it dies, I'll have time only to leap from the seat and run. Again I try and suddenly the tree gives. Slowly I topple it back into the flames. The fire answers the thunder with thunder of its own. A drop of moisture makes a cold burn down my cheek. Rain! In a moment a deluge hisses down into the fire. Hissing back in anger, the angry serpents of the fire strike back at the rain. Now comes the cloudburst, washing down the ruts of the old logging roads, making great brown rafts of pine needles, which catch on the exposed roots and heal the erosion with dams. The fire submits humbly, dies back upon itself, and soon there is only smoke and steam, rising into the torrent of the rain.

The forest and the meadows smell hot and fresh and sweet; ghostly ground fogs chase each other across the freshening green. Bathed in nitrogen from the rain, the grass seems to leap before our eyes. As the clouds lift, a light plane circles the steaming hills watching for fires. Out on the road, a low boy truck thunders by, taking a huge D 8 Caterpillar out to a fire. Tanker trucks rumble down to fill their empty bellies from my river; tired men thrust their soot-blackened faces deep into the tumbling water as they drink.

Rain falls steadily, saving the forest for another day, another time.

AS THE MONTH WANES, THE COWS and calves are scattered in small groups far and wide through the mountain meadows. In a long day's ride by saddle horse one is lucky to see forty head, and those are nervous as though afraid to be gathered up again, to be driven from this paradise of lush grasses.

In the heat of the day the thirsty cows head for water, leaving one cow as baby-sitter for a whole kindergarten of calves. Drinking as they do from the cows, the calves as yet have no need for water, and come to accept the disappearance of their only parent and her replacement by a protective nurse as part of the ritual of life. They quickly find, however, that even though this cow will protect the group from a coyote wandering by, her obligations end there. Let them try to suck and she sends them sprawling with a well-placed kick.

Water may be miles away, but the calves wait patiently, butting heads and frisking with the other calves. Then, as the afternoon wears, the baby-sitter raises her head and listens carefully. In the distance a cow bawls, and she knows the other mothers are coming back. She sniffs her own calf as though to reassure herself of its safety, then, abandoning her charges, she begins her own journey down the dusty trails to water. If danger were to threaten now, a bawl from one of the calves would bring the cows running, but now that they are near, the mothers lower their heads and graze slowly in.

At the first sight of a white face nodding through the trees, the calves stand up, stretch, take a few short steps, and watch with interest. A low bawl from one of the cows gives the signal, and pell-mell the thirsty calves rush for their mothers. Their tails flick back and forth eagerly, but their manners are atrocious. They butt the udders greedily to knock down more milk, and when the impatient mothers move away from such rough treatment, the calves crowd in front of them and force them to stand.

But soon the calves are full again, their ribs distended, and they suck less eagerly. A bubbling froth of milk falls to the ground. When at last the cows move off to graze, the calves follow them complacently. Night finds them over the ridge on another meadow, but the cows have no need for a formal camp ground. They bed down quietly wherever darkness catches them on the trail

The calves are growing fast. When born they might have averaged eighty pounds; now they weigh over two hundred, and weaning time is as yet four months away. But no rancher can ever be happy with them at this point, for, faced as he is with the constant economic strain of running a cattle ranch, the calves will always look to him far smaller than he had hoped.

CHAPTER 10

"DAD! DAD! COME QUICKLY! A BIRD just drowned itself!" Johnny and I are at the pond at the headwaters of the Williamson, ostensibly irrigating, in reality watching the myriad swallows, violet-green, barn, rough-winged, and cliff, work a busy caddis hatch, while acrobatic nighthawks cruise in open, bristly-mouthed pursuit through clouds of tiny flying ants. Rushing to John's side just as he plunges forward into the torrent to save the bird, I jerk him back.

And there it is. Swept by the current, tumbled over rock and rill, a small gray body flutters and bumps along the bottom stones, seemingly helpless but lively still, too active really to be drowned. On the clear bottom, unconcerned, it brushes a startled trout aside from where that silvery, freckled, rainbow-tinted wand poked at a caddis armor with his blunt nose and broke the clinging camouflage of bark and sand away, leaving exposed the poor astonished worm.

Seizing the yellow grub, the bird flies up, drenching our startled faces with its wing-flung spray, darts to the roaring waterfall, and tumbles fearless through as though the liquid were a mist, a cloud. While Johnny stares aghast, small, infant pipings sound above the roar. I smile and show him, behind the thundering waterfall, the bulky nest of grasses, roots, and twigs, show him the bird which perches nervous now upon a stone, and dips his head to settle out the water from his crown.

"It's a dipper, John, a water ouzel. Look at this faint line of whitish dots beneath his tail—look at how the membrane of his eye, working from back to front, pushes the water from its pupil. His oily plumage keeps him warm and dry, letting him feed along the bottom of the rushing stream where his pastures are his own." I pause, seeing on John's brow the faint, suspicious frown of doubt.

Water ouzels are rare around here. It was this culvert waterfall which made this one feel at home, but he isn't the first I've seen. In an autumn rain once I found a dipper cuddling for the night high in an empty swallow's nest inside the light plant room. That night when I turned off the plant I locked him in by mistake. In the morning I found him perched by the windowpane, and held open the door for him. When he flew out he swam in a puddle and I saw him pick up a rock between his mandibles and toss it over his shoulder like an anting bird. He ignored me and turned over soggy leaves and peered underneath them for insects like a hopeful gambler peeking under his last card. A dipper dips as surely as a wren must jerk its tail, a crane must dance, or Canada goose must nod its head.

"It's gone," John says, and so it is, off down the winding stream. We hear its piping flight call down around the bend, piercing above the tumbling tumult's roar, and leave it all alone to raise its brood in peace behind the summer waterfall.

Blessed with an abundance of July insects to supplement the laboratory wizardry of their commercial growing mash, the young sandhill cranes are changing fast. No longer do they appear like large buff goslings. Their long cinnamon-stick legs have sent them towering above their bantam foster mothers. When the first interesting sounds of morning begin, they rise to their full height, carrying the crouching hens higher and higher until they fall indignant in an ungainly heap. Our day belongs to them—they follow us about, allowing no private moments, superintending our every task. Theirs is the self-assigned task of guarding the children. As their reward for such vigilance they harvest the grasshoppers and damselflies we stir up as we walk, working us just as the cowbird works a cow.

The soft pinkish rubber of their bills has grown to gray iron, a formidable tool for creatures so young, capable of striking terror deep in the warm earth to a self-assured cutworm, or putting to flight a humanoid female in tight slacks. Delicately, they use their surgeon's tool to preen the flaking itch from their emergent feathers. The last bit of scraggly buff down has floated off with a summer breeze, vesting them in the pearly gray of the adult. But their feathered crowns still mark them as juveniles, as does their plaintive, intermittent whistle. It will be winter before the young birds lose their feathery crown for the bald rose caruncular skin of the adult. Voices grow rusty, shrill, and uncertain, before acquiring the stentorian rachet of the adult. By winter most young cranes can sound off with the old birds, although I have heard the immature call from young birds in the spring returning from migration with their parents.

Their emotional need of me is sad. Gradually they turn on their bantams, driving them off, preferring my upright stance. They spend their evenings on the front porch, croaking endearments to me as I read before the fire, then, when the light plant ceases to rattle and the dying house lights plunge the interior into darkness, they move off, groping for secure footing, to the stream to stand knee-deep in the glassy calm until morning, when they decide it is no time for me to be in bed.

I try to slip away without their seeing me, but each door shrieks its conspiratorial warning, and they run to dance with me.

Resignedly, I toss a twig. Choo-choo, the young female, hurls it high again, stabbing at it as it falls. Wings akimbo, tertial plumes trailing, they duck, bow, pirouette, and leap, flapping, in the age-old ritual of the sandhill crane dance. I glance around to see that no one is watching, then dance with them, measure for measure, leaping high, thinking a little sadly that I don't dance quite the way I used to. But the cranes are non-critics and squawk in delirious approbation.

But there is a time for work and a time for play. I must irrigate the pastures, raise my crop of grass for the season, or the steers will run short of groceries. I glare at the cranes as they destroy my small, humble earthworks with probing bills and let the water down the ditch again. There is no way to spank a crane. Wings outspread, they run flapping beside me, delighting in each worm they find in each spadeful as I send water coursing over thirsty fields. Choo-choo's probing bill unties my shoelace, and as I bend, Caruso, the male with a voice to shatter water glasses, hammers the copper rivets of my wallet pocket.

Off in the wild, the parent cranes teach their young to fly by running on ahead, wings outstretched, leading them into short, skimmering hops. Then, oft to the surprise of young and older birds alike, the right breeze kites them easily aloft, squawking with pride but oaring the wafting breeze a little desperately. They soon discover that the skill is not to go up but to descend and to land gracefully. They hurtle in too fast, long legs striding frantically like a human hurdler who has just tripped and is trying to catch up with his body. Since

Choo-choo and Caruso lack parents to teach them, it is my responsibility. One summer afternoon I take them up the hillside by the road then turn and rush toward home, flapping my arms like some strange, demented earthbound bird as they stare at me with interest, then quickly follow suit. How soft the wind slipping through my finger pinions. I am suddenly lighter, gayer, and once more a juvenile. The young birds catapult by me, skimming my head, squawking to me to join them as they gain the adventure of their first flight. Beating my arms desperately against their jet stream, I rush headlong on. I'm— almost making it. With the right headwind now *I could fly!* I reach a slope where the earth drops suddenly away, a sandpit mined by John and Taylor with a scattering of toy trucks. I *am* flying. For one long sweet beautiful second I am catching up with the cranes, then *crash!* I plummet headfirst into the pumice sand.

There is silence, then a cough of embarrassment. I remember suddenly that I never have gotten away with such antics without someone catching me in the act. My banker sits quietly in his automobile watching me. Beside him sits the Wheel from the Portland office.

"I was just teaching them to fly," I venture, because right at the moment there doesn't seem to be much to talk about. Gordon's face is splendidly masked. Only because I know him do I see embarrassment turning his sedate jowl to crimson.

"I've discovered a very interesting fact about sandhill cranes. The old birds run flapping their wings to teach the young to fly. It's *true.* I've watched it many times." I leap aside just as the young birds almost decapitate me with their wings, tumble into an ungainly landing, and come running back to tug on my trouser cuffs.

"Where are the steers you bought?" Gordon asks, by way of saying hello.

"I'll show you, but better let me drive the car," I offer graciously. Unaware that my face is gray with dust, and my clothes are making a disgrace of the immaculate upholstery, I pile into the driver's seat. The Wheel coughs fastidiously.

Questions pound so desperately through my mind, I almost scrape a white-headed woodpecker from the bark of a roadside jack pine. Why didn't they let me know they were coming? Why are they so grim? Is this the prelude to foreclosure? I pile out to open a gate, drive through, pile out again, close the gate, then, perhaps because I am

165

used to a two-door car, instead of this four-door, I pile in beside the men in the back seat. The steering wheel, the dashboard, the gearshift, are *gone!* I shuffle out and climb into the front seat as the bankers glance at each other in embarrassment. I am conscious that I need a haircut.

"Heh, heh!" I grin thinly. "Riding in this brand new automobile kind of reminds me of old George Hoyt. He had a ranch north of here years ago. Back in twenty-nine he arrived at the ranch with a brand spanking new Model A Ford he'd traded in his buckboard for and drove up to the house to show it to my uncle.

"'How do you like your car, George?' my uncle said, trying to be interested.

"'Why, Buck,' George said proudly, rubbing his hands in excitement, 'that's just quite an automobile. I drove her clear up here from Klamath Falls and never had to shift her out of neutral.'"

The Wheel never relaxes his death grip on his frown. "Hoyt?" he says. "Oh, yes, Hoyt. In 1928 he borrowed one hundred twenty-seven dollars to buy some hogs. Lost them all to cholera, he claimed. Probably bought that car."

Ahead of me a group of steers the bankers have come to see are lounging under a tree. Why aren't they out eating? Maybe they are sick with some rare deadly epizootic. There must be better bunches further down if I can skirt these, get the men interested in a story. Maybe George Hoyt can save me.

"They tell lots of stories about old George and how he liked to brag," I put in nervously. "One summer a professor from the university drove down to make a crop survey. He arrived at the Hoyt Ranch and started to question George.

"'Why, on this ranch we grow most everything,' George told him.

"The professor went through his checklist. 'Alsike Clover?'

"'Yep.'

"'Timothy?'

"'Yep.'

"'Tall wheat grass?'

"'Lots.'

"Finally the professor's credulity became a little strained— it had been a wearisome drive. 'Mr. Hoyt,' he asked. 'Would you happen to have some aspirin?'

"'Aspirin?' said George. 'Well, no, can't say rightly that I do—but next year I'm putting in a hundred acres.'"

The bankers have both been staring out the windows at the steers, which looked suddenly like drought cattle, but I know the Wheel heard. He fishes suddenly into his vest pocket and comes up with a couple of pills, which he gulps down dry. "I don't know where I'd be right now without aspirin," he says.

"Sure is too bad about those hogs," I venture, hoping to cheer him up. For a time we drive on down the ranch, looking silently out at steers whenever they graze near the car. If they had wanted to own better steers, why didn't they let me buy them in the fall instead of the spring when good animals were scarce? The least they can do is find one animal and say, "Now that one has a nice color," or a friendly face. The silence makes a hard knot of my stomach.

"Another story they tell about old George," I begin, "was one day he was setting around his little ranch when a car drove down through the pine trees. 'You own this ranch?' the driver asked.

"George swelled up with pride and said, 'Yep.'

"'How big is it?' the man asked.

"'See those mountains over there?' George asked.

"'Just barely,' the man said.

"'Well, sir,' said George expansively, 'my holdings stretch from them mountains you can't hardly see to the west, east to some mountains you can't hardly see either. One hundred thousand acres of the finest ranch and timber land imaginable.'

"'That so?' the stranger said, agreeably impressed. 'How much stock do you run?'

"'You'd never guess by lookin' at my hired man's quarters here, but I got a thousand head of hogs fattening on corn silage, four thousand head of cattle, three hundred head of fine Morgan horses, and fifteen bands of sheep. And right around that bend in the valley, I got me an eleven-bedroom house, and more sheds and barns than you can count.'

"The stranger nodded. 'That's quite a few buildings. Allow me to introduce myself. I'm Mr. Abrams, Klamath County Tax Assessor.'

"'That so?' said George. 'Well, allow me to introduce myself. My name is George Hoyt, lying son of a bitch.'"

"Let me borrow some of that aspirin," Gordon says to his superior. I pull off the road a little to avoid running over a steer which refuses to move.

Before I can get back in the road a big rock is swallowed by the car, bumps along beneath its low-slung elegance, and bangs against the universals as both men clutch their hernias. There is a horrendous silence, then a rattling crash as the rock tears off the muffler. The steers along the road all stand up and look thinner.

"Sorry about your car," I murmur.

"There is a good deal of frost in these upland valleys," my banker explains by way of nothing. "The land appears better than it really is. You can't raise grain, only grass, and the season for that is short. And it takes a ton and a half of hay to winter a cow. The one mistake I ever knew Buck Williams to make was to settle here."

Obviously both men are thinking that his second mistake was inviting me west as a boy, but I let it pass.

"Speaking of George Hoyt," I venture, spotting a dead steer up ahead. "Once in the old days, the Kittredge outfit was camped along the Marsh with about five thousand steers. Spotting the campfires, George drove his old hack and team over to be sociable. 'George Hoyt,' someone asked by way of introduction, 'have you met your new neighbor, Bill Kittredge?'

"'Nope,' George answered, 'but I understand he's a thievin' son of a gun.'"

Silence again in the automobile as the Wheel pales. "Mr. Kittredge was one of Oregon's great citizens," he says aghast, "a member of the Cowboy Hall of Fame, as well as a bank director."

"It's just a story," I explain, and fall silent. Bankers! What has he come here for? Surely not to listen to my poor attempts to give him the flavor of the land. In Portland he could get far better entertainment for the price of a martini. Maybe he should sense in me the pride and feeling for the past that comes when one loves one's land, and has a respect for its history. To understand what he has come to look at, perhaps he should see my children, faces bent to the manes of running horses; they learned to ride not by practicing in a ring but by helping. Maybe he should have known me when I walked straight and tall with youth, known me before my nails became broken with hard work, and my hands flinty from the rough horsehair of my reins.

Everything that sustains his life is done for him; here we do our own, proud that there is no one to do it for us.

That fragile peony in Gerdi's garden! Does he know what a triumph that was, how she labored to cheat it through the intermittent frosts of summer, the first peony to be grown at Yamsi *ever?* And that birch tree, growing in nothing but pumice, first girdled by mice, then as it rose again from the root gnawed asunder by a heartless porcupine with no regards for feelings or beauty. First a many-splendored bush; now a glory of a tree, its top finally reaching past the eves of the ranch house. It took not overnight but years of patient nurturing.

Can't he hear the children's happy laughter on the land? They are entertained and no one paid a dime for it, nor did anyone have to chauffeur them there and back or organize their play. And when have they ever been heard to whine, "What can we do next?"

I know a secret path I could show him that twists hard and unexpected through the woods. It leads to Ginny's and Marsha's world. There in that jack pine maze, sprawls the only ranch I know of that the bank doesn't own, a ranch in miniature, corrals, barns, fences far more neat than Yamsi's. Gates that swing. And animals galore. Plastic perhaps but real if you dream them real. The girls own the whole cow, the whole horse, not just the tail as does their father. Warm sunshine filters down through unpolluted air, and dapples through fragrant, needled greenery. The only vandals are a squirrel which borrows back some cones the girls had used as chimneys on their ranch house, and a chickadee which tried to upside down it on the fragile weathervane cut from a sardine can with their mother's best scissors. Is this the only ranch they will ever own, or a practice ranch to get them ready for a real one?

Gerdi and I both knew we were starting on a shoestring but then (and now) we believed perhaps naively in the old-fashioned America where if a man worked hard from dawn to dark he could make his way. Every year, by working a seven-day week, a sixteen-hour day, I have been able to go deeper into debt, losing ever more and more of my equity in the land. The casual visitor might say, "So what? You can always sell out for lots of money." But why should I have to sell if I want to stay? Why do I have to own a tool and dye corporation in Los Angeles or an oil field in Texas to raise my family on the land?

Reality brings me back to my bankers. The dead steer can hardly be ignored, for it is right in the middle of the road. Thousands of acres of hidden forest glades to perish in and he had to die right out in the open. Fat with bloat; feet sticking starkly out. "What did *that* steer die of ?" the Wheel asks.

"Hemorrhagic septicemia," I reply, which means I don't have the foggiest.

"I thought it was hemorrhagic septicemia," the Wheel comments. He drums his fingers on the ashtray thoughtfully. "Have you counted these cattle lately?" he queries. Which means that he figures if this steer is dead right out before God and everyone, then there are a few hundred more dead somewhere in the trees.

What can I say to distract his catastrophic thoughts? "That reminds me of a hired man I had once," I interrupt. "All he ever owned in his life he could have tied up in a red bandanna handkerchief. One day out on my range we found a bummer calf that was about dead from hollow belly. The old man picked the dogie up and carried him back in his arms, so I gave it to him. 'It's yours,' I said, thinking that the calf would never live.

"But the old man was that tickled he stayed up night and day and nursed the calf, and before I knew it the calf was not only still alive but was prospering on milk that should have been going to the house, and grain that should have been going to the chickens. In time, of course, given such treatment, it grew to be the loveliest heifer on the ranch.

"That young cow was his family, his whole life, the first real possession the old man had ever had. But one day as I was walking with him across the corral, we found the animal dead, shot by a passing carload of sightseers.

"I put my hand on the old man's shoulder. 'I know how you must feel,' I said. 'I'm sorry.'

"But the old man just shrugged. 'Wal,' he said, 'if you're goin' to be in the cattle business, you gotta figure on losing one once in a while.'"

The Wheel clears his throat. "I wonder if he had a mortgage with our bank," he muses, and the three of us lapse into silence. We can hardly keep from scanning the forest beside the road for more dead steers.

Evening fast approaches and the bankers are still on my hands. For the moment I have run out of George Hoyt stories. "How about a little fly-fishing on the river?" I stammer.

"I thought you'd never ask," Gordon says. "We just happen to have our rods along."

There doesn't seem to be a car on the place and their muffler is a disaster, so I pile them into the cattle truck. As the Wheel places his rod in back, he caresses it lovingly. "An English bamboo," he remarks, "given me by my father in 1903."

Thus encouraged, Gordon gives a long and detailed account of the origin of his own rod. I have wasted the whole day talking about George Hoyt when I should have talked fishing.

Once we have gained the stream the two men get out and make for their rods in the back of the truck.

"Where's my rod?" the Wheel suddenly asks. "My God, it's bounced out!"

"I'll get it. *Sir*," I volunteer, ramming the truck into reverse. Three seconds later there is a sickening crack I can hear in the cab, as I back right over his heirloom.

"Take mine," my banker offers. The Wheel's face is masked as he takes the other rod and puts the line up through the guides.

"Look out!" I cry, but it is too late. A sudden wind blows shut the door of the truck, shearing the rod off in the middle.

Dayton, John, and Taylor trudge ahead of us as we drive back to the ranch. They have their limits of trout, all caught on flies. The tail of Taylor's four-pounder almost drags the dust. Something in their father's eye warns them not to risk a comment. The sound of the broken muffler takes a long time dying out in the distance.

"Why do you have all that pumice dust on your face, Dad?" Dayton asks. I shrug. How do I explain my day?

"Haying season is coming," I say, "and I'm just getting ready for a season when my face will be dusty much more often than it is clean."

On the hay ranch on Klamath Marsh, the tall stems of the timothy bend with the weight of the ripening seed, and ripple with the afternoon breeze. The air is sweet with the scent of alsike clover, heavy and lush, with big pink blooms like strawberries, and the white Dutch clover, its small white blossoms growing low out of the wind, the favorite haunt of nectar-loving bees. Grasshoppers buzz busily in the tall bluegrass, which is so thick and heavy it has fallen over in a mat. Blackbirds scold from fence posts as I pass their nests on ditch bank, grass clump, and willow. In the rickety old barn, a late-nesting horned owl raises its brood. I would assume there was no male, except for the line of ground squirrels and mice laid side by side at the nest for the female by a silent nighttime visitor.

Marsh hawks sail plane lazily as they patrol the ditch banks for mice, while sparrow hawks and shrikes watch from the swaying hammock of the telephone lines. From a hole beneath an insulator bracket, small sparrow-hawk faces watch with curiosity as I go by as though they are seeing man for the first time. Already the growing brood of red-tailed hawks in a jack pine at the forested shore of the marsh have eaten over a hundred short-tailed ground squirrels that were raising havoc with my grass and my irrigation ditches. I would not trade my birds of prey for a ton of poisons.

As I zigzag out across the fields to inspect my hay crop, a peregrine falcon falls out of nowhere to dissolve a meadowlark in a puff of feathers. I have been used. The meadowlark was intent upon my approach and I was the last thing he saw. The falcon, so soon to be destroyed as a race by DDT, trusts me not, but carries the hapless bird to a distant fence post, where in the mirage he looks big as an eagle. White wing stripes flashing, a willet dive-bombs me and threatens me with his excited call; black terns scold and dive and scold again. From the blue abyss above, horned larks tinkle all unseen, sink, and are lost again somewhere in the indeterminate seas of prairie vegetation.

Above me to the west, I can see the cool snow fields of the Cascades, the flat-topped peak of Mount Scott, and the sharp horn of Theilsen. To the east the purpled benignity of Yamsay Mountain, and to the south Solomon Butte, part of its forested dome balded by the mange of a forest fire. The Marsh is like a vast, flat lake whose water the gods have turned to soil. Mirages shimmer and fade across the broad expanse. In the distance a rider and his horse trotting in for supper look like giants from some unknown land.

The hay is riper than I thought. Night and day I work on the haying machinery, replacing worn parts, tightening loose bolts, trucking it from Yamsi over the forest roads to the Marsh. My trucks are like scarecrows, rattling, flapping, faltering, backfiring, snorting demons of early vintage whose previous owners, in sequence, gave up on them long years ago, or died of old age and disrepair themselves.

Here a door missing, there a window. Parts made to open, welded shut, mysterious clankings in the bowels of gear boxes and trans-

missions. Motorists pass warily, as if they fear the whole crate will blow up and shower them with parts, as my trucks sidle sideways down the road and shimmy like go-go dancers with the heaves. My idea of prosperity would be to be able to buy a new truck when I need it; yet there is no depreciation left in them—every day I keep them out of the dump and on the road is money gained. Their route, winding through forest hills on bumpy, nerve-shattering roads from ranch to ranch, is thirty miles. Automatically, if the driver doesn't show up at nightfall we go looking for him.

In the early days, the hay was mowed with horse-drawn mowers, cutting a five-foot swath, raked into rows with a hay rake, gathered into bunches by a buck rake which pushed the hay toward the stack. Now a crablike modern complexity of wheel, pulleys, and V belts, called a swather, mows a twelve-foot swath of hay, devours the green river, augers it toward the center mouth, crimps the stems to facilitate drying, and fluffs the hay out into a windrow for drying and pickup by the baler. Allowing time for watching wildlife, hunting arrowheads, and being a boy, Dayton can swath upwards of twenty acres in a day.

When the hay is dry in the windrow I bale it into neat two wire packages with a hay baler towed by my old tractor. A revolving reel with steel fingers swallows up the windrow and it is then augured back into the bale chamber, where it is hit by the battering ram of the plunger and compressed in the four-cornered tube of the bale chamber. As it travels down the chamber it pushes before it two lengths of baling wire. When the hay reaches the desired density, the knotter, a miraculous synchronization of gears, wire knives, and twisters, goes into play. Giant curved steel needles whisk wire up through the bale chamber as the plunger moves ahead and retreats before the plunger can dash them to a thousand pieces. Twin fingers whirl, twisting the ends of the wire together; the wire is severed, and the bale is now complete. Allowing time for watching wildlife, and mending inevitable broken machinery, I can generally keep up with Dayton.

Together, man and boy, blessed with good weather and modern machinery, we put up as much hay in a day as Homer Smith or Ern Morgan did with ten men.

Now come endless days. We leave Yamsi early in the morning for the long drive to the Marsh. While we wait for the dew to vanish, we check our machines, add fuel and grease the myriad fittings. The operation is so integrated that the breakdown of one machine often ties up the whole crew. Constantly we check the bolts for tightness and the parts for signs of wear.

The baler is new and perfect; the tractor was old and disgusting when I bought it. It started perfectly the day before haying season, but now that there is no time to fix it, it requires cranking. Every time I start it I risk a broken arm as the crank whirls like the propeller of an airplane and throws me twenty feet away.

It is up to Gerdi to make the one-hundred-twenty-mile round trip to town for parts. She is having lunch with some friends in town and the car is spotless. But into the station wagon goes a scattered tonnage of broken, worn, dirty, greasy parts which she must somehow transport from the car to the parts counter without ending up looking like a vagrant. She swears that on one trip to town the sheriff sent her out to work in the potato harvest.

The parts men groan when they see her arrive. There isn't the slightest chance she will know what the parts are off of, or the serial number, and will be too embarrassed to know whether the parts are male or female, and besides she isn't about to discuss that with a stranger. She has no idea of makes; all she can swear to is that the baler is apple green, the swather fandango red, and the tractor is a faded puce with thingamabobs on the what-cha-ma-call-its, and she deals with borderline hysteria knowing if the part is not right her husband will snarl and send her winging back to town again.

In the line behind her there are a dozen harried farmers all with their alfalfa getting dryer by the moment who get into the act and confuse her further. In addition, the parts man is right in the middle of his most desperate season, and she expects leisurely, gracious, friendly attention as though she is trying to decide on a new girdle. On guard, she stands in constant readiness, if she isn't handled right, to storm out and take her business elsewhere. There are many places where she can buy a girdle; there is only *one* place in town that handles a 1935 Massey carburetor.

When she finally manages to communicate, the parts man looks through endless dusty books mumbling, "I thought I saw that thing in this book a coupla years ago. Maybe you better tell the old man to buy a newer model, or else why don't you check the junkyards?" When he finally comes up with a right number, he comes back with the cheery message, "Sorry that part is obsolete" or "It will have to be back ordered at the factory back East. Take three weeks."

Before her luncheon date with her friends, she spends half an hour down in the lady's restroom, where she is interrupted by a young hoyden who dashes back up the stairs announcing to the dining public, "*Mom, Mom!* Some woman's down there taking a sponge bath in the toilet." She finally gets the grease off her hands only to find that her dress is dusty, her hair is a fright, and there is a squashed and dried mosquito trailing across her cheek like a painted comet.

Her friends spend most of their time talking about their cabin at the lake, golf scores, and the latest story in *Redbook,* and wonder why she sits with her hands beneath the table instead of eating such a yummy salad.

Meanwhile back on the Marsh Ranch, the baler is stopped waiting for the swather to be fixed or the swather is waiting so as not to get too far ahead of the broken baler. I pace the windrows nervously, knowing that the hay must be dry but not too dry, battling the swarms of mosquitoes that are angrily berating me for having destroyed the ecology of their tall grass forest. And now the watchful storm cloud that has been peering from the rim of the Cascades moves overhead and dumps a scattering of rain on my hayfield, ignoring my neighbor's dry pasture where it is desperately needed.

Rained out, we head in for the old ranch house along the shore to eat our sandwiches, now curled like dried scalps, on the warped picnic table beneath the grove of aspens. For a moment we enjoy the lazuli bunting on the fence, the orioles flashing in the cool, nervous greenery overhead. Then comes the thunderous rumbling of a mainline freight train racing for Seattle with a load of new trucks and pickups for some suburban farmer who can afford them. The house shakes and the dust clouds whirl into our food as the great mass of mud gourds of the cliff swallow colony shiver from the eaves for the umpteenth time this week, and the swallows take vengeance on us innocents until we retreat into the house.

I have a moment of relief when the crew of indigents who are supposed to haul the hay by means of my ancient trucks over the hills to Yamsi arrive, but it ends when I find that they have left the attachment for the hay loader at Yamsi, as well as the spare tire for the truck with the flat, and they allow as how they might just as well start tomorrow instead of today. I sigh, for out in the fields the bales are already starting to mold on the bottom and the weatherman has just announced a ninety percent chance of rain.

When at my insistence they finally get a load loaded, they lose half of it while attempting an irrigation ditch. Then as they head in toward shore with the rest, the radiator overheats and they find they have nothing in which to carry water. Once this is remedied, we find that the barrel of gas I stored for emergencies like this has been drained by some passerby.

Synchronization is of the essence, but usually Dayton is too far ahead with the swather or not far enough, the baler is too far ahead of the trucks, or the truckers are grumbling unhappily as they wait for the broken-down baler to turn out the bales they need to finish their load.

Happiness is seeing a truck load of hay disappear into the blue haze at the far end of the Marsh, and to find out that night that it got safely into the ranch and has been unloaded in the pole shed by my wife and children.

Youth or sex give no indemnity when a hay truck arrives at the ranch to be unloaded and sent on its way again. Even John and Taylor drag what bales they can off the truck and act as errand boys to pack water for the thirsty crew. Between truckloads they roam the woods looking for mice to feed the voracious appetite of Alexander, the great gray owl.

John and the owl are inseparable comrades. On his perch, the owl bounces up and down, peering excitedly to see what delicacy John brings him this time. Walking upon the lawn as the boys play, Alex leaps and pounces playfully on imaginary prey, seizes my buckskin glove and carries it up to the top of his favorite perch, the kitchen chimney.

And instead of the owl acquiring mannerisms from John, John takes them from the owl, bobbing his head as though to bring his eyes into focus, flapping his wings to strengthen his flying powers, staring at everyone and everything with round, unblinking eyes, and abandon-

ing the English language for the series of whistles, hisses, beak-snappings, and hoots that are owl talk. My wife calls to John from the door to tell him that his bed hasn't been made in three days, but there is no answer. He is up in the tree on a perch next to his friend, Alex, where he has been sitting visiting the long morning. "John!" my wife shouts, seeing one small tennis shoe out of place in the treetops. "Answer me this instant!"

"Who," says John.

CHAPTER 11

THE HAY SHED IS A VAST, STARKLY empty cathedral abandoned by its congregation or too new to have acquired one. Six hundred feet long, and thirty-six feet high at the ridge, it is little more than a roof floating at treetop levels, held aloft by three naked ivory columns marching in aligned perfection, from end to end, giant trees, debranched, debarked, chosen from the multitude of lodgepole pines, each matching the others in size and straightness.

The trucks come groaning and limping in from the Marsh with great fragrant loads of bright green hay. Our heads swing as we unload the trucks now looking back gratefully at what is already stored, now looking ahead gloomily at the staggering emptiness which is ours yet to fill.

In any haying operation disaster is only a machine failure away, and the very complexity of the equipment precludes an uneventful season. As with any job staggering in its immensity, one gets it done only by wearing away at it, chip by chip, day after endless day. One loses perspective, finding little more to life than endless drudgery, feeling that one is condemned for some forgotten sin to an eternity of hauling hay into the shed in blazing summer, and hauling it all out again in frigid winter. Year after year after year.

Down on the ranch, the fields are left to irrigate themselves, with a touch here and there by my frantically busy wife who now cooks meals for an average of twenty, trots hell-bent about her matriarchal domain, gathers, moves, doctors, and sprays the cattle, taxis children, runs back and forth to town for parts, referees other people's fights, wins her own, handles everything on the ranch her slothful husband forgot to do, hosts a constant stream of company from all over America who are determined not to do a blamed thing on their vacation including take care of their children, and yet she finds time, somehow, to wage a

178

constant war against the grass, which flourishes far better in her garden than in the meadow.

She keeps both the ranch house and the town house psychopathically clean on the grounds that she might get killed on the road and doesn't want another woman coming in to find dust in her closet. Her idea of fun would be to clean my blacksmith shop, which is an acknowledged disgrace, fostered by my dual premise that one of the world's greatest triumphs is to avoid a trip to town by making the part off one old abandoned machine perform a completely different service on another, and that nothing, however insignificant, should be thrown away. There is no task on the ranch that women can't do and it is a constant challenge to her inventiveness to disguise from me the fact that she can really do almost anything far better than her husband. Surely the rural wife is the great unsung American.

But there is only one of her so that down on the ranch the steers are left pretty much to their own company, the fields to irrigate themselves, broken fences unmended, cattle mixed, the mail left unread, the trout uncaught, and most emergencies ignored until that indeterminate time known as after haying But the ranch somehow survives, just as it has survived neglect in every summer since men first put up hay here for the winter.

Since predation, pesticides, and the perils of migration have not yet taken their voracious toll of the production of summer, the birdlife in the valley is staggering to behold. Each pair of swallows, including the chittering forked-tailed barn swallows that built their nest in an abandoned stirrup Homer Smith left hanging in the carpenter shop a quarter century ago, has raised two broods, sending each unit population from two to a dozen. Near the house, the telephone wires belly down desperately with the weight of the gathering hordes and sometimes one wire scissors against the other to catch them all by the neck. "No, Operator, that banging noise isn't always on my line. Today it happens to be perching swallows. And last night it was a pair of great gray owls visiting my son, John. Ring me back tomorrow and it may be eagles."

It is sad when the swallows leave. There is ample food for them until September, yet one day in August they will be gone, save for a few confused birds abandoned to wing friendless and alone over the deserted ponds.

Down along the valley, as morning frosts turn the mature grasses to buckskin, the young sandhill cranes keep their parents carefully in sight as though they fear to be left behind when the age-old tocsin of migration chimes. Now that their young have achieved mobility to run or fly from danger, the cranes no longer limit themselves to the wet marshes. They move together up the draws, searching out the gathering hordes of egg-laying grasshoppers, shredding a thousand hapless insects for every one they swallow, and by this year's action providing against next year's epidemic.

Yellowheaded, Brewer's, and red-winged blackbirds gather like black storm clouds, feeding here, feeding there, yet ready on an instant to quit a feast of plenty just because one nervous individual leaps into the air. The work they do for me I could not hire done, nor is there an insecticide so safe and cheap. Admittedly, modern insecticides would wreak havoc with my insect population, but next year my birds would not be back to help, and to the end of time I would be committed to an expensive spraying program. It takes little carelessness on the part of the rancher to upset the desperately important balance.

One year when the government swore up and down that DDT was safe, I sprayed my cattle for horn flies, and the few animals that strayed across the river were enough to sterilize the waters downstream from that point at which they waded. It was a sad, sad time. Near the stream banks, flycatchers anchored to the locale by nests of growing young waited patiently for insect hatches along the river, while, nest by nest, strident youngsters gaped their yellow mouths even at the passing wind, and soon were forever silent. Swallows worked past their perching hours, then, pair by pair, deserted their silent nesting holes for new territories far up the river. On the needled floor beneath the jack pines, baby nighthawks, camouflaged so perfectly against danger, fell to starvation, one enemy to which protective coloration was no matter. If any insects hatched along the river bottoms they seldom escaped to the surface but were gobbled by desperate trout who fed now at all hours, and who soon resembled not fat pumpkinseeds but snakes with heads all out of proportion to their bodies. All this done by a fool who had yet to understand.

Man has been guilty, in years past, of causing destruction through failure to understand the far-reaching effects of his acts. His guilt is now compounded, for he knows what he does is wrong, and yet goes right on doing it.

Insecticides were a technical advance, and, caught up as he was with the excitement of new tools solving age-old problems, Man overdid himself to use them. Pesticides were often a miraculous answer but they were seldom the answer. And some of the problems they solved had been compounded by Man himself, who had unwittingly upset the balance of Nature.

For years after the drainage of the marshes, and the subsequent reduction of natural predators, grasshoppers overran the land at Yamsi in multitudes. The flats were a rattling, dry grass sea of them; gentle horses panicked, whirled and bolted rather than let themselves be ridden through the hordes. Flying with the wind, a grasshopper could raise an angry welt on a man's face or put out an eye. They traveled at a slow creep across the lush meadows, turning green grass yellow, then brown and sere; then when they had grown to maturity they began to travel, a vast insect army living off the land, waves overleaping waves in short, purposeful flights. They piled like snowdrifts against the obstacles of buildings, filled the ruts of country roads so that cars spun as helplessly as on ice.

We cowboys were grounded from our horses for the duration of the emergency. We spent endless days mixing arsenic with sawdust and bran, scattering it in the face of the advancing hordes with a primitive propeller powered by the rear end of a Model T Ford. The score was a handful of grasshoppers, thirty-nine Hereford heifers, and one mischievous dapple gray draft team some idiot tied to the poison wagon while we human bug catchers were having our own lunch.

Discouraged, we built miles of tin fences across the lines of travel and V'd the insects into pits for burning. Nothing really worked and while I was waiting for the pits to fill, the grasshoppers ate my Stetson hat and my woolen jacket.

Some control came, of course, with modern insecticides, but those chemicals were shotgun remedies which sterilized the land with lasting effect. It was quite by accident that I achieved desired control, not by insecticides, but by restoring the marshes and thus the feathered flocks which once more brought Nature into balance. In the decade since, instead of losing a quarter of our annual forage to insects, the forage lost has been negligible, without an ounce of spray.

But due to the public apathy we fight a losing war. To control invasions of timber beetles, the Forest Service sprayed its forest lands and killed the fish life in Five Mile Creek and in the North Fork of the Sprague. Trappers put out 1080 on my private land, and a light plane tossed strychnine bait over my meadows within a mile of the house killing fourteen coyotes and my English setter. I had lived in harmony with the coyotes and had never lost a single calf to them, but someone just couldn't stand the thought of them being there. Some predator control is needed, of course, particularly in those lands where food supplies are cyclic or out of balance, but let the dollars be spent there instead of in areas where control is neither needed nor requested. This would free more dollars to control predation where the need is urgent.

OUT ON THE MARSH A TRUSTING coyote pup trots behind the truck as the side loader picks up the bales from the ground and sends them up to the man loading. He has learned to use Man to provide a meal, for the fat meadow mice must dash for cover as each bale is moved. With one stiff-legged bounce, the pup is on them. The voles are fierce, angry fighters; the pup yelps as one grabs his nose with sharp little teeth and holds. He flips it into the air, pounces as it falls, and next time is more careful. As the last bale goes up on the load and the ropes are stretched taut over the load, the coyote retreats to the cool of a shaded ditch and is lost from view. He has learned to use the ditches as escapeways. While the loaded truck creaks and lumbers in toward the shore of the Marsh we catch sight of his pointed ears and head as he watches us depart.

One evening as I drive back toward Yamsi after a long day of baling hay, who should I meet on the road but Biddy. Bucking and playing, she comes up, hoping to be scratched, while her calf watches suspiciously from the bushes. Perhaps his mother has set a bad example and he will trot up to be friendly to the next human he sees, and it will turn out to be a cattle rustler.

If Ginny were near, I would manage all sorts of deprecating remarks about the calf and its ridiculous mother, but alone with her now I am proud. Ginny will never know the visits Biddy and I have together, and how hard I work to make sure Biddy is bred to the best herd sire I own. But now, thankless vixen that she is, she blocks the road as I try to drive away, scratches her rear against one shattering headlight, then deposits a great, steaming mass of organic matter on the hood of my car as though sending my wife a present for her garden. I make a mental note that come autumn Biddy will bring a top price for hamburger.

At every bend of the road, I expect to come upon my hay trucks, stalled and useless. Miraculously, the old battered trucks keep bumping their slow, grinding, steaming way along. The trucks are loyal to me, but not the crews. Yesterday the men departed for town, taking with them the tools from the tool box, fueling their cars with gas siphoned from my tanks.

Even the old-timers had their compulsive quitters, though with more honesty and flavor. The Klamath country had Walkaway Burns, who could work anywhere he chose, but who often left in the middle of the day without ever bothering to pick up his check. He had his own form of Social Security in the form of back pay coming from half the outfits in the country.

One day as he was driving a team of horses through the frozen woods, his young helper asked, "Just why do folks call you 'Walkaway'?"

"Son," said Walkaway gravely, "I'd be glad to show you." Handing the boy the reins, Walkaway disappeared into the woods.

Desperate for help, I buy a hauler a truck, permitting him to pay me for it as he hauls. Soon I discover that he is hauling my hay to town and selling it. He is convicted and given five years' probation. Next, my best hauler turns out to be wanted for assault with a deadly weapon, and departs hastily.

It is easy to become frantic, for thousands of bales litter the fields unhauled, and white mold forms on the bottoms as they soak up moisture from the soil. Storm clouds rim the Cascades, and in the morning there is frost on the machinery, and everywhere the sharp scent of autumn.

Searching out warm bodies on the streets of Klamath Falls, I find a likely one, but by the time I get him to the Marsh he has passed out from drinking the shaving lotion I had just purchased in town. Just as I am about to despair, a truckload of men arrive from town wanting work, but what they really want to do is hide out. The boss is seized for insurance fraud, the driver can work only two days before he is due in court to answer charges of statutory rape, and the remaining scarecrow of a man suddenly breaks and runs shouting across the Marsh, "Dere's snakes in the bales!" He is last seen almost three days later trudging into the city limits of Klamath Falls, headed for the nearest pub. The truck is deserted on my place and turns out to have been stolen from an Indian woman one of the men met in Klamath.

All I can do is shrug off my troubles and wonder if somewhere in all those unemployment statistics there isn't a boy who would like to earn enough in a summer for a year in college. I feel a real sadness for those who can't find work, a real anger against those able-bodied parasites who won't. Along the swift advance of years, what happened to human pride, to the feeling that in working we were part of the life blood of America and that, however humbly, as individuals we really mattered?

The last bale is baled and my hand trembles as I turn off the baler engine for the last time this year. But we are not done yet. Stretching out before me is the vast sea of bales, and there is no one to haul it. For a few days the children pitch in and help me, then school starts and I am alone, cooking my own meals, doing my own chores, and appreciating all over again how much the family adds to my life to make my way easier.

At night I toss and turn, dreaming of endless rows and no help coming. In my dreams, the autumn rains come flooding down to turn the bales from green to buff to black. In their sogginess, they heat, smell of rampant mold, and steam in the cold air. My banker sits on a rotting bale reading a list of ranchers whose notes are up for renewal. One by one he checks off each name; through mine he draws a line with a red pencil, and sadly shakes his head.

But day by day I keep on plugging. The children come out weekends and pitch in to help without my asking. At the Marsh the fields are becoming bare; at Yamsi the hay shed is bulging with eight hundred tons of hay. Suddenly we are loading the last loads. Johnny steers the truck, Taylor lines the bales, Marsha helps me load, while Gerdi, Ginny, and Dayton crew the other truck. The road to Yamsi seems longer than ever; the truck overheats and I pack water in my hat from a seep spring on the hillside. A rear tire blows; there is no spare and I keep on driving.

The last bale goes up the elevator and we fall back on the hay, not cheering, but silent with the immensity of what we have accomplished. The hay is actually in. Let it rain.

THE STEERS ARE FAT AND SLEEK. On arrival at the ranch last May, they averaged five hundred pounds; now they weigh upwards of seven hundred. We gather field after field, working them slowly south up the ranch, and ease them into a holding field for the night. We prayed for a warm balmy night; instead, frost coats the grass and the cattle will not feed until it has melted off. Ellington Peek arrives in the dawn to take delivery for the feed lot man to whom he has contracted the steers.

Down the long hill from civilization to the west rumbles a great shining fleet of modern, sanitized, split-level cow apartments, which will take them south to a feed lot in California. Having driven through the long night, the drivers are red-eyed and stare vacantly about as they wait, hunched against the cold. Longingly they glance in the direction of the ranch kitchen, not realizing that my wife is also chief buckaroo and has better things to do than to serve them coffee.

Silent in our thoughts, we mount our horses in the early light and ride down the long lane to the holding field. As we approach the steers rise lazily from their beds, sag their backs to stretch, and move toward the far end of the field. As quietly as possible we shape them into a herd. It is a nervous time for us all, and even the greenest hand senses that to speak too loudly is to be fired. If the herd spooks and runs, the effort can cost me thousands of dollars in lost weight, for the disaster loosens bowels and every time a steer raises his tail I lose a dollar, which makes for pretty expensive fertilizer.

The dog, which was nowhere to be seen when we left, now stands barking, guarding the gate to the corral, and to curse him aloud would break my own strict rule for silence. Peacocks shrill loudly as the truckers choose that moment to start their engines and jockey their trucks into position. The sandhill cranes tip back their heads and hurtle a strident challenge into the thin, cold air. As the steers begin to mill and throw up their heads to stare nervously about, a driver slams his truck door, whistles merrily, and shouts back to one of the drivers in the rear he hasn't seen since yesterday, four hundred miles away. In the lane, the column of steers stops flowing, fences on either side sing with strain as the steers bunch up, plunging over each other's backs, and drowning in the sea of flesh. I leave the drag to ride through the restless jam-up, trying to force the leaders out of their stalls so that the river may flow on.

When somehow we get them in, and ease them through the network of corrals without tearing off their hipbones on the gates, we hasten them across the scales, load by load, twenty at a time. After every five loads we pause and check the balance of the scales, adjusting to the accumulation of debris. Weights and numbers are inscribed carefully in our record books, for later totaling over coffee in the ranch kitchen.

Cattle bawl, men shout, dust rises, metal slams on metal, as we herd the steers in groups up the loading chute into the bowels of the truck. Truck after truck is filled, then suddenly the great aluminum caravan is gone, the rumbling roar fades into the distance, the corrals and fields

are stark and empty as though the steers had never been. Over coffee we add up the long columns of weights, deduct three per cent of the total for shrink, as per contract, so that the buyer doesn't have to pay thirty cents a pound for that long drink of water the steers sucked this morning from the river.

The gains have not been enough this year to warrant my investment; like any other livestock man I've taken a gambler's chance at making a fair profit and lost, coming out with little more than a pasture bill for all my risk and hard work. For a long moment I hold the draft which Peek writes out for me; never before have I been so impressed with the vast difference between gross profit and net. I glance trembling at the figures and the dreams run rampant in my head. Then Gordon shatters the illusion by taking the draft quietly from me, and heads for town before I can head for Mexico. I worked so hard for the bank this year, why can't they be friendly?

Deep in the curling river, the great trout lie shadowy, rose-hued, scarcely moving, lazy now from feasting on the frantic fly hatches of summer. Where June was a month of frothing action, July one of swirls and darting wakes in glassy moonlight, August of dimpling disinterest amidst still rampant plenty, September is moody silence and glop-eyed somnolence. The sulking wraiths, swollen monstrous from greed, now strike only in anger, frustrating the angler, for if the leader is delicate enough to fool the fish, it is also too fine to hold him.

Throughout the forest, the squirrels and chipmunks scamper in frenetic haste, gleaning from the pines whatever harvest has fallen with the most recent fingering of the autumnal wind. Weathered and barkless, the gray, curling silk of the fallen pine is tracked with bloodlike footprints of rodents stealing the scarlet-juiced seed of the bitterbrush, thus marking, telltale, each scampering route from bush to winter storeroom.

Yesterday, the short-tailed ground squirrels looked fat and puffy as they stood like driven tent pegs to watch me pass. Now deep beneath the earth curled at tunnel's end in a puff of summer's grass, they sleep the half-year's mate away, while far above, the red-tailed hawks circle the cooling sky in bewilderment. With hibernation, the scampering plenty that raised the brood of hawks is gone, shifting the hunt to winter denizens, the wood mouse, pine squirrel, and the snowshoe hare.

Biddy stands in the right angle made by the junction of the Bull Pasture with the Kay Davis field, noses the gate, rubs her monstrous, itching head briskly against the gate latch, collapses the gate and lets herself in off the range. Her calf stands amazed at his mother's powers, but hangs back as though fearful that the gate will somehow snap back up and grab him.

It's gathering time, and Biddy seems to know it to the day. She moves jauntily off across the meadow, leaving her calf to follow if he will, forget her if he must. He makes a brave run at the snarl of barbed wire that was the gate, ducks back in sudden fear, leaps high to clear it, and lands squarely in its middle. With a startled bawl he plunges ahead, twisting the wire into a desperate mess. He leaves the fly swatter of his tail hanging on the wire, but once free, as though amused at his success, he bucks and scampers off across the meadow to where his mother, satisfied at last to have achieved the meadows which have been off limits to her the summer long, buries her head in a patch of clover unharvested by the steers.

At length she remembers her bovine allegiances, raises her head, looks off toward the distant wall of pine forest, and bawls long and low. It is the signal to gather, and soon from here and there out of the hidden glades of the forest come the nodding, shining faces of the range cows, startling motion from the painted silence for the dark green trees. For one long moment, the cows stand and watch, elevate their nostrils as though they hope to smell some sentimental scent from spring. Then quickly, they see the downed gate, and trot briskly forward, glad to be home once more.

By the time I come scrambling along on my sorrel horse, Tunic, eager to gather the first cows of the season off the range, fifty-nine cows and three bulls are already in. Biddy gives me a fat, triumphant, chewing, bovine look as I try to straighten the tangle of the gate. I can just smell great, juicy, Biddy steaks cut from her loin, dripping juice into the hissing heat of the barbecue, splattering hot grease into the gray-ashed cubism of the charcoal.

If I could just open the gates and let the cattle in off the range it would be easy, but I need to keep accurate count so that later in the fall I am not looking for cows that are already safely in the fields.

Eager for work, my horse moves out at a long trot, eats up the miles, up the long Bull Pasture draw, across the Buckhorn Springs road, on toward the head of Telephone Draw. We noon at the ruin of John Cole's old deer camp. I slip the bridle off my horse, loosen the cinch, and water him at the spring which trickles from the willow clumps and gurgles into the first of a series of beaver dams. Years back, I brought the beavers here in burlap sacks tied to the back of my horse; they have paid me for my trouble by building dams, not only healing the erosion, but providing water for cattle and wildlife.

The past is ever present. I find an arrowhead as I drink from the spring; here and there are rusty bedsprings, old cans, an insulator, and a piece of telephone wire from the line that ran through here in the thirties and gave the draw its name. As I rest, five cows and calves drift down off the bitterbush ridges, drink thirstily from the beaver pond, then stare at me in surprise as I catch my horse. I start them down the draw and they disappear into the masses of willow and aspen. Only the faint crackling of the brush lets me know they are still ahead. When miles later I see them in the clearing of a meadow, my herd has swelled to thirty cows, twenty-five calves and two old bulls.

They move well under their own power. Now and then a lead cow bawls a greeting as the herd flows into another group of cows scattered across the meadow, and absorbs it. Nutcrackers and gray jays scream at us as we pass and leave them once more to solitude, just as a flash flood moves quickly down a canyon and is gone.

But as the miles go by, the cows tire under the Indian summer sun and now seem reluctant to leave their summer ranges. The milk-fat calves drag to the rear, tongues hanging, drooling zigzag lines on the dry earth. One calf has lost his mother and I let him go back to find her. He slips past me warily, not sure whether I am letting him go or have failed to see him. Small black flies buzz about my nose and mouth, the same tiny flies that drive the mule deer bucks to seek the open burns in the heat of the day. As I pass a burn, I see for a moment only emptiness, then beside a rotten, charcoaled log, I catch the flick of motion, the geometric contours of spoonlike ears, as the flies molest a five-point mule deer. He seems to fade into the ground shadows as I pass, his antlers frozen like dead limbs, thrust into the scrub of a dying aspen.

As I herd the cattle down the draw, I zigzag back and forth behind them. Every foot is a struggle. Two bulls fight out of pure cussedness and the whipped bull keeps veering off to stand in the trees on first one side of the draw and then the other, hoping to be overlooked and left behind. My saddle lacks much of the comfort that it had when I was younger. Overcome for the moment with being forty-four, I stop in the shade of the trembling aspens, and stretch out to give my saddle a rest. Through the constant motion of the fanlike leaves I can see blue sky, and an occasional drifting cloud. I cradle my head on my hands and think back on the past.

The old cowboys who rode this range are gone. Only I am left. Why can't I bring Homer Smith back to life out of the past, if only for the fall gather? Once more I hear the gruff bass of his voice, catch the small mirth in his faded blue denim eyes, see him fold one great cabbage-leaf ear against his cheek in thought.

FAR UP AHEAD A COW BAWLS forlornly for her calf. I begin to wish I hadn't let that calf go back, but soon I hear the click of bovine hooves from up the draw, and calf and mother come nodding down the trail to join the herd. The mother has been up on the ridge in the bitterbrush; a forked twig still hangs jauntily from her ear.

The glade in which I rest looks familiar and suddenly I have the feeling that I have lain in this very spot, thought these very thoughts before. Here it was twenty—no, thirty years ago I first saw Big Red. He was a magnificent red sorrel with a white zigzag of lightning down his face, and three white stockings, shining like red gold among the wild horses as they came charging down the bluff to water. In seconds they had winded me and were gone, scattering dust clouds as they thundered across a burn and flung themselves into the virgin pines on the ridge. They were no sooner gone than I heard a mare nicker from up the draw and Charlie Lenz, a slender halfbreed who owned a ranch below Mamie Farnsworth on the river, came trotting down the draw. His face was blade thin, eyes suspicious, and he would have flung back into cover had not I glimpsed him.

"Charlie," I said, brashly for a kid. "There's a blaze-faced sorrel horse in that bunch of wild horses I'd give anything to have. I'd pay you to trap him for me."

Charlie glanced in the direction of the ridge where a faint puff of dust still lingered prisoner of the trees. From his dismay it was obvious that he had been hunting the very horses I had spooked, and his chances at them were over for the day.

"What's it worth to you, kid?" he asked, as though wondering where a skinny kid like me would get money.

"I'll give you seventy-five bucks and I'll promise not to tell anyone I found your still and three barrels of hooch in those willow bushes above your place on the river."

Charlie rode on ahead of me without an answer and I would have ridden the rest of the afternoon behind him in sheer persistence, had not his buckskin mare kicked at my horse and hit me right in the knee.

But he'd heard me all right, for less than a month later he came by Yamsi with my sorrel horse, already broke to lead. The horse was freshly castrated, his tail bobbed off square, and on his left stifle was Charlie's iron, a fresh lightning Z.

Big Red was the first horse I ever owned, and like most wild horses he broke out lots easier than a barn-raised colt. Within a week I was riding him out on the range. Seeing my success, Charlie got the idea he might get some of his own outlaws broken at the risk of my body. He offered me a job trailing a herd of two hundred horses eastward across the Oregon Desert to Idaho, roping colts to ride out of the herd. But if a fellow got bucked off just once way out there it was a long walk home, and somehow my good sense prevailed, much to my regret in later years.

I glance up the draw, half expecting Charlie to come riding by again, but there us only silence now and emptiness. I swing my leg over my cantle and ease my horse on after the cows, feeling suddenly more alone than ever. When I finally reach the gate into the Haystack Draw field, I count one hundred forty-seven cows and seven bulls.

Day after day I scour the range for cows, riding through meadows I haven't seen all year, checking the trails for tracks of cattle I've missed, planning my trips to high noon it at the waterholes. Thirty head out of the Wildhorse Meadows, ten head out of Deer Draw, and a hundred and ten from the Teddy Powers' country. I am getting nervous now, for there are only four days left until the beginning of deer season and then it will be suicide to a ride a horse in the woods. There are fresh tracks near the salt, but the cattle are gone.

Of all the year, this is perhaps the time I enjoy most. No pressures now that really matter; only the day-to-day relationship of a lonely man and his horse, drifting from one wandering meadow to another over the intermittent ridges of yellow pine. Dropping off the ridges into Bear Draw, I rest for lunch in a thicket of bog birch and bush willow where the only water is from ponds I've dug with my tractor. Resting on one elbow, chewing a twig, I watch bemused as a host of nuthatches, creepers, warblers, finches, and tanagers come in from the arid forests to bathe and drink. They hardly notice me as I laze in the shadows. Tired from a hot, dusty thirty-mile circle, my horse stands quiet, lip hanging vacantly, eyes half closed, hip sagging, hoof cocked, dreaming of home. As a good-natured coyote trots to the pool to drink, camp robbers scold. The coyote laps up water with a long pink tongue; for one moment he cocks his head as an Audubon warbler bathes on a half-submerged log, then resumes his panting as he trots away. As I ride down the draw looking for cattle, I surprise him in his bed, where he has lain curled in a soft hill of a deserted ants' nest.

As I enter the house for supper, the telephone jangles persistently as though it has been ringing since morning. A neighbor has seen four YZ cows twenty miles to the south. I thank him and tell him about fifteen head of his heifers I saw on a scab rock flat north of the Black Hills. The woods are filling up with deer hunters; dust clouds hover in long strips over the forest roads. Five hundred deer camps within a mile of my fence. What foresight my uncle had so many years ago when he built his house of stone.

CHAPTER 12

ALL SUMMER LONG THE FINICKY
steers picked at the feed, ignoring the coarser grasses along the poorly
drained sections of the ranch. Now this works to my advantage, for
the cows are less selective, and tear into the rushes and sedges as
though they are bluegrass and clover. Throughout the summer the
cows have drifted restlessly from one part of the range to another;
now with feed, water, and salt under their noses, they seem to enjoy
staying in one place.

Just as the flocks of blackbirds are swelled with this year's production, so is my herd of cattle swollen by the calves, who now, in the
distance, seem almost as big as their mothers. Now and then a handful of cows and calves drift out of nowhere to pace the fence, hoping
to be let in, but lacking Biddy's resourcefulness. I open the gate for
them, wondering how I could have missed them in the gather, then
gratefully add their numbers to the tally sheet posted in the kitchen.
They have made it in off the range to safety just in time.

Outside my fences, the hunters are in a frenzy. One car impales the
next with lurching headlights. All night long they drive in to the ranch,
some lost, some out of gas, some wanting to know the way to the
nearest buck, some wanting to see the cranes in the middle of the night,
some wanting to know if the water is good to drink, or if I will let
them escape the crowds by camping among the cattle where they will
be safe. I am a reasonable man; I am glad that they are enjoying our
beautiful land, but I wish that some of them had done a better job of
preparing themselves for the ordeal.

I am still missing cows and calves but they will have to fend now for
themselves, for to ride a horse out into that shooting war would be
unfair to the animal. It is a nervous time. All my earthly goods are not
locked in a vault somewhere, but exposed to thieves and vandals.

All it will take is one hunter on a Honda roaring through their midst
to stampede my wary cows and calves right through my fence and

out into the open range again, from which there would be no gathering them. The dumped garbage, broken bottles, cut fences, downed gates, wounded livestock, rustled calves, warming fires left burning in the trees or dried grass, are all things the rancher is expected to take in stride. If most city dwellers had to live as vulnerable yet so far from police protection, they would be terrified. All that keeps the rancher calm is his faith in his fellow man. Year by year, he loses a little more of that faith.

It is a sad thing for wildlife. Bewildered by population pressures, more and more ranchers and farmers are draining their marshes and ponds, plowing up cover, discouraging wildlife because all these things attract people, people cause trouble, and trouble they have plenty of already. Eighty percent of wildlife depends not upon public land but private for the food it eats, especially in the critical periods. Add up a host of Yamsis scattered about the country, protected from vandalism by public understanding, and you would have a refuge system vastly superior to any public money could buy. In private agricultural land we have the greatest hope for the future salvation of our wild resource, yet so far no one has asked the farmer to help. And he cannot help, of course, until he is protected from overt acts from a miniscule lawless segment of the public. In most cases laws already exist against vandalism, but laws are ineffectual when not backed firmly by public understanding.

The woods explode with shots. I was in the Battle of the Bulge, the Ruhr Pocket, and the Rhineland Campaign, and never heard more than this. There is no open season this year on females, but the wounded does, burning with fever, head naturally for Yamsi and the river. Does and fawns, riddled horribly by irresponsible, excited shooters, lie helpless along the marshes. They seem to plead with me with big, dark eyes to end it for them. There are too many deer for the range; left unchecked, they would destroy the plants for all time and starve. I know of few conservationists who do not agree to a harvest. But I know of no conservationists who are not made sick by the agonies caused by careless greedy shooting.

The family lies low for the first week of the season. If I have to go out I whistle a constant tune whenever I enter the forest. My mouth dries and I can hardly speak. And a hunter actually stops me and asks me to whistle a different tune. "White Christmas" is making him nervous.

194

But eventually we are forced out of hiding by the very urgency of the tasks we must do. Keeping to the open meadows, we ride the length of the valley. It is not a pleasant feeling. I see a man sitting on a log, watching me through the scope of his rifle. My calm comes near being ruffled.

Gingerly we gather the long meadows, pushing the cows and calves south to the Kay Davis corrals for working, or separating as we attempt to classify the cattle. First we cut out the dry cows, those giving no milk. These will be pregnancy tested to make sure that they are carrying calves. There could be various reasons for a cow's dryness. She might be physically incapable of carrying a calf, or might have lost her calf last spring while calving. Perhaps rustlers shot her calf during the summer; perhaps it simply died of disease. If she is a fine young cow and is now, as determined by the veterinarian, sure to be carrying a calf, we give her another chance in the herd. It is good business to sell dry cows no matter how pretty they look, for they are already one-time losers.

Once the drys are out and driven to a separate field, we pick out those replacement heifers good enough to improve the quality of our herd. The decisions are tough to make, since, in a range operation, good records are hard to keep. We pair the calf with its mother, making sure the mother is of the type we need and a good milker. We judge the calf on size, bloom, uniformity, heaviness of bone, straightness of back, smoothness of tail, head, color, and general conformation as a high-yielding meat-producing animal.

Tradition demands that the man doing the cutting uses his own judgment without comment or help from the holding crew. The crew sit quietly on their horses, holding the herd together, each man helping the cutter out of the herd with his animals whenever they head his way. If there is communication between men it is only to whisper or bum a cigarette, for excessive noise is discourtesy which distracts the man concentrating on his work. Men have been fired for less.

I ease my horse quietly into the herd, staring intently at the cows, following my horse only by the feel of him between my knees. Suddenly the horse lurches sideways and in my relaxed concentrated state I almost end up on the ground. I glare about just in time to narrowly escape being run over by Ginny who, unbidden, is cutting out a superb heifer calf. "Best calf in the bunch, Dad," grins Ginny. "It's Biddy's, you know."

With a sidelong glance at me, Biddy tiptoes out of the herd. I have never seen her look so grotesque. She walks stiffly, head low as though expecting a torrent of abuse, waiting for me to call her back but a little smugly too, knowing if I do my female buckaroo will quit.

I am about to ride over to Ginny to tell her that I happen to be the one doing the cutting here, when a sudden jolt sends my hat spinning into the herd.

"Get out of my way, Dad!" Marsha shouts as her horse runs right into mine. She ducks and dodges, sending a cow and calf trotting from the herd. "But, Dad," she protests even before I can. "It's Kay, she's the greatest calf and look, her mother's a registered cow from the Day herd. And besides, Ginny's got a calf and I don't. You wouldn't want to foster any old sibling rivalry around here, would you?"

I collect my horse beneath me, straighten the saddle, and ride back into the herd. I am about to cut out a good pair when Ginny trots over to me. "Don't you remember that one, Dad? Take another look. She didn't raise much of a calf last year, and if that calf weren't fat he'd have a high tail bone." Suddenly, I feel awfully old, and headed down the skids to retirement. I hear again a slim fragment of a conversation I had with a booming-voiced Ora Summers, whose voice on a windless morning can be heard five miles away. "Why, those girls there know lots more than that guy!" Ora was referring to Whisky Jim's daughters, and the "guy" was one he'd hired from town, but the words stick as though the shoe fits.

I shrug and ride out to hold the herd. One of the cowboys gives me a strange look. "If anything happens to me," I reply, "I want those girls to know how to run the place." A thrill of elation goes through me to have thought of such a reasonable excuse. Once more, though, the old depression hits. They are not only doing a good job, they are doing it *better.*

When we have cut out the top twenty percent of the heifers, enough to replace those which will be culled from the herd or lost through death, or pregnancy testing, we lock them in a separate field and hope against hope that no one will leave the gates open and mix them up again. Next spring the calves will be culled again, as yearlings; then, in July, the heifers will be bred to Angus bulls, for calving the following April, as two-year-olds.

The hot days of Indian summer combine with the chill of the nights to produce a twenty-four-hour pneumonia, which kills a number of fine big calves. I carry a syringe on my saddle, slipping up on any calf that might look sick and shooting a dose of medicine into its hip. It is a relief when the first of November comes and we can deliver the calves to die for the next owner.

We have contracted the calves to Ellington Peek, who has sold them on commission to someone else. As we did the steers, we gather the cows and hold them overnight in the Pond Field. At dawn we bring them up the lane to the corrals.

Perhaps the cows sense that they are to see their calves for the last time, for as the gate closes behind them, the bawling starts. Bunch by bunch, we work the cattle, letting the cows rush out through the gate, holding up the calves. When all the cows are in one corral and the calves in another, we pick out any calves too small to wean, and turn them back with their mothers.

The calves in their distress are losing weight every moment they stay off the scales. Quickly we separate the steer calves from the heifers, then put both bunches across the scales. On the average the heifer calves weigh about twenty pounds less than the steers and bring less money per hundredweight, so there is a marked difference in what they bring. If a steer calf weighs 420 pounds, and sells for $36 per hundredweight, then he brings me $151.20. The average heifer weighs 400 pounds, sells for $30 per hundredweight, and thus brings $120. Buyers justify the spread by claiming that the steers gain better than

197

heifers on feed. If the housewife were loyal to her sex she would demand heifer beef and the price would rise, putting an end to such discrimination. All the rancher can do is hope that all his calves will be males.

I would do almost anything on a ranch rather than add up figures, for my profits never total what I told the bank to expect. As long as food costs are tied to the cost of living and a political pawn they will never get better, yet as far as the housewife is concerned, the farmer will always be a villain. She should consider that, in 1946, she spent 26 percent of her take-home pay on food; in December 1969, only 17 percent. In 1951, one hour of labor bought 3.2 pounds of chuck roast, or 4.2 pounds of hamburger. In December 1969, 1 hour of labor bought 5.3 pounds of chuck roast, or six pounds of hamburger. On the ranches our products bring 1947 prices, while our costs have gone up more than 110 per cent.

Using actual 1969 figures, the economic picture of Yamsi is equally dramatic and frustrating. Out of five hundred cows, we have an 80 percent calf crop, which is about average for a range operation. The calves are worth an average of $138.60. Thus the four hundred calves I sell bring the huge amount of $55,400. But before I rush out and buy a new pickup, I must remember that this is gross profit, and cars are purchased out of net. I must first deduct the costs.

900 tons hay at $25	$22,500
Interest on owning 500 cows	11,250
Range costs	4,100
Taxes	3,000
Insurance	2,000
Cost of owning land (interest)	6,000
Bull costs ($10 per cow)	5,000
Salt and veterinary expense	1,000
Labor	3,800
Commissary	4,500
Business telephone	1,000
Total expense	$64,150
Sale of calves	55,400
Losses on cow operation	$ 8,750

These figures were for the cow and calf operation alone. Now let's add in the total operation, including the steers I ran on the meadow.

900 tons hay	$22,500
Interest on 500 cows	11,250
Range costs	4,100
Taxes	4,000
Insurance	2,600
Cost of owning land (interest)	8,450
Salt and veterinary expense	2,000
Labor	3,800
Commissary	4,500
Business telephone	1,200
Bulls	5,000
Transportation (pickup and gas)	4,300
Total expense	$73,700
Income from calves *and* steers	75,400
Total profit	$ 1,700

Of course all this is based on the assumption that there are no breakdowns on the machinery or death losses in the cattle. *Actually* . . .

Obviously I am raising five children who are properly clothed and fed, which I could not do on an income of only $1,700. Like most farmers and ranchers I can live only by going deeper and deeper into the land. The average indebtedness of the ranching industry within the past five years has doubled.

The calves that are sold from Yamsi go often to California to winter on grass. When they have reached seven hundred pounds or so, they will go to a feedlot, where they will be fed a grain ration, scientifically balanced, for about a hundred and twenty days, after which time they will weigh about a thousand pounds and bring close to $29 per hundredweight.

Why, then, does a sirloin steak cost the housewife $1.50 per pound? When an animal is slaughtered he is not all beef. Of a thousand-pound animal, only 590 pounds will be beef. Take off 125 pounds for bones, fat, waste, and shrinkage, and that leaves 465 pounds of retail cuts, and of these retail cuts only 140 pounds will be in the form of steak and of this steak only 40 pounds will be in the form of sirloin. Beef may not get any cheaper, but it will continue to be an adventure in good eating, and the first choice for the housewife who is having her husband's boss over for dinner. Somewhere in the course of every single day I should pause to be proud that Yamsi produces so much joy for so many total strangers.

As the brand inspector counts the last calf into the last truck, and the driver roars off in pursuit of the others, the cows bellow themselves into a frenzy. We work the herd carefully, cutting out old cows, cows with bad feet, bad eyes, or udders. These we ship off to the local auction. If we find strays, we keep them in and notify the owner.

The bulls are separated now from the cows and will remain isolated until the following June; the replacement calves are weaned, vaccinated against pneumonia, and put on hay and grain for the winter. The cows are turned back down on the river. For a few days they bawl plaintively and make frequent trips back up the lane to the corrals, but soon they accept the fact that the calves have gone forever, and devote themselves to the primary concern of getting their share of the grass. When the children gather the two-year-old heifers from Calimus and drive them back over the hill, the ranch is once more under control.

FROST HAS TURNED THE WILLOW leaves to gold and sent them skittering and tacking like fairy boats upon the quiet stream. The aspens, which last week shone of hammered gold, stand naked and modest, their brilliant shrouds flung carelessly at their feet.

High above the valleys, the sandhill cranes group, circle, and glide, summoning all who will go with them into the vortex of migration. Their calls fall faint and sad upon the lonely marshes and draws which were their eight-months' home. Tiny specks now in the sky, their circles take them ever higher; then slowly the circles widen and drift southward, their voices fade, and they are gone to the California marshes until spring.

Down on the brittle brown marshes, nests of blackbird, marsh wren, yellowthroat and rail turn soggy beneath the autumn rains. A miracle of a white Canada goose sails all unconcerned about his rare plumage amongst his normal fellows. He is a buffy white, without the black wingtips of the snow, and faintly through his creamy neck feathers shows the marking of the Canada. He had better stay with me; he will not last long over the guns of California.

My resident Canadas are barely tolerant of the great flocks of inter-lopers from the north that pause to rest. Necks stretched low, hissing their angriest, they fly at them and drive them a few short feet away at best, then return to their own feeding. Year round they stay with me, and have never seen a stubble field or flown high over city lights.

The Wilson snipes are silent now, standing grouped in the shallows, as unmoving as an Audubon print. Stirred up by a diving eagle, skeins of ducks, mallards, teal, bufflehead, scaup, and gadwalls drift like float-ing cobwebs gray against a gray sky, but soon land. Each river bend hosts a hundred resting ducks, glad to have found this chance to rest on their long journey south. A few feed quietly on the drifting lemna, a tiny waterweed that floats its two padlike leaves upon the water and trails its roots beneath; the rest sit quietly, bills hooked back un-der their feathers.

Tomorrow, next week, depending on weather or some stirring in their breast, they'll drift on south again, much refreshed, island hop-ping, refuge to refuge, over the waiting guns.

Neck still swollen from the rut, a mule deer buck stands defiant at the timber's edge. A group of does goes traipsing by on their way to salt, but he stares past them as though he's had his fill. Tricked by her summer habit, a cow bawls for a calf she hasn't seen in weeks, then plods, head drooped, on down the valley.

For the moment the life blood of the valley seems congealed as though by frost. The drifting water is silent, murky, dark. The land goes dormant as though resting from the fury that was summer.

CHAPTER 13

DURING THE ERA WHEN I MANAGED Yamsi for Buck, he was always out to improve my character with hard work, and it may be the only job he ever undertook in his lifetime at which he failed. I'd come in from sixty hot dusty miles in the saddle hoping my day was over, and relishing the fact that his automobile was nowhere to be seen, when up he'd drive as if he'd been hiding in the brush waiting for me. His mind jumping with projects, he'd amble my way, turning right, then left, as though steering himself with the thumbs he kept hooked in his suspenders, clearing his throat whenever I started away as though to rivet me to the spot. I wanted badly to buy the ranch from him, and I patiently courted his favor.

He'd spend his day in the kitchen making the cook nervous with his watchful eye, peering up at her intermittently over the *Saturday Evening Post*, the one magazine to which he was addicted. By evening he'd be ready to expend the energies he'd built up during those long hours I'd been working.

"Come on," he'd say. "As long as you're not doing anything important, ride along and open gates for me." It didn't matter to him that my wife had fixed a nice supper and was just setting it on the table. "Always remember," he'd say, sensing her disapproval, "work comes first on a ranch. A rancher can't worry about food." But when he did finally settle at the table, he'd be the first to sniff if the food wasn't exactly piping hot.

"Do I need rubber boots?" I'd ask, not wanting to ruin a good pair of tailor-made Bluchers by getting them wet.

"Hell, no!" he'd growl indignantly. But the first thing he'd do when we got down to the fields was walk out over a meadow, shin-deep in water, expecting me to follow. If I planned ahead by wearing rubber boots, he'd avoid water like a coyote with rabies, and would lead me on a foot-blistering five-mile forced march through the woods.

202

His walk was as unpredictable and erratic as his sequence of thoughts. He carried an irrigation shovel over his shoulder like a rifle-toting soldier and every time he stopped short or changed course, he accidentally clouted me alongside the head with it. If I dropped back far enough to avoid the shovel, he'd talk so low I couldn't understand him. A Lorelei luring me within range to destroy me.

There aren't too many ways to open or close a gate, but my way was always wrong. And the disgrace was that I'd spent twenty-five years learning. To listen to the man, one of the seven deadly sins was not handling a gate properly.

Once, coming along behind him, I found where he'd left the gate to the Bull Pasture open and the steers were already filing out to the open range. The next time we passed the gate I twitted him about leaving it. He didn't like the rub. "Why, the wind blew that gate open," he protested. "Look, I can make the latch swing back with my hat." He spent the next five minutes beating his Stetson to a pulp, but the gate stayed shut. I was smart enough to avoid further comment.

One by one, the men who had been his companions on the ranch, Homer Smith, the Erns, Paddock and Morgan, had drifted away, leaving me to inherit their listening post. I was lucky to get in one word for his thousand. To argue a point was useless for his hand slipped habitually to his hearing aid to shut out controversy. If he had been thinking about something, he naturally assumed that he had been discussing it aloud, and often his monologue started right in the middle of one thought only to trail off in the middle of another.

Both my uncle and I knew that I had foolishly shaped my whole life around the dream of someday owning Yamsi. He dangled the ranch before me like a plum, knowing that as long as I had hope I was helpless in his hands. My desires gnawed at me like a man's fruitless hankering for a beautiful woman. Across the West there were larger acreages, richer, more productive lands, better cattle operations, but Yamsi, the lonely valley at the headwaters of the Upper Williamson, paradise for bird and beast, was a unique and irreplaceable feudal barony.

There were times when I think Buck almost understood my love of the land, even respected it. But there were other times when I would catch him looking at me sadly. One day he'd agree to sell me the ranch; the next he'd change his mind and put the ranch on the market. He was ever willing to sell, but to someone who could afford to pay for the land without regard for what the land could produce.

Once, he phoned to say, "I'm sending a guy named Guber to look at the ranch. Big industrialist from California. Sold some land down south for twenty thousand an acre, and has a year to re-invest or pay the tax. The price doesn't matter to a guy like that. He'll go a million, I'm sure."

In due course, Mr. Guber arrived and drove his big car over the sugar pines I'd just planted, while his boy erupted from the car, trampled my wife's iris, and swept down upon my tame sandhill cranes, showering the poor astonished creatures with sticks and stones.

"Hyar!" I roared in my best cattle drive yell, while Mr. Guber looked surprised, then pained at my impertinence.

From his car he took a huge auger and proceeded to drill soil test holes all over my virgin meadow, holes that to this day look like the work of a badger gone berserk in a prairie dog town.

Just one of Mr. Guber's problems was that his education in the cutthroat world of big city business had made him a cynic. Since I had introduced myself as the owner's nephew, he assumed that I was getting a handsome commission for selling the ranch. If I said something favorable about the property he took it as gross exaggeration. If I panned the ranch, he took it as a slip of the tongue, and the gospel truth. When I told him it went to thirty below zero in the winter, he assumed sixty, and when I told him the snow got so deep only the tops of the giant pines showed, he assumed that they became completely buried.

And so I confided to him that a mysterious disease was causing the cattle to abort, that my uncle was selling because the state was putting in a summer camp for wayward boys right next door, that we were having trouble with the wives of the hired men, who sometimes got so lonely on rainy days that they hung themselves in the closets. I mentioned that whatever he had heard about the glories of Yamsi trout fishing had certainly been true—in the past—but that erosion caused by logging operations had so clogged the river with silt that it was ruined forever. While I wanted my uncle to sell the ranch since my fourth wife was suing me for divorce, it would really bother my conscience to see him trick a refined gentleman like Mr. Guber. As a finishing touch, I told Mr. Guber that if he would give me a hand cleaning the septic tank, which had been clogged for several months, when we were done I would cook him lunch.

When he left, Mr. Guber threw his arms about me, telling me that there were no honest men like me in Los Angeles. For some reason when Mr. Guber passed my startled uncle on the road to town, he stuck his fist out the window and made an impolite gesture. The old man never could figure why we never heard from Guber again.

Those who worried me most were the heavy construction types, men who *actually* move mountains. "I'll have to apologize," I admitted to one. "The river winds back and forth so much that the ranch is actually nothing but swampland."

But instead of looking worried, he beamed his Texas best. "Boy," he said, his forty years lording it over my thirty, "I've got thirty-seven DW 21 carry-alls and fifteen D8 Caterpillars that could chew this whole ranch up timber and all and regurgitate it out on a level with a hundred-foot drainage canal right down the middle."

"But the river!" I protested, startled out of my cool. Suddenly all I could think of were my trout, my sandhill cranes, my wild, beloved land.

"Son," he said. "That river will be easiest of all. We'll just chain the head end to that butte over there, hook up about a dozen of those D8s to the downstream end, and we'll pull that river channel out so straight it won't even have a bend in it."

I took me a little while to simmer down enough to find a chink in that one's armor. As he leaned to drink from Wickiup Springs, he took out a bottle of assorted pills and helped himself to half a handful. Back in the car, I began to shiver and shake, asking him if he'd mind rolling up the windows and turning up the heater.

"In summer?" he asked suspiciously. "What's wrong with you?"

"I don't know the name for it," I answered quite truthfully. "Don't let my uncle know I told you, but it's a strange fever transmitted by our local mosquitoes. The doctors can't seem to find a cure."

Year after year went by; potential buyers came and went. Rumors ran rampant on Main Street, Klamath Falls, that one celebrity or another had agreed to buy the ranch. Even though my uncle knew that the rumors were completely unfounded, they served to send his asking price spiraling upwards.

Gerdi and I went on raising our family in uncertainty, wondering privately, and with anguish, if, at thirty-five, I didn't owe it to my family to go off to promote the fencing machine I'd patented, which had prospects of doing well.

Loving Yamsi as we did, we couldn't bear to see it fall into disrepair, but worked side by side with our children the long days through, making the ranch glow. For all the horrendous lies I told potential buyers, the fences marched straight through the woods, the cattle gleamed with the prettiest color one can show a visitor—fat—and the shining meadows were ever more lush and green. But clearly something had to be done about my future; at the first possible moment, I had to catch the old man with his hearing aid turned on and tell him that I had to leave.

Gerdi watched with apprehension as Buck got out of his car, touching his chest to indicate that his hearing aid was shut off, and that he wasn't about to turn it on. Tall, straight, young-man lean, hair white as a country snowdrift, silent in one of his shy, leave-me-alone moods, he drifted about, looking at the profusion of Alpine flowers Gerdi had cheated through the frost, at the new fence she'd built of jack pine poles, at the carefully barbered lawn where there had been only dust when we came.

He wandered through the big stone house, thirty years old, built for him by buckaroos long dead. Perhaps he saw how the rooms shone with Gerdi's love, for he stared dreamily at the rugs, if threadbare, fresh fluffed from a morning in the air. Drifting out again, he watched the children as they galloped bareback on a flashy mare, smiled at the muddy rivers sweat made upon our cheeks as Ginny, Dayton, and I came in from driving a herd of cows over the long ridge of Taylor Butte to the Sycan and Teddy Powers meadows.

Hoping for an audience, I grinned at him as I rode up, sitting the storm easily as my horse snorted and flung himself sideways in a half sunfish. The old man only shrugged and indicated that he was in no mood to hear what I had to say. For a time, he stood at the fence before the house, lonely, trammeled by the years, then he turned, drove off to town, and never again returned.

An hour and a half later the telephone rang, angry and insistent as a locust, in the ranch kitchen. I lifted the receiver, half expecting to hear Mamie Farnsworth's voice from the grave. Instead I heard the voice of Buck's accountant and those incredible words, "Buck wants to know if you still want to buy the ranch." Had his hearing aid been on earlier in the day, I would have blurted out to the old gentleman that I was about to leave his service, and for that he would never have forgiven me. It was as close as that.

The price turned out to be such that the mortgage would be the only thing we would ever have to pass on to our children, but we were all too happy to care. And once the thorn of the ranch had been removed from our relationship, my uncle and I became better friends. Attending respectfully the long swinging draft of his reminiscence, I sat out many a long afternoon with him in Klamath Falls, smiling in abstraction as he attacked the system, and the failures of modern man.

In his own mind he had justified his treatment of me. "There's nothing that builds a young man's character better," he advised, "than having to struggle."

"You ruined mine by giving in so easily," I said. "Know what I did yesterday? I went out and splurged. I bought my wife her first new pair of Levis in fifteen years."

"Make sure she doesn't throw the old ones away," he suggested. "The way the cow business is, she may need them for underwear."

One afternoon he took a long drive around Klamath Lake. "Canoed thirty miles once across Klamath Lake to see a red-haired girl named Alice," he told me. "Never married her though. Too much religion in the family." That night, still in control, he passed to his reward as though he had planned it that way. He was still trying to avoid spoiling my character to the very last when he left all his money to charity. If he feared that prosperity would spoil me, he was probably right— had it ever come my way.

TOMORROW. TOMORROW BRINGS December again, the coming both of winter and the time of reckoning, when I balance this year's profits against this year's losses, and take a cold, hard look at next year's prospects. Agricultural forecasts predict an oversupply of beef will quickly materialize to depress prices unless cattlemen, working as an industry, agree to market their beef animals at lighter weights. No chance. Since the beginning of the livestock industry, it has been every man for himself. Even if the general economy is healthy, even if poultry, pork, and mutton are in short supply, even if the markets are not flooded with foreign beef, the prospects for next year are grim. All I can be sure of is that the costs of running my ranch will go up.

My only choices are to sell the ranch or go deeper into debt, borrowing still further on my land until my equity is eroded and gone, and a sale is inevitable.

I am Yamsi's last link with the past; with a change of ownership out of the family the shadows of all those who have gone before will fade away. Without me, a uniquely primitive and irreplaceable environment will die, the lonely sanctuary, the home of owl and eagle, osprey, kingfisher, and crane. The pulsing riot of wildlife now living in safety along my pristine and timeless river will be homeless. It is a hard fact of agricultural economics that change of ownership brings need for new efficiencies of operation brought on by pressures of financing. At Yamsi, it would mean drainage of marshes, cutting of forests, increased use of fertilizers and pesticides. Worse yet, it could mean use of the land for its highest, short-term monetary return, the chopping up of the ranch for subdivisions, a hated thought to anyone who loves the land. Once land like Yamsi has gone that route it is gone forever. In my hands lies the fate of sandhills, of sora rails, tule wrens, yellowthroats, goshawks, and great gray owls. In my hands is the fate of five hundred brood cows, the last of the Bar Y herd my uncle spent a lifetime building. In my hands, the future of my children, and of theirs; in my hands the decision that will keep them on the land or send them scratching for survival in the cities. History has appointed me. I am the crossroads.

But I am not alone. In rural areas all over America, parents face the same sad choice of whether to quit or tough it out, to keep their patrimonial lands out of the clutches of corporate farming. Children face the decision of whether to stay on facing a life that can promise only a continual struggle for survival or to head for the cities. These are painful determinations, yet few decisions will be more vital to the future of America.

What will our military do when they no longer have the capable, inventive, athletic farm boy as a source of leadership? Many a general has found to his delight that they seem to come from the soil almost pretrained to the disciplines of a soldier. What will industry do when it can no longer recruit the farm boy with his long history of thinking for himself, of using his hands and wits, of making decisions? Industry has learned sadly enough that there are far too many urban youths who have yet to make their first important decision even at twenty. Within the next decade, the government may well be forced to mount a massive, costly, artificial program to send youth back to the farms for training. It would be far cheaper to find a solution *now* to help youth stay with the land.

Historically, America has always looked to the land for her leaders. For here, young people are trained from earliest youth to make decisions; they work without supervision at an early age, and solve problems for themselves. The sad flow of youth from farm to city is one of the great sociological problems of our time, and one which must be reversed if we are to continue strong and free.

The bankers are not ogres; they are merely realists, professional economists whose job it is to assess financial capabilities without taint of sentimentality. They are not sociologists. Against the banker's will, he is pitted against the farmer, a nonrealist, who will be lost in discouragement at that economic point where he is no longer able to dream.

The young ranch-raised men and women of today, more sophisticated, better educated than their fathers at all levels of education, are too smart to blunder along in the footsteps of the generation before. All sorts of fascinating careers are open to them, vocations which will offer more pay, more leisure time. If they do decide to stay with the land, it will be because they have been able to find sufficient challenge, the excitement of new ideas, new crops, new profits, new uses for the land never before imagined.

Perhaps the wheat they harvest from their tired lands will no longer be in the form of grain but recreation. The bottom lands their grandfathers wrested from the forest may no longer be cultivated in the usual sense, but become a refuge for wildlife, a fish-producing lake. Perhaps for a fee they will host the children of the city executive, teaching them basics not taught in schools. If they stay with the land it will not be exactly the life they dreamed of. In all cases it should be better than the ghetto; in most cases it should be a life full of unlimited challenge, a life that exceeds their dreams.

Nor are my children an exception. For them there must be a new challenge to bind them to the ranch. It will be up to them to find new incomes for the land to supplement the grazing income, new uses which will be in harmony with the land and preserve rather than destroy its special loneliness.

Within the decade, Calimus will no longer be a sagebrush bottom surrounded by pine woods, but a lovely recreation lake, designed by environmental planners, who will turn a drab, low-yield landscape into a thing of rare beauty, a quality environment. I see marshes for wildlife, islands with trees, and sheltered coves, designed by man to screen one user from another, managed trout production of a quality no public agency could match, a degree of recreation far exceeding its competition, the national forest which surrounds it. The national parks and forests are destined always to be open to mass usage. The Calimus development would be open to regulated usage, limited solely to that number who could utilize the land without destroying the very loneliness for which they had paid their fee.

In coming years Yamsi will no longer be a cattle ranch as such, nor will it be cut up into subdivisions. It will be a unique refuge which furnishes loneliness to humans on demand, a place where men can flee the pressure of the teeming cities, heal their tired brains in harmony with nature. Nor will government agencies be able to destroy it. It will not be another National Park, its beauty trampled by a multitude whose unconstrained mass destroys the very thing the park was set aside to preserve.

Private land like Yamsi, with controlled access, can be managed on that quality basis soon to be lost forever from public resources as the population burgeons. Here man will rest side by side with wildlife which will have found a refuge where they do not fear the gun. Surely for my children there will be no limit to the challenges and satisfactions such management offers.

In California, more than five hundred acres of prime agricultural land go daily out of production, covered with roads, houses, factories. Forever. Agriculture performs a vast service for those who follow us, by fighting to preserve the land in a good healthy condition for our children. A lovely, lonely, pristine block of land like Yamsi is even now a rarity; it may be as early as this decade that the public finds out—too late—that it has lost such treasures forever.

Once an alternate income for Yamsi is established, then its agriculture commitments will decline in importance. The marsh lands will increase because the profits will be in the call of a sandhill crane, the wing music of teal, precision flying along the river, the therapeutic joyousness of marsh wrens ringing from the cattails.

I believe in the industriousness, the inventive ingenuity of the American farmer, his ability to adjust, and his penchant for productivity. Once he understands how to develop his recreational potential as a crop to its full earning capacity, he will produce a quality and quantity of recreation now only dreamed of. But he does not have much time.

Already, with pressures of population, and the shifting of the vote to urban areas far from the land, the whole concept of private land is being rapidly eroded. If agriculture is to retain possession and control of its land resource, it must make the land contribute more than just the production of food. It must contribute vastly to recreation and wildlife or be lost. Moreover the industry must make the public aware of the contributing role of private agricultural land to conservation and wildlife. Only when the public is aware that private land can contribute a gift that public land can never match will the concept of private land ownership be on firmer ground.

Gordon Barrie stands beside me as I lean on the rail fence and stare out over the frozen meadows. I hardly heard him drive up. Banker to three generations, reality is his job, yet here he is a friend. He, too, has had his struggle with vision.

The shadows of the Yamsi we both love pass before us. A scattering of sleek Bar Y Herefords moves restlessly across the meadows as cowboys out of the past drift them into a herd for the long annual drive to the hay stacks of the Bly Valley. Ash Morrow, Jack Morgan, Buster Griffith, Tommy Jackson, Harold Hatcher, Oliver Little, Slim Fields, Ern Morgan and Ernie Paddock. How many of them are dead now or forgotten!

Sunning herself in her rock garden, cascades of white hair drying on the gray lava rocks behind her, Margaret Biddle closes her faded blue eyes and tips the wrinkled ivory of her face to the mountain sun. How many years she has been gone! Out on the meadow Homer is having a vocal bout with his cranky gelding, Tune. In the corral drowse ghosts of horses my children have only heard about. Yamsi, Sleepy, Whingding, Yellowstone, Roany, Buttons, Ginger, Bleuch, Goosey, Freckles, Moose, Badger, BK Heavy, BK Jimmy, Spade, Steel, and Spot.

Buck wanders erratically across the meadows, now watching his cattle form into a herd, now digging in the frozen earth. The vision fades and they are gone.

Destroying the shimmerings of the past with the focus of the present comes the laughter of my children. Marsha and Ginny ride past us, mounted on handsome colts they've broken themselves. Towing her lead rope proudly, Mickey the cow dog drags the reluctant donkey, Hominy, almost hidden by her loaded pack. Perched snugly in his nest of bedrolls on her back, with one hand raiding a hidden can of tomorrow's cookies, Taylor shows his merry, freckled face and waves good-bye. They are bound for a chilly campout in some lonely glade they know about, a secret paradise.

Working with the tractor out in the fields, Dayton is building a new pond for wildlife. John scampers across the meadows, his faithful great gray owl, Alexander, flying on behind like a kite without a string. My patient wife readies the garden for winter, while beside her the tame sandhill cranes probe the frosty earth for one last worm lingering after summer.

"The Bank was wondering . . . ," Gordon Barrie begins, his voice trailing away because we have been friends a long time and to say more would be an indecency.

To stay or sell! High above Taylor Butte, a pair of wild sandhills are sailing their last circles of the year, drifting ever southward, leaving my valley behind in perfect faith that their fiefdom on my marshes will be here next year, and the next, as long as there are cranes to fly.

Somehow, it's hard to explain to a banker, a realist, the real profits of the year. The way the children are growing up, healthy, happy, capable, no problems—the wild things I made a home for in my valley—none of this can quite be transmitted into dollars for the Bank to understand. Their thoughts are expressed in numbers, mine in adjectives. How can I represent in cash for them my responsibilities to history, to my children, to Nature, and to the land?

I lean on the front fence staring off across the meadows, aware suddenly that it was here my uncle leaned before me to make decisions. He called it his "trouble spot." Now it's mine.

There's lots to do. There's an old slough down in the Kay Davis field that, with a little tractor work, would make a dandy marsh, maybe make a home for one more pair of cranes. And I'll need the tractor down there anyway when I skid in logs for the new corral. I'll have to have that project done by May, in time to brand the calves.

"I've got a real feeling," I remark to Gordon, "that next fall, cattle prices will be better. And say, not to change the subject or anything, but I saw a rainbow trout today down in the river, in your favorite hole, that must have weighed fifteen pounds."

The young Forest Service engineer seems uneasy as he strolls toward me, glancing all directions but mine in an attempt to appear nonchalant. Intent upon my troubled decisions, I scarcely heard him come. Silently, he hands me a map showing a projected road system for the country west of me. The map shows a spaghetti plate of roads, leaving no thicket untouched.

I am sad. Angry sad. What does it matter now that I managed to defeat Road 3190 through this very land? They have made my victory a hollow one with a substitute tangle of roads which will destroy the land for all time.

Why do they so hate the forest? What is there about a blank spot on the map that sparks the bulldozer syndrome in an engineer? Why doesn't the Forest Service be blunt and honest and change its name to the Forest Engineers? A service organization they are not. Why can't they realize that the land involved is the very watershed for the Williamson River, whose fragile volcanic pumice soils, which float away with water and blow away with wind, have finally been stabilized by vegetation cover only after many thousands of years.

Of limited commercial value as wood chips or cores for veneer, these lodgepole pine thickets are worth far more as a haven for wildlife under pressure. It is these very thickets that have made a productive wildlife unit out of the vast, open, bitterbrush-rich, ponderosa pine forests to the west. Even with heavy logging pressure, these lands have remained productive because the animals and birds were able to find a thicket sanctuary.

Remove even a percentage of the lodgepole cover, and the heavy winter snows, melting too swiftly under the fierce, high altitude sun, will bury the Williamson River in a deluge of moving sand, filling in spawning beds, trout holes, and wildlife marshes. Without shade, the trees will fail to reseed themselves on the hot dry pumice flats and hillsides.

It took Nature six thousand years to stabilize the volatile soils of this unique ecological niche with a covering of lodgepole pines. Short-lived, they grew, died, and rotted away, slowly building a slim supply of organic matter in the barren pumice. Vastly inferior as lumber, they were shunned by the lumbermen; their best economic function still is as a cover for elusive soils.

In a proper spring, with snow melting slowly in the shade of thickets, the pumice layer absorbs the water like a sponge. But when the snow melts too fast, freshets gut the hills, flooding the valleys with heavy layerings of floating pumice, choking the rich bottoms with a sterile shawl through which even grass cannot penetrate.

The acreage involved is small, perhaps six or seven miles square, yet it is perhaps the most important great gray owl sanctuary in America. Once the roads have been built and the timber harvested, the owls and goshawks will be gone from its thickets, and the sandhill cranes from its lonely draws. Rodents and grasshoppers will own the land.

It is a small watershed, inhabited by no one, from whose bosom well forth crystalline springs in delicate hydrostatic balance. How can Man predict the effect of his actions upon the springs themselves, which trickle slowly down, held in check by field and forest, to make up the might of the Williamson? It has no glamorous name, this land, to attract the fancy of the public. If I leave there will be no one left to defend it.

Alex, the great gray owl, sails across the lonely meadows on silent wings, and lands on the post beside me. Gently he lays a gift of a fat meadow mouse in my hand. Temptation has allowed him to consume part of it; the remainder at the moment is all he possesses to give. He cocks his great shaggy head at me as though he asks a favor in return, as though he asks me to stay on and fight for his last domain.

The mouse? Maybe it is the owl's small gift to me to lend strength in the battle against the bureaucracy, his small way of doing his part. Maybe after all—maybe that's what it's all about. Each one of us who cares doing his small, whatever-he-can-do thing in one last fight to save the land. I must not let him down.

Epilogue

Since this book was first published in 1971, I have had thousands of letters from readers curious to know if the Hydes still live at Yamsi, at the headwaters of the upper Williamson. There is an old bronc rider's expression, "Hang tough and rattle!" The Hydes have done just that. We are still there.

What has saved the ranch, in part, has been our willingness to diversify, to change with the times and look for other incomes. With a thirteen-year-old son, Taylor, driving a thirty-five-ton tractor, fifteen-year-old John driving a huge earthmover, twenty-two-year-old Dayton running compaction equipment, and with me cracking the whip, we dammed up snow-water runoff at Calimus to create a lake with three and a half miles of shoreline. My uncle would have had a fit at the very idea.

Hauling in gravel for spawning beds, re-vegetating the banks, we turned the river flowing through the ranch into a fine trout fishery. Now fishermen come from as far away as Africa to cast a fly for trout, bringing in an income which supplants that from cattle. Since I finished this book, I have written thirteen others, including a near sequel to the Yamsi story, *Don Coyote*.

We have had our share of tragedy. In 1979, our daughter, Marsha, at twenty-two, recently married, graduated from Oregon State University, and with a new job teaching high school, died on the ranch in a horse accident. Swiftly, with no pain, and with her boots on.

Dayton Jr. is working on a ranch at Black Butte, near Sisters, Oregon. Taylor finished his long studies in veterinary medicine and is a practicing veterinarian. Son John and his wife help Gerdi run the cattle operation at Yamsi, while Ginny and her husband host the fishermen there. Like Thoreau, I have a rude cabin on my own Walden Pond, contemplate Nature, and write.

And, suddenly, I'm seventy-one—not quite knowing where the years went, telling stories better than they were, stiff jointed from every horse I ever met, a little bewildered that the children are grown now, and that kid I was just snappish with is a grandchild. My thirteenth!

Aware that I proposed to the right girl for the time and was damn lucky she said "yes." Otherwise where would all those nice kids be?

And she snappish too, not quite able to forget being taken for granted or, for all the hard work and worry, that we were better off when I was thirty. We went the way we went, warmly human.

My old part-Indian friend, Al Shadley, gone to the happy hunting grounds. I phoned him once when he was in his late seventies, and joked, "Al, are you getting any loving lately?" and he replied, kind of wistful like, "Oh, I was too old last spring." The harness hanging dusty in the barn has long outlived Al's old work teams. Our last old draft horse, Perch, now rests among the pines.

Slim Fields is gone too. Groundhog Day was always Slim's big day. He was worried he couldn't saddle a horse much longer, and did just what he told me he'd do thirty years ago rather than be a burden to folks. A brave man.

Old age is when you finally throw away a few things nobody else would care about, when your children no longer remember how hard you used to work, and you realize, suddenly, that despite all the books you've written, there will probably be a few stories you will take with you.

Three o'clock in the morning, yet already in the distance the rumble of trucks, the drivers driving hearses for the last of the great pines as the Forest Service services the forest. I've lived closer to the stars here than most and been damn lucky. Above Calimus Butte, to the east of Hyde Lake, I can see the faint glimmering of first light. I can tell from the fading stars that it will be quite a day.

Dayton O. Hyde
Chiloquin, Oregon
July 1996